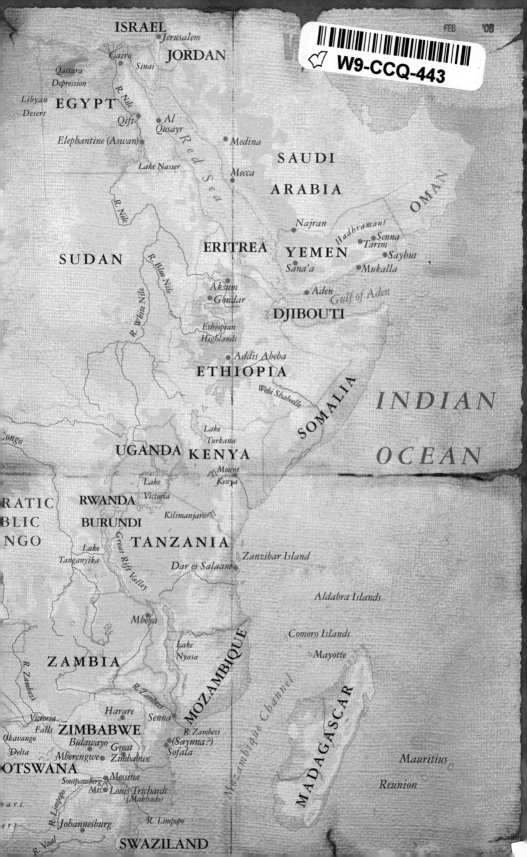

FEB '08

W9-CCQ-443

ISRAEL
Jerusalem
JORDAN
Cairo
Qattara
Depression
Sinai
R. Nile
Libyan
Desert
EGYPT
Qift
Al
Qusayr
Elephantine (Aswan)
Lake Nasser
Red Sea
Medina
Mecca
SAUDI
ARABIA
OMAN
R. Nile
SUDAN
R. Blue Nile
R. White Nile
ERITREA
Najran
Hadhramaut
Senna
Tarim
Sayhut
YEMEN
Sana'a
Mukalla
Aksum
Gondar
Aden
Gulf of Aden
DJIBOUTI
Ethiopian
Highlands
Addis Abeba
ETHIOPIA
Webi Shabeelle
SOMALIA
INDIAN
OCEAN
Lake
Turkana
Congo
UGANDA
KENYA
Mount
Kenya
Lake
Victoria
RWANDA
Kilimanjaro
RATIC
BLIC
NGO
BURUNDI
TANZANIA
Lake
Tanganyika
Great Rift Valley
Dar es Salaam
Zanzibar Island
Aldabra Islands
Mbeya
Comoro Islands
Mayotte
ZAMBIA
Lake
Nyasa
MOZAMBIQUE
R. Zambezi
Mozambique Channel
MADAGASCAR
R. Zambezi
Harare
Senna
Victoria
Falls
ZIMBABWE
R. Zambezi
(Sayuna?)
Sofala
Okavango
Delta
Bulawayo
Mberengwe
Great
Zimbabwe
OTSWANA
Soutpansberg
Mts.
Messina
Louis Trichardt
(Makhado)
Mauritius
Reunion
ari
R. Limpopo
Johannesburg
R. Limpopo
R. Vaal
SWAZILAND

THE
LOST ARK
OF THE
COVENANT

Solving the 2,500 Year Old Mystery
of the Fabled Biblical Ark

TUDOR
PARFITT

HarperOne
An Imprint of HarperCollinsPublishers

For my brother, Robin Parfitt, 1946–2006,
and his sons, Adam and Ifor Parfitt,
and his granddaughters, Poppy and Ella Parfitt

Author Note
Some of the names of the people mentioned in this book
have been changed, as have some of their personal details,
in an attempt to conceal their true identity.

All images are copyright of the author other than the following
from the insert sections:
Images marked 2, 4, 17, 18, Alamy; 23, 24, 25, 26, 27, 28, 29, Kevin Evans;
1, Griffith Institute, University of Oxford; 15, Piet le Roux;
3, Scala Archives photo library; 5, Superstock

Maps courtesy of HarperCollins Publishers, London

HarperCollins books may be purchased for educational, business, or sales promotional use. For information please write: Special Markets Department, HarperCollins Publishers, 10 East 53rd Street, New York, NY 10022.

HarperCollins Web site: http://www.harpercollins.com

HarperCollins®, 📖 ®, and HarperOne™ are trademarks of
HarperCollins Publishers

FIRST EDITION

Library of Congress Cataloging-in-Publication Data is available.

ISBN-13: 978-0-06-137103-5

08 09 10 11 12 RRD(H) 10 9 8 7 6 5 4 3 2 1

CONTENTS

1 The Cave 1

2 The Sign of His Kinship 23

3 Protocols of the Priests 45

4 The City of the Dead 81

5 A Key to the Past 99

6 Opposites Are One 121

7 The First Cataract 149

8 Legends of the Queen of Sheba 177

9 The Tomb of Hud the Prophet of God 199

10 The Moses Gene 233

11 The Fire of God 247

12 The Sacred Fire Pot 279

13 Watchdogs of the King 313

14 The Dust of Its Hiding Place 335

Epilogue 367

Index 373

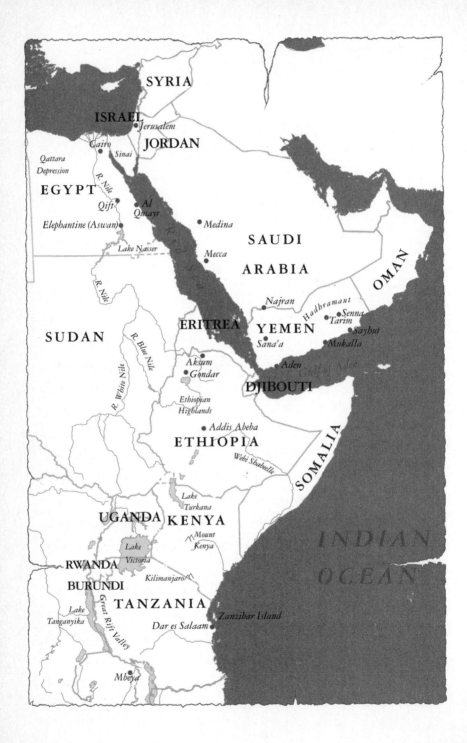

THE CAVE

I t was a time of drought.

In 1987 my home was a grass hut in a dried-out tribal area of central Zimbabwe in southern Africa, completely cut off from the outside world. I had been doing fieldwork on a mysterious African tribe called the Lemba. This was part of my job. At the time I was Lecturer in Hebrew in the Department of Near and Middle Eastern Studies at the School of Oriental and African Studies (SOAS) in the University of London and for a while now this tribe had been my main academic subject.

How had I spent my time in the village? In the blistering heat of the day I would wander over the hills near the village and poke around the remains of the ancient stone-building culture, which, the Lemba claimed, was the work of their distant ancestors. With my little trowel I had discovered a few bones, pieces of local pottery, and one or two iron tools of uncertain age. Not much to write home about. Then I would read, write up my notes, and spend much of the night listening to the elders' narratives.

The Lemba harbored an astonishing claim to be of Israelite origin, although the presence of Israelites or Jews in central

Africa had never before been attested. On the other hand, since early medieval times there had been rumors of lost Jewish kingdoms in darkest Africa. What I had heard was that the tribe believed that when they left Israel they settled in a city called Senna—somewhere across the sea. No one had any idea where in the world this mysterious Senna was located and neither did I. The tribe had asked me to find their lost city, and I had promised to try.

What I knew about the 40,000-strong Lemba tribe in 1987 was that they were black, they spoke various Bantu languages such as Venda or Shona, they lived in various locations in South Africa and Zimbabwe, they were physically indistinguishable from their neighbors and that they had a host of customs and traditions identical to those of the African tribes among whom they lived.

They appeared to be completely African.

But, on the other hand, they also had some mysterious customs and legends that did *not* appear to be African. They did not intermarry with other tribes. They did not traditionally eat with other groups. They circumcised their boys. They practiced the ritual slaughter of animals, using a special knife; they refused to eat pigs and a number of other creatures; they sacrificed animals on high places like the ancient Israelites; and they followed many of the other laws of the Old Testament. The sighting of the new moon was of cardinal importance for them as it is for Jews. Their clan names looked as if they were derived from Arabic or Hebrew or some other Semitic language.

During the months I had spent in the village trying to unveil their secrets, I never found the absolute proof—the smoking gun, demonstrating that their oral tradition, which linked them with ancient Israel, was true. I never found an inscription on stone, a fragment of a Hebrew prayer, an artifact from ancient Israel. Not even a coin or a shard of pottery.

Before arriving in Zimbabwe I had spent a couple of months with the large Lemba communities in the neighboring country of South Africa. Here the leaders of the tribe had given me a good deal of information. I had hoped to build on this in Zimbabwe and asked the local Lemba chief to facilitate my research. Chief Mposi called a meeting of the elders of the Lemba clans and, tempted by my promise to try to find their lost city of Senna, they formally agreed to permit me to research their history.

But subsequently they did not tell me nearly as much as I had hoped they would. They were tight-lipped about anything to do with their religious practices. It was only my willingness to sit around late into the night, until my whisky had loosened the old men's tongues, that had enabled me to hear something of their remarkable cult.

The following day they would regret their nocturnal indiscretions and mutter that the clan elders shouldn't have authorized my research, that white men had no business meddling in their affairs, and that I should stop trying to penetrate the cloak of secrecy that veiled their religious rites.

Others tried to frighten me into leaving by telling me lurid tales of what had happened to previous generations of researchers who had wandered too far down forbidden paths. One of them had been forcibly circumcised after daring to walk on Dumghe, the tribe's sacred mountain. Another had wandered too close to a sacred cave at the base of Dumghe, and had been stabbed with a traditional assegai and badly beaten. He had narrowly escaped with his life.

As my hopes of finding the critical clue regarding their true identity began to die, so did the crops in the fields around the village. It had not rained at all for months. There was some thick muddy liquid at the bottom of the boreholes. Every morning the women brought water in rusty old oilcans balanced on their heads. When that was gone, there would be nothing left to drink. Except beer from the bottle shop, for people with money. And there weren't many of those.

This morning, early, before the sun had risen, the chief had called for a rain ceremony. The chief's messenger had arrived just as the household was beginning to stir. The cooking fire was being blown into life and water was being heated for tea and the washing water, which was brought every morning to my hut by the daughter of my gentle host, Sevias. The messenger told Sevias that his presence would be required that evening. This was a last desperate throw of the dice.

There had been drought for so long that the streams that once had brought life and the occasional fish to the village had completely disappeared. They now looked like goat tracks filled with deep, fine dust. With no water, life in the village would soon become impossible. The tribe would have to move elsewhere. But where? The drought covered the whole land.

Toward evening the elders and notables congregated in the chief's large hut at the center of his *kraal*—the group of huts that formed his property. They had been invited to drink *chibuku*—home-brewed maize beer, the consistency of porridge, dance the night away, and to entreat the ancestors for rain. This was deepest Africa.

Sevias invited me to accompany him. We walked together across the parched earth as he told me about the great herds he had once owned, of the trees groaning with fruit, of the maize that used to be as big as pumpkins.

We were among the first guests. I sat next to Sevias on a baked-mud bench circling the hut and watched the preparations for the ancestor party with keen interest. I had never imagined I would be permitted to observe anything as close as this undoubtedly was to the heart of their cult.

I had a camera, tape recorder, and notebook. I was fairly sure that this evening would provide me with the material for at least one academic article, and an impressive one at that.

Chief Mposi sat alone. He was in poor health and gave the impression of being preoccupied. He stared at the mud floor, resting his head on the knop of his stick. With a sudden movement he bawled at his wives to serve beer.

"It's sitting there and it's not doing any good to anyone!"

"I'm serving it," snapped his oldest wife, lifting up the beer pot with her muscular arms.

"Too late," he growled.

The *chibuku* pot was passed from hand to hand, from right to left, with no unseemly show of haste, like a decanter of Madeira after a dons' dinner at Oxford.

The silence was broken by the chief calling out the names of his four wives. They were singularly different from each other in age, size, and beauty. They answered in turn, knelt side by side, and started to clap. They turned away from the chief, rose to their feet and lit candles, as the other women began ululating and whistling.

A long antelope horn was thrust through the opening into the hut and a triumphant blast silenced the shrill sound of the women. The man blowing the horn was tall and well built. He was wearing a skirt made of strips of black fur and around his head he had a strip of leopard skin. He was the witch doctor. His name was Sadiki—one of the Lemba clan names—an unmistakably Semitic name whose presence in central Africa was a mysterious anomaly. He led the ceremony. *Magagada* rattles made of dried marrows were tied to his ankles with bark fiber thongs. He stamped his feet on the earthen floor of the hut and blew a long haunting note on the horn.

Four elderly women sitting together on the mud bench that went round the hut started pounding on wooden drums. The rest of the guests were clustered behind the witch doctor, propelled into the small, juddering movements of the dance by the rhythms of the drums and the *magagada* rattles, barely moving, lost in concentration.

Sadiki stood at the epicenter of the storm of sound, directing its movement. He had an overpoweringly regal air, and looked arrogantly around him. Suggestively he moved a foot. Then a hand. His body followed and, positioning himself in front of one of the drums, he danced, like David before the Ark, pausing to blow the ram's horn similar to the *shofar* that had once been blown in the Temple of Jerusalem. The drummers looked far too old and frail to be able to produce such a sound and yet they were to drum for hours without a pause.

The beer started to circulate faster. Poverty had taken its grip on the village. It had been a long time since the beer pots had been passed around so liberally. Some of the men, no longer accustomed to drinking, were already inebriated.

The chief's oldest wife was apparently already possessed by the spirits of the ancestors. Staring from side to side she fell to the ground weeping. Looking around in an unfocused way she pulled her long, western-style dress up over her fat marbled buttocks and over her head. She danced naked, positioning herself in the space in front of the women drummers vacated by Sadiki.

The pulse quickened again. Sadiki, sweat pouring down his broad, muscular chest, placed a headdress of black eagle feathers on the naked woman's head. Sevias told me that this was to show respect to the ancestors. She danced on, casting great shadows on the candlelit walls. She fell to her knees, sobbing, in front of the old chief and tenderly placed the headdress on his head.

The chief was dying. Everyone said so. He looked gray and ill. He gestured to me that I should join him. He took my hand in his and whispered in my ear, "The ancestors have come from Israel: they have come from Senna. They are here with us. Good-bye, *Mushavi*. Perhaps we shall see each other in Senna." Senna was the lost city from which they had come and it was also the place they expected to go when they died.

His face, illuminated by the flickering light of the candles, was corrugated with lines of age and illness; his eyes were concealed by dewlaps of mottled light-colored flesh. He peered at me and then indicated that I should rise and leave him. Saddened and mystified by his words, I went back to the bench to my notebook, camera, and recorder.

I had been here in the village so long I was beginning to feel at home, one of them. I had drunk a good deal of their *chibuku* beer. After the first few swigs it becomes more or less palatable and after a while positively acceptable. It struck me that this was no time for sitting in a corner taking notes and recording Lemba music. There were more important things to do. This was more a time for observer participation: I removed my shirt in order, as I thought, to blend in with the half-naked men and women whose ghoulish shadows were leaping wildly on the walls and who were falling into a kind of trance all around me. The chief's oldest wife crossed the hut, leaned over me, her withered breasts brushing my shoulder, and whispered something incomprehensible in Shona, the language of the dominant Shona tribe among whom the Zimbabwe Lemba lived.

I started to dance to the pounding rhythm of the drums. One of the chief's younger wives was dancing topless in front of me, swaying drunkenly, supplicating the ancestors, running her hands over her breasts and down over her belly and legs.

The women drummers quickened the rhythm of their drums.

Another woman in a bleary-eyed trance slid out of her clothes and moved into the center of the hut. Men stood around her admiring her slim body and full breasts, urging her on.

"She is speaking to the ancestors," Sevias bellowed in my ear. "Soon they will reply. When their voices are heard it will be better for you to leave."

Toward midnight there was a change in the atmosphere. I imagined that the time had come for the cultic incantations and secret prayers to be offered up. These were the closely guarded things. These were the oral codes that governed their lives and that no doubt held the clues to their past that I was seeking. These codes and incantations were for me the heart of the matter. This is what I wanted to be part of. This is what I had come here for.

My arms were raised; my face was turned up to the straw roof above. Sweat was pouring off me. I felt a great sense of excitement. I had been accepted. I was one of them. The ancestors were about to descend and I would be there to observe what happened next. No one from the outside had ever observed this before. Inside my head I could feel a kind of channel opening that seemed to be a channel of communication with the Israelite ancestors of the tribe.

I was rejoicing in the efficacy of my five-star research methodology when I felt a fist driven into the side of my face. It was the fist of the chief's oldest and sturdiest wife. I fell to the ground on top of the recumbent and malodorous body of Mposi's greatest drunk—a sort of tramp called Klopas whom I had met and smelled many times before. For a few seconds I lost consciousness. I was pulled out of the hut by some of the men and propped up against the side of the chief's hut.

"Er, I upset the chief's wife," I said. "I'm sorry."

I did not feel at all sorry. I felt bloody furious.

"*Mushavi*," said Sevias leaning over me. "You did not upset anybody. This blow was just a welcome from the ancestors. Perhaps it was also a little warning. Just a little warning. If the ancestors had not wanted you here at all they would not have given you a light blow like this but they would have torn you into pieces. Now you must go because the ancestors are coming among us. The uninitiated must leave."

The spirits of the ancestors would not be happy to see me there, he explained. Secrets would be shared. There were things I should not know. Truculently, I thought to myself if I don't get to learn the secret things, here, tonight, the chances are I never will. It was now or never.

Outside the hut, a group of elders were looking anxiously at the night sky, hoping for signs of rain. Sevias sat down next to me against the wall. His kindly lined face betrayed signs of concern. His concern was not only for the rain, or lack of it, although this was as critical a matter for him as for the others—indeed his own life and the life of his family depended upon it—but also for me and my disappointment at not being admitted to all the tribal secrets. I had already told him that my fieldwork had not yielded as much as I had hoped.

Head cocked, his hands held in a gesture of supplication, he asked with just a hint of a smile, "*Mushavi*, have you found what you were looking for in your time with us?"

He often honored me with the tribal praise name *Mushavi*, which the Lemba generally use solely among themselves and which I thought could perhaps be connected with *Musawi*—the Arabic form of "follower of Moses (Musa)." Perhaps he was trying to flatter me by calling me *Mushavi* but the rest of his question was incomprehensible. He knew full well that the tribal secrets for the most part were still intact.

I smiled and with as much patience as I could muster said, "You know very well, Sevias, that there are still many secrets you have not told me. And don't forget the elders of all the clans agreed that I should be given access to *everything*."

"Yes," he replied gravely, "but many times I have explained to you that no matter what was said at that meeting of the clans, there are things that *cannot* be told outside the brotherhood of the initiated. Prayers, spells, incantations. Many of our secrets *cannot* be revealed. We told you that. My brother, the chief, told you that. The others told you that. They would have to kill you, *Mushavi*, if you learned those sacred things. That is the law."

His lined face became almost a parody of concern and anxiety.

Sevias was a good man. In all the months I had spent in his *kraal*, despite the drought and the uncertain political situation both within the tribe and in the country at large, despite family difficulties, he had always been calm, kind, and dignified. I realized now that I had never been happier in my life than sitting writing under the great tree in Sevias's *kraal*.

He shuffled his bare, calloused feet in the parched earth.

"But how about the tribal objects?" I insisted. "Those things you brought with you from the north, from Senna. I've been told about these but I've still seen nothing of them."

"It's true," he said. "We brought objects from Jerusalem long ago and we brought objects from Senna. Sacred, important objects from Israel and Senna."

Senna was the original lost city that the tribe maintained it had once inhabited after leaving the land of Israel. Professor M. E. R. Mathivha—the scholarly head of the Lemba tribe in South Africa—had already told me a good deal about their Senna legend. The tribe had come from Senna "across the sea." No one knew where it was. They had crossed "Pusela"— but no one knew where or what that was either. They had come to Africa where they twice rebuilt Senna. That was the sum of it.

"Sevias," I insisted, "can't you at least tell me what happened to the tribal objects?"

He studied the sky and said nothing. Then he murmured, "The tribe is scattered over a wide area. You know, once we broke the law of God. We ate mice, which are forbidden to us, and we were scattered by God among the nations of Africa. So the objects were scattered and are hidden in different places."

"And the *ngoma*? Where do you think that may be?" I asked.

This was a wooden drum used to store sacred objects. The tribe had followed the *ngoma*, carrying it aloft, on their sojourn through Africa. They claim to have brought it from Israel so many years ago that no one remembered when. According to their oral traditions they carried the *ngoma* before them to battle and it had guided them on their long trek through the continent.

According to Lemba oral tradition the *ngoma* used to be carried before the people on two poles. Each pole was inserted into the two wooden rings that were attached to each side of the *ngoma*. The *ngoma* was intensely sacred to the tribe, practically divine. Sacred cultic objects were carried inside. It was too holy to be placed on the ground: at the end of a day's march it was hung from a tree or placed on a specially constructed platform. It was too holy to be touched. The only members of the tribe who were allowed to approach it were the hereditary priesthood who were always members of the Buba clan. The Buba priests served and guarded the *ngoma*. Anyone who touched it other than the priests and the king would be struck down by the fire of God, which erupted from the drum itself. It was taken into battle and ensured victory. It killed the enemies of its guardians.

I had first heard of the *ngoma* months before in South Africa. Professor Mathivha had told me what he knew about it and I had had a detailed account from an old Lemba man called Phophi who was steeped in the history of the tribe. Phophi had told me how big the *ngoma* was, what its principal properties were, and what traditions were associated with it.

I also knew that some forty years before, an ancient *ngoma* had been found by a German scholar called von Sicard in a cave by the Limpopo, the crocodile-infested river that marks the border between Zimbabwe and South Africa. He had photographed it and the photograph had been included in a book he had written on the subject, but apparently the *ngoma* had long since disappeared without a trace. Mathivha, Phophi, and other Lemba elders had told me that the artifact found by the German in its remote cave was without doubt the original *ngoma* that the Lemba had brought from the north.

One night, a few weeks before the rain dance, sitting up late around the fire with Sevias and other old men, I heard a little more of the legend of the *ngoma*.

"The *ngoma* came from the great temple in Jerusalem," said Sevias. "We carried it down here through Africa on its poles. At night it rested on a special platform."

It suddenly occurred to me that in form, size, and function the *ngoma lungundu* was similar to the biblical Ark of the Covenant, the famous lost Ark that had been sought without success throughout the ages. The biblical description of it, which I knew from the years I spent as an undergraduate studying classical Hebrew at Oxford, was etched in my mind:

> *an Ark of shittim wood: two cubits and a half shall be the length thereof, and a cubit and a half the breadth thereof, and a cubit and a half the height thereof [...] thou shall cast four rings of gold for it, and put them in the four corners and two rings shall be on one side of it and two rings in the other side of it. And thou shall make poles of shittim wood and*

overlay them with gold. And thou shalt put the poles into the rings by the sides of the Ark, that the Ark may be borne with them. The poles shall be in the rings of the Ark; they shall not be taken from it. And thou shalt put into the Ark the testimony which I shall give thee.

The Ark, like the *ngoma,* had supernatural powers. It was never allowed to touch the ground. It was practically divine. Like the *ngoma* it was carried into battle as a guarantor of victory. Sacred objects, including the tablets on which the Ten Commandments had been inscribed and the magic wand of Moses's brother Aaron, were kept inside it. Anyone who as much as looked at it would be blasted by its awesome power. A priestly caste founded by Aaron, the brother of Moses, guarded the Ark. The priestly clan of the Buba founded by an individual called Buba, who was thought to have led the Lemba out of Israel, guarded the *ngoma.*

The functional similarities were striking. But the differences in form were significant. The Ark was apparently a kind of box, coffer, or chest, while the *ngoma*—although it also carried things inside it—was a drum. The Ark was made of wood but it was covered in sheets of gold; the *ngoma* was made of just wood.

Most critically, there was no connection in ancient times between the world of the Bible and this distant and remote inland corner of Africa. And there was no proof at all, in any way, that the Lemba guardians of the *ngoma* were of Jewish ancestry. Nonetheless, the area of overlap between these seemingly very different objects attracted me and turned my mind toward the strange story of the Ark of the Covenant. It was an interesting comparison but, I thought, no more than that.

* * *

Outside the chief's hut, with the tumultuous din of the drums crowding out all the night sounds, I leaned against the mud-and-straw wall of the hut and slowly felt the pain of the blow recede. Sevias looked ill at ease. He took my arm and raised me to my feet, guiding me farther away from the groups of men who were standing around, enjoying the cool of the night air before returning to the frenzy of the dance.

"Talking about the *ngoma* and the things that were brought from Israel is too dangerous, *Mushavi*. This is part of the secret lore of the tribe. I cannot tell you any more about this than we have already told you. We told you that we call ourselves *Muzungu ano-ku bva Senna*—'the white men who came from Senna.' We told you that the *ngoma* came with us from Senna. We told you what the *ngoma* used to do. And we told you that the *ngoma* has not been seen by men for many, many years."

Sevias was about to turn away when he hesitated and put his hand on my arm.

"The old men say it was the *ngoma* that guided us here and some people say that when the time is right the *ngoma* will come to take us back. Things are getting worse in this country. Perhaps the time is coming."

"Sevias," I asked. "I know this is one of the great secrets of your tribe and I know that there are many in the tribe who do not wish to share their secrets with me. But I am leaving soon. I don't want to leave empty-handed. Could you just tell me, please, if you have any idea where the *ngoma lungundu* might be?"

Sevias paused, looked around, and fell silent. He glanced up at the disappointingly bright night sky and again shuffled his feet in the fine dust of the *kraal*. "Where it is now I do not know. But some years ago the very old men used to say it was hidden in the cave below Dumghe Mountain. It is safe there. It is protected by God, by the king, by the "bird of heaven," by two-headed snakes and by the lions, "the guardians of the king." It had been taken there, so the old men said, by the Buba from Mberengwe. They are the clan of Lemba priests and in those days there were some of them who stayed down on the Mberengwe side. But, as you know, that is the one place that you should not go. Not on Dumghe Mountain."

He bade me good night and walked quickly back to join the elders.

I took Tagaruze, the policeman who had been instructed by the local police headquarters to act as my bodyguard (and to keep an eye on me), and walked the couple of miles back to Sevias's *kraal*.

I felt a pang of regret that I would soon be leaving this beautiful place with its rugged hills and great rounded boulders, molded and shaped by aeons of wind and rain, sun and drought.

The next day, I was planning to move on north toward Malawi and Tanzania, following the trail of the passage across Africa of this enigmatic tribe, in search of their lost city of Senna. It seemed a long, lonely quest and all of a sudden I found myself yearning for home.

I had had a letter from Maria, my voluptuous, salsa-dancing Latin American girlfriend. It was tender but firm. She wanted me to go back, to leave this self-indulgent quest of mine for what she called the nonexistent Senna. She wanted me to marry her and lead a normal life, the conventional and sedentary life of a scholar and university teacher. If I didn't want to marry her there were plenty of men around who did.

"Men," she said, "there are millions of them. You are an *imbecil* if you do not take the chance now when you have it. Others would."

And it was true. Every time she walked down the street there were very few men who failed to notice her. She had a way of walking. I tried to put her out of my mind. She would wait. Probably.

I was still feeling tipsy from the *chibuku*. If what Sevias had told me was correct there was perhaps some chance of my actually finding their *ngoma lungundu*. This would perhaps reveal something about where the tribe had come from. It would perhaps help me find the lost city of Senna. Perhaps there was some writing on it, or secret, sacred objects inside it, which could help me on my quest. All I needed to do was to go to Dumghe.

I felt a tremor of excitement. The sacred mountain of the Lemba is situated a couple of miles away from Sevias's *kraal*. It was a beautiful rounded hill, east facing and covered with the characteristic rounded boulders of the region and was sparsely wooded. There was open country between the *kraal* and Dumghe. There were no villages or *kraals*—and no noisy dogs to alert the tribe to my activities. There was no dangerous wildlife, save packs of jackals and the occasional leopard, and I was too drunk to be overly concerned about them.

Following a sudden, *chibuku*-inspired urge, I decided to walk to the sacred cave, the one place where the tribe had forbidden me to go. A no-go area. In the past anyone daring to go there not of the initiated would be punished by death.

The elders would be dancing and drinking for hours to come, I thought to myself. The rest of the tribe were asleep. No one would ever know I'd been there. I knew that the cave was situated at the base of two massive rocks that had sheared away from a cliff that formed the eastern side of the mountain. It is covered with great, smooth round boulders created over the millennia by wind erosion. The rocks behind which the cave was hidden had once been pointed out to me, and I had been told that behind the sacred cave there was another cave even holier than the first. That was perhaps where the *ngoma* was protected, as they said, by its guardian lions and polycephalous snake.

It was about two o'clock in the morning when I arrived—along with Tagaruze, my tough police bodyguard—at the great *meshunah* tree where I had encountered the Lemba guardian of Dumghe during my first days in the village. From the tree all paths leading to the cave could be seen. The official guardian was reputed always to be on duty but that was difficult to believe and, in any case, as far as this occasion went, I had little to worry about for I had seen him at the rain party, drunk like all the others.

We paused for a moment and then made our way up the side of the mountain toward the rough track that led down to where the cave was. To one side the path hugged the rock face; to the other there was a sheer forty-foot drop into the void. It was a treacherous descent and stones kept plummeting into the abyss.

Even Tagaruze was scared. Tonight he was going way beyond the call of duty. He was as fascinated by the Lembas' stories as I was. But he was beginning to regret having agreed to accompany me this night. He was not much given to words but finally he muttered, "Why are we doing this? What are we looking for?" I was scared too, and did not reply.

I thought I heard a noise in the trees and brush above the stone face of Dumghe. We fell silent. One of the elders had seen a lion, a white lion, he had said, on the mountain, a few days before. The elders had told me that the *ngoma* was always protected by lions. These were the lions of God, the guardians of the king. We pushed on, slithering down the path that led down to the cave at the base of the rocks, pausing from time to time to listen for signs of danger. Tagaruze took the gun from its holster and stuck it into his belt. There was a damp, acrid smell in the air. My hands were wet with sweat from the effort of the walk and from fear.

Suddenly, the path fell away under my feet and it was only Tagaruze's swiftness in grabbing my arm that prevented me from disappearing over the edge. Loose stones fell over the cliff in a tidy avalanche. A flat, neat echo sounded below us. We paused and looked down into the ravine. I could just make out the outline of the final stage of the descent that led down the cliff opposite the great wall of rock.

Carefully we edged our way down. Once there was a crack of branches; once the sound of a large bird and of rushing air, then silence. I wondered if this was the "bird of heaven," the creature Sevias had claimed was one of the protectors of Dumghe.

We reached the base of the two great rocks. There was another sound of a branch snapping. Perhaps the Lemba *did* keep someone posted here all the time to guard their treasures, after all. There was only space for us to walk one abreast. I led the way, flashing my flashlight around until we reached what appeared to be the entrance to the cave. This, I thought, must be the Lemba holy of holies. Between the boulder and the cliff face there was a mound of loose scree. I placed my desert-booted foot on it, holding the flashlight with one hand and resting the other against the side of a boulder. There was nothing to be seen. Encouraged, I went through the narrow entrance and pointed my flashlight straight ahead. All I could see was a wall of rock.

But I could hear something: a sort of rasping sound, a cough or a snarl, and then a louder sound—a snort, perhaps, which became a deafening roar as it bounced off the surrounding rock face. My hand gripped the flashlight in terror. My legs turned to jelly. The gun, I thought, shoot it whatever it is. Tagaruze had the gun but when I turned around I realized that Tagaruze was no longer behind me. Tagaruze had disappeared. I was alone.

I retreated through the opening, back first, keeping my face to the sound, and then scrambled up the narrow track after him and fled through the wooded slopes of Dumghe. The noise followed us, rising through the natural shaft made by the great rocks high into the mountain. It was a terrifying sound—it could have been a lion or a leopard or just about anything else. We did not wait to find out. We ran as fast as we could until we got to the *meshunah* tree.

Breathlessly we sat down at the base of the tree. As my rump hit the ground I felt something slithering away under me into the undergrowth. Shuddering, I stood up quickly.

"What the hell was that?" I asked.

"That was just a snake," Tazaruze said offhandedly.

My blood turned cold and I felt like throwing up. I had been told that one of the guardians of the *ngoma* was a two-headed snake. I was a million times more afraid of even the smallest, most inoffensive grass snake than of any cat, great or small, on the face of the earth.

I shuddered. "And how about that thing in the cave?"

"It must have been a Lemba ancestor in the body of a leopard or a lion. Or it was the protectors of the *ngoma*, the lions of the Almighty, the guardians of the king. Everyone knows they prowl around this mountain. This was a terrible, big mistake."

What the policeman had said was undoubtedly true. It was a mistake. I was to rue that mistake for many years to come. We did not find the elusive and mysterious *ngoma lungundu,* the strange artifact that played such an important role in the imagination of this remote African tribe, but the events of that night were to change my life and lead me on a quest that would be resolved only many, many years later.

2

THE SIGN
OF HIS KINSHIP

"Sorry. It's a forgery!"

It was my very first meeting with Reuven. The year was 1992, half a decade after my adventure at the mouth of the cave at Dumghe. We were in my vaulted study in the Old City of Jerusalem. A weird light seemed to be coming from a yellowing document, which was spread out on the table.

Reuven ben Arieh was a financier and diamond merchant, a highly orthodox Jew and a highly unorthodox everything else. He lived mainly in Jerusalem but also had homes in Paris, London, and Miami. He was a tall, full-bearded, well-built man. The first thing I noticed about him was his eyes. Those eyes were something. This man was something. He had a beautiful, soft-spoken wife, Clara, admired by everyone, and a life-absorbing mission.

His mission was stark in its simplicity and bound to fail: it was to end gentile hatred of Jews. To terminate anti-Semitism. For once and for all. It was as simple as that.

Hatred of Jews was a subject about which he had some personal experience: most members of his immediate family, including his father and mother, brother, and sister had been murdered at Treblinka. Reuven, who was about ten years older than me, was born in Holland in 1935. During the Nazi occupation, he spent three years hidden in a neighbor's garret. In 1945 he emerged to discover that he was an orphan. Later that year he was claimed by some elderly and wealthy childless relatives of his mother's who brought him up. They died in the early 1950s, leaving him their fortune. He studied chemistry in France, took up his father's trade of diamond cutter for a few years, and then in 1953 moved to Israel.

By the time I met him he had fought in three wars against Arab states: the Sinai Campaign of 1956, the 1967 Six-Day War, and the Yom Kippur War of 1973.

It was the hostility of Muslims and Arabs toward Israel and Jews that was of most concern to him. It was this hostility, particularly, that he wanted to eliminate from the world. Whenever I subsequently met him—and wherever I met him—it was Arab and Muslim resentment of Israel and how to combat it that he really wanted to talk about.

A few days previously Reuven had purchased the manuscript from Anis, one of the Jerusalem dealers. It could be dated more or less to the time of the Prophet Muhammad. So he said. It was going to change the world.

When he arrived at my house in the Old City that late summer's day, clutching his tattered manuscript, Reuven was as excited as I have ever seen him, before or since.

He was wearing a very stylish version of the black hat, long dark jacket, and trousers worn by observant European Jews.

But everything was subtly wrong. Despite the heat and dust, his clothes were spotless, and immaculately cut by a Parisian tailor. The tropical weight woollen cloth of his suit was a very dark blue worsted with a herringbone pattern. He gave off a slight suggestion of Chanel *Homme*. As I was to discover later, he usually had his hair cut in New York, went for regular manicures, and his handmade shirts came from Turnbull & Asser in London's Jermyn Street. Although I am not Jewish, I had lived in Israel for many years and was familiar with many aspects of the Jewish religion and culture, and it was clear to me that Reuven looked like no other orthodox Jew in Jerusalem—and I told him so.

Grinning at me he said, "I want people to say—Hey! Reuven that handsome guy! That beautifully dressed orthodox Jew!"

He had "returned" to Judaism just after the Yom Kippur War. Before that, he had been a completely secular Israeli. He was now what is known as a *baal teshuvah*—a sort of born-again Jew. He maintained a fastidiously kosher home but elsewhere he would occasionally eat in a nonkosher restaurant. Since his conversion to Orthodox Judaism, he had immersed himself in the Talmud—the great Jewish collection of religious law—and the Jewish mysticism of the kabbala.

However, he also had what he referred to as his "principal interest." For many years he had been scouring Islamic texts trying to find something that could be exploited to neutralize—or better, eradicate—Muslim hatred of Israel and Jews. What he was looking for was some ancient, unknown Islamic text praising the Jews or foretelling the return of the Jews to Palestine, something that would make the settlement of Muslim land by Jews seem ordained by Allah, something that would legitimize Zionism in the eyes of the Arab world, something that would destroy Muslim hatred of Israel. It was an extraordinary idea.

As he put it: "No peace will ever come to the Middle East until both sides—Jews and Muslims—reorient their spiritual relationship. We need some document from the past that could allow us to put conflict aside and respect each other!"

And today, it seemed, he had found that document.

At first glance it appeared to be a letter from the Prophet. The astonishing thing about it was that it set out not to vilify and condemn the great enemies of Islam—the Jews—but to praise and defend them. In fact, the Sons of Israel, the *Banu Israil,* as they are called in the Quran, are lauded to the skies.

He explained to me that Muhammad had never, ever had the idea of trying to create a new religion. He wanted simply to introduce the older faiths of Judaism and Christianity to the polytheistic people of the desert. The original direction to which Muhammad's first disciples prayed—the *qibla*—was actually toward Jerusalem. It was only after the Jews of Medina—one of the oasis towns near Mecca—proved to be disloyal and fought against him that he turned against the Jews and started to pray in the direction of Mecca.

"What's this got to do with changing the world?" I asked.

"Everything, my friend, everything. You could say that the Jews' disloyalty to the Prophet was the beginning of the conflict between Islam and the West. You know the Middle East scholar Bernard Lewis?"

"Yes, he used to teach at SOAS."

"Lewis calls this "the clash of civilizations." This was the great fissure between the cultures."

"Yes," I acknowledged, "that is true in a way."

"But just listen! What I've got here could easily reverse all that. That's why I wanted to meet you. I need you to authenticate it. This manuscript gives a radically new perspective on what the Jews of Medina really got up to. It's explosive. Muslims could soon be joining Jews and even Christians in prayer. Can you imagine that? They could all be praying together toward Jerusalem. Praying in the same direction is the first step to *thinking* in the same direction."

Reuven's eyes were shining with the splendor of this vision. "This document is like a news broadcast from ancient times," he continued, "from the time these troublesome religions were spawned—a tattered fragment from the past that will permit us to put aside our conflict and actually try to love each other. Armageddon could be postponed for a century or two!"

This was the gist of the document he held in his hand: Muhammad swears in the letter that it was the Jews of Medina and the other oasis towns of Arabia who had always come to his aid in his many battles against the heathen tribes of the desert. The Jews were even ready to desecrate their holy Sabbath to help him. They never left his side. They never betrayed him. During a single bloody campaign, the Jews killed over 20,000 heathen enemies of the Prophet: 7,000 knights, 7,000 regular horsemen, and 7,000 foot soldiers.

"*This* is what the Prophet *actually* promised the Jews," declared Reuven reverently, raising one finger for emphasis. "Not centuries of contempt and persecution!"

"Just listen." He put on a pair of reading glasses, scrutinized the document, and read aloud. "'O men of the Children of

Israel, by Allah I shall reward you for this ... I shall grant you my protection, my covenant, my oath and my witness for as long as I live and as long as my community shall live after me, until they see my face upon the Day of Resurrection.'

"Did you hear that?" he asked, his voice suddenly shrill, thrusting the document in my face and revealing an immaculately laundered cuff. "If the Muslim world knew about this, they would change their attitude to Israel overnight! There'd be no more Arab–Israel wars! No more terrorist attacks!"

Unfortunately, there was more to the letter than met the eye. It was probably quite old, I could see that. The body of the text was in Arabic and there was a short introduction in Hebrew. I knew something about Hebrew palaeography—the study of the form of ancient writing—and I could see this was a medieval Hebrew Yemenite script. This much was genuine.

Then I recalled that once in the Yemen I had seen an almost identical document in the home of an antiquarian in Sana'a, the capital of the Yemen. It was called *Dhimmat al-Nabi* (The Protection of the Prophet) and was an ancient Jewish fabrication, an old forgery, which the Yemenite Jews had created to counter the animosity of their Muslim neighbors. There was no Jewish community in the Muslim world quite as wretched and persecuted as the Jews of the Yemen. They needed all the help they could get. However, this document would not persuade many Muslim scholars to turn their received opinions upside down. It would not change the world.

"It's a shame," I said, "but it is a forgery. A very old forgery."

A yellow *hamseen* wind was blowing in from the desert. It was stiflingly hot. Reuven's face fell when I gave him my assessment of his document, and he grew silent. He just sat there grimacing, rubbing the side of his head where he had been grazed by an Egyptian bullet in the last of his wars.

Had it been genuine, the document he had just shown me could have served this purpose pretty well.

"Are you *absolutely* sure it's a forgery?" he asked trying to keep the disappointment out of his voice.

"Quite sure," I replied flatly.

One cold, damp Jerusalem evening, some months later, we were walking back to my house in the Old City. Reuven had just flown in from Miami. He was suntanned and exquisitely dressed as usual, but he seemed agitated and I wondered what was troubling him. We had just passed through the Jaffa Gate, one of the main entrances into the walled city of Jerusalem, when he said, "Redemption. That's it, redemption."

"What do you mean?"

He said nothing. We walked silently down the alley leading to the Armenian Quarter. After a few minutes he turned to me and murmured, "Redemption is what it is all about. I think I have found what I have been looking for. I now know what to do."

"You've not bought another ancient document from your dealer chum, have you?" I asked in disbelief.

Stroking his beard, he smiled.

"I have found it."

"Found what?" I asked.

"You'll see," he said. "Wait until we get to your place."

We passed Zion Gate, another of the historical entrances to the city, and walked in the shadow of the medieval walls toward the Western Wall, one of the great retaining walls built by Herod the Great to enclose the area of the Temple, and sacred to Jews ever since.

It had been a bitterly cold winter and was close to freezing when we arrived back at the house. I lit the Friedman paraffin stove in the study and put a match to a pile of olive wood in the sitting-room grate.

Finally when we sat down, he could no longer contain himself.

"I think that I have found what I have been looking for," he announced quietly. "I think the solution is the Ark of the Covenant."

We talked late into the night, huddled around the fire, drinking Israeli 777 brandy. He started by telling me about the efforts going on throughout the world to locate the ancient Temple treasure in Jerusalem. He explained the global religious importance of the Ark and its deep significance for mystics, kabbalists, and freemasons. He explained the history of the Ark as the Bible relates it.

The Ark had been made at God's command shortly after the exodus of the Jews from Egypt around 1200 BC. It was essentially a coffer containing the tablets of the law that God had given to Moses on Mount Sinai and was believed to be the home of the Israelites' invisible God. It was placed in a tent-like sanctuary called the tabernacle and could be approached only by priests of the tribe of Levi. The Ark punished by fire those who disregarded the strict rules that governed the way it should be treated. It was carried before the Israelites as they advanced through the desert and was said to have generated some kind of energy that blasted a dry path across the River Jordan.

The Israelites had to destroy Jericho if they wanted to conquer their Promised Land and the Ark was somehow, in some strange, mysterious way that has never been satisfactorily explained or understood, instrumental in making its walls come crashing down before the besieging Israelite horde. The first important religious site the Israelites created in Canaan was at Shiloh, not far from Jerusalem. The tabernacle and the Ark stayed here for hundreds of years. During the battles against the Philistines—the great enemies of the Israelites—the Ark was used in battle.

It was seriously dangerous.

Finally, at the time of King Solomon, the son of King David, it was placed in the magnificent new temple created to house it. From this moment on we hear precious little about the Ark and the assumption is that at some point over the next few hundred years, and probably before 587 BC, this fabulous artifact disappeared.

As Reuven was speaking, my mind was transported back five years to my perilous night on Dumghe and the vague associations I had imagined between the *ngoma* and the Ark. But Reuven was unstoppable.

The more he spoke about the Ark the more excited he became. "The Ark radiated mystical energy from the center of the world," he said. "For Jewish mystics the Land of Israel—*Eretz Yisrael*—was in the middle of the world. Jerusalem was at the center of *Eretz Yisrael*. The Temple was at the center of Jerusalem. The Holy of Holies—the *devir* was at the center of the Temple and the Ark of Moses was at the center of the holy of holies. Directly beneath the Ark," he continued, "was the *even Shetiyyah*—the foundation stone—a stone drenched in mystic power. A kind of cosmic battery for the universe!"

Reuven's face had taken on a strange radiance and his voice grew louder. "This," he boomed, "was the place where Adam was buried. *This* is where the patriarch Abraham was prepared to sacrifice his son Isaac. *This* is where Muhammad ascended to heaven. *This* is where the very creation of the world took place. The foundation stone was the critical element that separated the upper world from the pit of chaos below, and the Ark incorporates that elemental centrality."

Breathlessly he described the construction of the Ark by the Israelite craftsman Bezalel shortly after Moses had led the Hebrews out of Egypt. He spoke of the exquisite golden cherubim that were placed on its golden lid—the Mercy Seat—which was nothing less than the actual throne of the Almighty. To be honest, all these mystical and supernatural references left me cold.

"Oh, come on, Reuven," I groaned. "Anyway, according to the book of Deuteronomy it was Moses who made the Ark, not Bezalel, and it was just an ordinary wooden container. If you remember, God commanded Moses to make two stone tablets and an acacia Ark. He made the simple wooden Ark and took the stone tablets to the top of the mountain. The law was duly inscribed upon them and Moses brought down the tablets and put them into the Ark he had made. No gold, no cherubim, nothing.

"Modern scholars think that the more elaborate description of the Ark with all its gold stuff was probably a scribe's attempt to make the Ark match the glories of the Temple and was written hundreds and hundreds of years after the period when it was made, which would have been about 1300 BC."

"Don't try to diminish it," growled Reuven, seizing my arm. "The Ark was the holiest thing in the world, ensconced in the holiest place in the world. It was where the *Shekhinah*—the divine presence of God—lived. The combination of the holiest place in the world and the holiest *object* in the world radiated its own force and the world is still trembling! My Kabbalistic teachers taught me that the Ark existed and still exists in a kind of hyperspace. It defied all physical laws. When it was put in the Holy of Holies it was attached to its carrying poles. We know that the space available was too small for the length of the poles yet the Ark still fitted in. It is as close to heaven on earth as the world has ever seen. The Ark was constructed on a heavenly original."

"So it was kind of fake, like your document. Not even an original," I said grinning, hoping to deflate him a little or provoke him into a more rational discourse.

For a few minutes, he appeared to be lost in thought and then he plunged back into the magical and mystical aspects of the Ark that seemed very far from his central interest, his mission. He told me that his kabbalistic teachers drew an analogy between the Ark, with the two tablets inside, and the brain and its two hemispheres. In the same way as the brain was central to the working of the body, so the Ark was central to the working of the people of Israel.

"Reuven," I said patiently, "this is all undoubtedly of great interest, but how can the Temple treasure and the lost Ark possibly help you in your mission to placate the Muslim world?"

"Because I have found this!" he said triumphantly. "I have found an amazing passage actually in the Quran and *this* is no forgery." He took a copy of the Quran from his briefcase and read aloud in his faultless Arabic.

Their prophet said to them, "The sign of his kingship is that the Ark of the Covenant will be restored to you, bringing assurances from your Lord, and relics left by the people of Moses and the people of Aaron. The angels will carry it. This should be a convincing sign for you, if you are really believers."

"Muhammad considered the restoration of the Ark to the Jews to be a sign of the kingship of Saul, the first king of Israel. I have no doubt that contemporary Muslims would see the restored Ark as a convincing sign of kingship and political legitimacy today. *This should be a convincing sign for you, if you are really believers.* The Ark seen in the context of this verse from the Quran would be better than any manuscript. In any event, who can say if the kind of manuscript I have been seeking really exists? But the Ark once existed and if I can find it, it would guarantee peace in our time between Muslims and Jews."

I had never noticed this verse from the Quran. He went on to tell me what Muslim theologians and scholars had to say about the Ark. The Muslim version of events was based loosely on the well-known story in the Apocryphal second book of Maccabees, a late Jewish text, which relates that the Biblical prophet Jeremiah carried the Ark out of the Jewish Temple just before the Babylonians seized Jerusalem and destroyed the Temple in 587 BC. Jeremiah took it across the River Jordan into what is today the kingdom of Jordan, hid it in a cave on Mount Nebo, the mountain from which Moses had gazed upon the Promised Land before the Israelite conquest of Canaan, and then sealed up the entrance to the cave. Some of the Prophet's followers tried to find the path that Jeremiah had taken in order to find the Ark. He rebuked them and said that the Ark would remain hidden until God gathered his people together at the end of time.

Here the Arab historians take up the story and this was new to me. According to them the Ark was subsequently discovered on Mount Nebo by the Jurhum tribe. They took it to Mecca and there it stayed. According to some Muslims the Ark is still to be found beneath the Ka'aba—the construction at the heart of Mecca that is the holiest place in the world for Muslims. Reuven told me of other Muslim theories concerning the fate of the Ark. Abbas, a cousin of Muhammad, maintained that the Ark was hidden in the Sea of Galilee, *Kinneret*, in Hebrew—and would be found just before the end of time by the *Mahdi*, an Islamic Messianic figure.

Reuven's handsome face was glowing as he added that Islamic scholars believed that relics of Moses and Aaron would be found inside the Ark, including the tablets of the law, Aaron's rod, the scepter of Moses, and Aaron's turban.

I smiled skeptically at this piously enunciated list. "Did Aaron *have* a turban?" I asked.

He looked at me steadily. "You don't get it, do you? Don't you understand that if I can find the Ark I can bring peace and redemption to this part of the world? I'm not going to leave it for the *Mahdi* to find! Muslims will accept the legitimacy of Israel and this country will become what it was meant to be—a land of peace, a land flowing with milk and honey!" His voice was hoarse with excitement.

I could see that Reuven was in the grip of a genuine passion and realized that there was little to be gained by teasing him.

"Well, it's a very interesting idea. In fact in some ways it's an interest that we share. We just have different ways of expressing it. I've been fascinated by the Ark, in my own way, since my African days. What I find compelling is that the *idea* of the Ark has sent ripples throughout the world. I discovered what I think was the end of one long, sinuous ripple when I was in Africa and I imagine there are others."

Reuven nodded solemnly. "Yes, its rays penetrated every corner of the earth as the Kabbalists teach us. Its impact upon the world when I find it will be overwhelming."

"*When* you find it? Come on, come back down to earth, Reuven. You have no idea where it is. You don't really know if it ever *existed*. I don't think it did. Personally I think it was an idea more than a thing. This is not, my friend, what I would call a realistic project. Anyway," I continued, "the Quran says that angels will bring it. You don't look much like an angel to me. But you could work on it."

Brushing aside my objection and sarcasm with a dismissive movement of a manicured hand, he looked me straight in the eyes and said doggedly, "I have spent years combing the Islamic texts for the forgotten passage that would change the world. Thus far, I have failed. So now, realistic or not, I am going to broaden my search to include the Ark. The Ark, if I can find it, is going to give real legitimacy to Israel. It will give our spiritual sovereignty back. It will redeem us. It will redeem the world!"

I felt a shiver running up and down my spine. The firelight flickered on the vaulted stone ceiling. Next to the passionate Reuven I felt prosaic. For me, the story of the Ark ensconced in its tabernacle tent took me back to my childhood in Wales and to the little chapel called Tabernacle where I had gone with my father. And when I had mentioned the Ark to my father *en passant* on my previous trip to England his eyes had lit up with interest.

But nonetheless *my* interest in it was historical, pragmatic. Reuven's apocalyptic vision was quite the opposite. I wanted to deflate his rhetoric, bring him down to earth, but I couldn't. It was as if his intoxication and passion had paralyzed me. I began to sense that his passion was taking me over too. I refilled his glass and my own and stared into the flames. He pushed his well-shod feet closer to the fire and leaned back, his hands clasped behind his head, then began to intone in a tense, menacing rasp:

> From the ashes a fire shall be woken,
> A light from the shadows shall spring;
> Renewed shall be the blade that was broken;
> The crownless again shall be King.

"That's Tolkien, isn't it?" I asked.

"Yes," he replied, "from *The Fellowship of the Ring*. It just seems to catch my mood. Just think: political and religious redemption for the Jewish people. 'The crownless again shall be king.' The redemption of Israel will be brought ever closer by the discovery of the Ark. For thousands of years it has been hidden somewhere, probably broken, crushed, worm-eaten. But 'renewed shall be the blade that was broken.' I have a strong sentiment that in my lifetime that blade—the Ark—will indeed be renewed. I have a strong sentiment that the final redemption of the Jewish people is not far distant."

He stopped short and continued in a dry reflective tone, "I don't know why the redemption of my people has taken such a hold on my life. But it has."

Reuven soon plunged back into his new obsession. He told me how the third-century anti-Christian Roman emperor Julian the Apostate had planned to help the Jews rebuild the Jerusalem Temple but as soon as the work commenced the workers were frightened away because great balls of fire gushed out of the ruins. This was some sort of proof, thought Reuven, that in the third century the Ark was still there.

He told me about the destructive, murderous power of the Ark as it is described so graphically in the Bible. He told me about Templar knights who are known to have thoroughly excavated beneath Temple Mount during the Crusades and according to some unsubstantiated rumors taken the ancient treasures of the Jews back to the Languedoc.

With increased intensity he went on to describe more recent secret excavations to locate the Temple treasures. He told me about an eccentric Finnish scholar and poet, Valter Juvelius, who had organized a covert dig on the Temple Mount in 1910–11. Juvelius claimed to have discovered a secret bible code in a library in Istanbul, then the capital of the Ottoman empire, indicating where the Temple treasure, including the Ark, lay hidden. He raised funds for an expedition and persuaded a captain in the Grenadier Guards, one Montague Parker, the thirty-year-old son of the Earl of Morley, to lead it.

At Juvelius's insistence, the team was accompanied by a Danish clairvoyant who directed their labors. One night, in April 1911, under cover of darkness, having first bribed the governor of Jerusalem, Azmi Bey, Parker and his team, disguised as local Arabs, climbed into the compound and started digging directly under the cupola of the Dome of the Rock itself, the holiest place on earth.

The sounds reached the ears of a Muslim attendant and the alarm was raised. Violent riots flared up throughout the city and Parker and his team beat a hasty retreat to their expedition yacht moored off the coast near the port town of Jaffa. When they got back to London the headlines of the *London Illustrated News* blazed: "Have Englishmen discovered the Ark of the Covenant?"

Whether the discovery of the Ark would indeed bring about peace between Israel and the Muslim world I had no idea. In 1992 the political situation throughout the Middle East was far worse than it had ever been. The First Gulf War had been fought a year before and Jerusalemites were still recovering from the fear of attack from Iraqi scud missiles tipped with bio-logical or chemical warheads. Reuven spoke of this a lot. He was terrified of what might happen to the Jewish people in the future. He thought another holocaust was entirely possible. I often tried to reassure him that this was not really very likely, but he wouldn't listen. It was this fear and his dread of extreme Islamism that drove him.

In January 1991, just before the scuds started falling on Israel, I had been to see my old friend Lola Singer. I had first met her when I was working in Jerusalem for the British Voluntary Service Overseas in 1963 (it was that year in Israel that had, in fact, originally made me decide to study Hebrew at Oxford a year later). While doing VSO I was assigned to an institution for handicapped children where Lola was a social worker. Some of the children were the offspring of women who had been the subjects of sterility experiments in the concentration camps. They were all grotesquely deformed. Once a week for a year I went with Lola to visit the parents of the various children in different parts of Israel.

It was through endless conversations with Lola and the kids' parents that I began to understand something of the tragedy of recent Jewish history. Lola's own story was dreadful enough. A Polish Jewess from Radom, Lola had lost most of her family members during the Holocaust: they were gassed at Auschwitz. In 1939, before the war, she was a beautiful and talented young woman, studying to be a doctor. For a Jew to be admitted to a medical faculty in Poland in the years before the Second World War was virtually impossible. The entrance exams she wrote were literally faultless. They *had* to admit her. She was a young genius. After the German invasion, Lola's world fell apart. Her young husband, kicked out of Germany as a Jew, was shot by the Russians as a German. She managed to escape from Poland via Russia and arrived in Jerusalem in 1943.

The day I visited her she was all alone in her small apartment. Like many Jerusalemites she was afraid that Saddam Hussein would launch poisoned gas missiles against the city. Now an old woman, she was standing on a chair trying to tape plastic sheets to the window in the vain hope of making them impervious to gas attack. Of all the people I knew, she was the last one upon whom I would have wished this futile activity.

As I helped her down from the chair, she said between clenched teeth, "They gassed my mother and my father, they gassed my aunts and uncles, and cousins. They gassed my friends from school. They gassed my childhood sweetheart from next door. But you know, they are not, they are *not* going to gas me."

She slumped into a chair and burst into tears. I finished taping up the plastic sheeting. There were places where it would not stick on the window frame and you could feel the draft coming straight through. This protection would not keep out a medium-strength breeze let alone a poison gas attack.

By the time I went to Oxford I knew a great deal more about Jewish suffering than most gentiles and like all sane people I wanted to see an end to it. Like Reuven I also passionately wished to see Jews and Arabs reconciled. Maybe, I thought, a crazy idea like Reuven's was worth considering. Even a lavishly funded worldwide search for the Ark would cost less than even a couple of American smart missiles.

Reuven left at about two o'clock. I stayed up for another couple of hours staring into the embers of the olive-wood fire, dreaming about my friend's quest. When, finally, I went to bed I couldn't sleep. The whole house stank of paraffin. To get some fresh air I pulled on my old brown Arab *jalabiyyeh* and went on to the roof terrace of my house.

Jerusalem was bathed in cold white moonlight. Looking toward the Temple Mount, I could see the great golden cupola of the Dome of the Rock shimmering in the pale light. On this night, the city was breathlessly beautiful. In the Talmud it is written, "God gave ten measures of beauty to the world: nine measures he gave to Jerusalem and one only for all the rest of creation." It was here that the Temple had once stood. The rocky outcrop over which the golden cupola of the Dome of the Rock had been constructed once formed part of the Holy of Holies where, according to Jewish mythology, King Solomon had placed the Ark.

It seemed to me that the stories that surrounded the Ark were the stuff of fairy tales. In much of Jewish tradition there was something ineffably improbable about the Ark. The texts maintained that when the Ark was brought into the Temple by Solomon, the very wood and gold with which it was made came alive and formed trees that yielded abundant harvests of fruit. The Ark breathed life into everything. It was only when the faithless Israelite king Manasseh, hated by Jewish tradition, brought a foreign idol into the Temple that the miraculous trees dried up and the fruit withered on the branch.

This was strange, I thought, as I gazed out at the night. The Ark at some level was the secret weapon of the ancient Israelites. It meted out death, yet it breathed life into everything. These properties seemed to carry a powerful mystical message. Reuven had explained that for the Kabbalists this dualism expressed different and opposite forces acting in the Universe. When the two properties of the Ark were finally in harmony, the Messianic era would arrive. Whatever the Ark expressed symbolically, it was pretty extraordinary. But had it ever been a real, objective *thing* or was it just a powerfully symbolic multilayered, multitasking myth?

I stayed on the roof for a long time, huddled in my rough woollen cloak, gazing at the sleeping city.

But what, I asked myself, if the Ark were more than just an imagined, mythical construct—the legend of a visible little home for an invisible big God?

Some had said that the Ark was still buried in a secret passage beneath the Dome. Others had claimed it might have been secreted away to the Judean Hills, which I could see all around me on the distant horizon; or farther still to the

Arabian Desert; alternatively, in the murky depths of the Kinneret.

I had even heard rumors from starving refugees when I had been in Ethiopia a few years before at the time of the great famine, that the Ark had been taken to Africa by the first Ethiopian emperor, Menelik. And I had heard about a strange Ark-like object when I was in southern Africa. As I thought of where the Ark might be, I could feel a growing, irrational excitement course through my veins.

The words of Kipling that I had loved as a boy came into my mind. "Something hidden. Go and find it. Go and look behind the ranges—something lost behind the ranges. Lost and waiting for you. Go!"

But had the Ark ever really existed? Was there anything hidden? Anything to look for? I had my doubts.

My mind turned to Reuven. Sometimes when I looked at him I could sense an awareness of things that few people had. His eyes, which had been trained to discern the slightest flaw in gems, seemed to see farther and with greater clarity than normal eyes. However, I wondered if he was as capable of seeing flaws in arguments as he was of seeing flaws in gems.

I could see that if his quest ever delivered this enigmatic object, as an actual object, in some physical manifestation, its discovery would achieve more than a thousand unread monographs.

But was there any earthly way in which I could help him? Could I help him change the world? Did I want to?

3

PROTOCOLS
OF THE PRIESTS

The sirens howled all night. Groggily I faced a new Jerusalem day and realized that I had a growing obsession. Reuven's infatuation with the Ark had now taken over my dream time as well as a lot of my waking hours. It seemed absurd but I couldn't get it out of my mind.

When he had come round to my place a week before, Reuven had asked me to provide him with a scholarly reading list and this day would be spent achieving that goal.

It was the day when the scales fell from eyes and I saw the Ark for what it was.

I had made an appointment to see a distinguished academic in the field of ancient Semitic studies: Chaim Rabin, professor of Hebrew at the Hebrew University in Jerusalem. Many years before, Rabin had taught at Oxford, where I had studied. His successor, David Patterson, who had been my teacher, had often urged me to look him up. To ask Rabin's help in compiling a bibliography was a perfect excuse finally to make his acquaintance. He was a quite outstanding scholar even though by now he was getting on in age and I had heard that his mind was beginning to wander from time to time.

I walked from the Old City across town to the modern quarter of Rehavia and found the old scholar waiting for me in his neighborhood café. Rabin was a balding little man with bushy eyebrows, keen probing eyes, and an infectious smile. As we sat drinking a lemon tea in its silver-rimmed glass, I explained the background to my visit, without saying anything about Reuven. I wanted hard facts about the Ark from a wise, unbiased source.

"Is there any chance at all," I asked, weighing my words carefully, "that the treasures of the Temple of Jerusalem and Ark of the Covenant will ever be found?" I grinned at him in what I hoped was a disarming way.

Frowning uncertainly, he scratched his forehead. "Oh, not *another* treasure seeker! Don't tell me that Patterson has sent me a *treasure*-seeker!" He spoke English with a pronounced German accent, which failed to make his tone any more agreeable.

I was embarrassed and confused by this little barb and muttered that I had a sort of marginal interest in the topic and wanted some help in preparing a short bibliography. Briefly, Rabin looked the picture of contrition.

"Yes, well, I am sorry. It's just that there's been so much talk recently about the Temple treasure and quite a few odd characters have beaten their way to my door to pick my brains and waste my time. It's quite true—they *waste* my time! A lot of individuals and institutions are looking for the Ark. Some are charlatans and some are downright sinister! There's a rather overly enthusiastic American gentleman by the name of Mr.

Wyatt from Tennessee who claimed not long ago to have actually found the Ark in a cave just outside the city walls. No proof, of course. And Wyatt is not the only enthusiast of this kind."

"But why are people so *fascinated* by it?"

What Rabin told me opened a small window into the past and changed my view of the Ark forever.

He thought the reason people were interested in it had something to do with its *unmythical* nature. It was a simple object with strange properties. It had great symbolic importance both for Rabbinic Judaism and for Kabbalists, but it had started off as a *real* object.

There were so many improbable stories about the powers of the Ark in the Bible that I had failed to perceive it as a truly historical artifact. The historicity of the Ark was substantiated, he said, in the most factual biblical chronicles. If it still existed, I did not know; but on the basis of what Rabin, one of the greatest scholars in the world in this field had to say, there was little doubt that it had existed *once*.

In addition Rabin explained that the Ark still exercised an enormous amount of power. He told me, in the hushed tones of someone who had difficulty believing what he was saying, of an extremist Jewish organization called Ateret Cohanim (the Crown of the Priests), which was planning the reconstruction of the Jewish Temple. They believed that the world was in End Time: the period before the coming of the Messiah. Restoring worship in the Temple after a gap of 2,000 years would further accelerate the coming of the Messiah.

Rabin told me that some of the rabbis of Ateret Cohanim believed that the Ark still existed and had been searching for it behind the Western Wall in the Old City. After Israel's fateful victory over the Arab states in 1967, this area of the Wall came under Jewish jurisdiction for the first time since the destruction of Jerusalem by the Romans in AD 70, and a small prayer hall was soon constructed in a tunnel to the left of the Wall. From there, members of Ateret Cohanim and their sympathizers secretly excavated under the Temple Mount at night and penetrated into a system of ancient tunnels that they considered to date from the First Temple. There had even been rumors that the Ark had actually been discovered.

"If ever they *do* find the Ark," said Rabin, "the Temple will be rebuilt. Without a doubt. If the Temple is rebuilt, the Dome of the Rock, you understand, will have to go. You see it is *rather* in the way. The Temple would be rebuilt on its foundations. On its smoldering ruins. As it is Islam's third most sacred site, it would be a reasonably efficient recipe, I believe, for the next world war. They want to eject Islam from the site: a couple of attempts by Jewish zealots to blow it up have been foiled. The next time we may not be so lucky."

Rabin looked at me, one bushy eyebrow raised, his lips pursed in disapproval.

"You seem almost to be implying that finding the Ark is a possibility," I said.

"Perhaps I am. Well, *you* know, theoretically," he murmured, smiling in a conspiratorial way. "As you know, serious scholars don't pay much attention to it. It is rather a topic for a certain kind of adventurer. Along the lines of the film, that popular American confection, *Raiders of the Lost Ark*." Again he pursed his lips.

"But perhaps, briefly, we could put our scholarly reservations to one side and for a moment enjoy a bit of speculation." He sat back in his chair and smiled, not unkindly.

Rabin's main argument for the possible continued existence of the Ark was that it would never have been allowed to fall into enemy hands. The priests would have removed it long before a besieging army was knocking at the gates of Jerusalem. Both in 587 BC, when the Babylonians took Jerusalem, and in AD 70, when the Romans destroyed the city, there was adequate warning before the city eventually fell.

"In those days," he said, "armies traveled slowly and noisily. And in any case, before the Roman attack there were horrifying warnings and portents: the most prescient being that a sword-shaped star hung over the Temple, which it did in a way in the form of a Roman sword—the *gladius*."

"So you think it would have been taken?"

"Yes, no doubt. They would never have just left it in the Temple to be defiled by the enemy."

"Who do you think could have removed it?"

"Certainly priests. A possible line would be to follow the trace of the priests. If they left a trace."

Rabin took a sip of his tea and looked out onto the busy street. He reflected for a moment and said, "It could be that the prophet Jeremiah, who was of a priestly family, had it taken out just before the Babylonians came, as later Jewish tradition suggests. After Jerusalem fell to the Babylonians in 587," he continued, raising his hand to attract the waiter, "we hear nothing more of the Ark. If it was hidden somewhere, it was probably hidden just before the destruction of the city. Alternatively, possibly some time before. But probably not later."

Rabin seemed to pause for breath and briefly regarded his gnarled hands. Then, thoughtfully, he continued. "No *Jew* would ever have destroyed the Ark, and if the Egyptians or Babylonians or Romans had destroyed it or stolen it or taken it away, there would be a record of it. They would have boasted about it. For the Jews it would have been the greatest possible national disaster—a calamity even greater than the destruction of the Temple—and they would have chronicled it and would still be writing about it and lamenting it! How we Jews love to lament! We have a whole three-week period of lamentation from the 17th of Tammuz to the 9th of Av—but there are plenty of other days of lamentation throughout the year. However, we have no festival of lamentation for the Ark. Instead, history provides us with total silence."

I felt embarrassed about asking the next question. How could anyone really have any idea at all where it was after so much time? But I asked it anyway.

"Mmm ..." he replied, smiling enigmatically and rubbing his hands together. "Somewhere in the Middle East or Africa, I suppose. There is some outside chance it was taken to Egypt in the ninth century BC by a certain Pharaoh who is called Shishak in the Bible. Or it could have been taken later. And if it were hidden somewhere in Egypt there is some chance it might have survived because of the hot, dry conditions. However, if you want further precision there are a number of serious possibilities. Even one or two, well, let us call them clues."

In spite of himself, I could see that Rabin was enjoying the conversation. Over my protests, he paid for our tea, took my elbow in a firm grip, and ushered me across the bustling Rehavia street to the apartment where he lived.

In his book-lined study, he took out a dusty volume from a shabby wooden cupboard. "You know the Hebrew word for cupboard?"

"Of course," I said. "*Aron.*"

"That's right. *Aron* means chest or cupboard, anything that stores things. It is a very simple word, nothing very fancy or spiritual about it. It is the same word we use for the Ark—*aron habrit*—Chest of the Covenant. In English, 'Ark'—which ultimately comes from the Latin *arca*—sounds, how would one say it, rather romantic or mysterious, does it not? In Hebrew it's just a good old word for 'chest' or, even more prosaically, 'box.'"

"Could it have any other meaning?" I asked. "Is it connected with cognate words in other Semitic languages?" As I asked the question, the word *ngoma* flitted briefly through my mind but I dismissed it instantly. There was no connection between Semitic languages and Bantu languages that I knew of.

"The cognate word means coffin in Phoenician and second millennium Akkadian, and could be a wooden container in first millennium Akkadian if I remember correctly."

"The meaning 'coffin' seems a long way from the dwelling place of the living God," I remarked. "On the face of it, it even seems a little absurd."

"I don't know," he said, wrinkling his nose, in the charming way he had. "No, I think we can be fairly sure that in the classical Hebrew of the Jewish Scriptures the word means what it appears to mean, which is to say, well, yes, something like coffin—it does *actually* and *literally* mean coffin once or twice in the Bible—but more generally box or chest. Now where could that good old box be? What clues do we have?" he asked with a boyish smile.

He told me that in the writing of the Jewish sages and even in the Bible there were a number of clues as to the Ark's whereabouts. In early rabbinic works, for instance, it was thought that King Josiah, who came to the throne of Israel in around 639 BC—the precise date is debatable—hid it somewhere in the Temple under the instructions of the prophetess Huldah. This was probably the standard Jewish belief over time. The sages wrote that the Ark was hidden "in its place." This presumably meant somewhere in the Temple. Specifically it is sug-gested that it was buried under the floor of the part of the Temple where the wood used for sacrificial fires was stored.

"Putting aside political problems, is the Temple where you would search if *you* were looking for it?"

"If I were looking for it, I would always start with texts. That's what I always advise my students: *Go to the text*. There's more to be found in dusty old tomes than people imagine. In this case, I think, the text of the Dead Sea Scrolls could provide us with some enlightenment."

The story of the discovery of these remarkable documents started on a rugged Palestinian hillside in 1947, as the violent conflict between Jews and Arabs in Palestine grew out of control and the British, who had governed Palestine for the previous twenty years, were preparing to pack their bags for good. A lean, unkempt Bedouin goatherd was searching the rocky hills along the Dead Sea for a lost goat. He threw a stone into a cave. Instead of the bleating of a frightened animal, he heard the unmistakable sound of breaking pottery.

Further investigation revealed a number of terracotta jars filled with manuscripts. Seven of these manuscripts were sold to a Jerusalem antique dealer and cobbler called Kando, who in turn—and at some profit—sold them to clients in the Holy City: three to a scholar at the Hebrew University and four to the metropolitan of the Orthodox monastery of St. Mark.

Between 1947 and 1956, a total of more than 800 manuscripts or parts of manuscripts were found in eleven caves.

Once the press found out about them, the scrolls became a sensation. What would they reveal about the origins of Christianity, the person of Jesus and the authenticity of the Bible? Scholars soon established a collective view that the Jewish Essene sect, which lived in this desolate place but about which very little was known, had hidden the scrolls as the Roman army was advancing toward them in search of Jews involved in the First Jewish Revolt (AD 66–70) against the Empire.

One of the most remarkable finds was the Copper Scroll. Discovered in the third of the Qumran caves to yield its treasures, this scroll records a list of sixty-four underground hiding places of valuable items: gold, silver, aromatics like frankincense and myrrh, and manuscripts. Initially a number of scholars refused to believe that this list of lost treasure was genuine. Some thought it was no more than a kind of literary collection of lost-treasure stories. I asked Rabin about it.

He shrugged. "The Copper Scroll was a bit of an embarrassment. Look at this." He reached for a file in the bookcase behind him and took out a yellowing clipping. "This is what the *New York Times* wrote when the scroll was first published: 'It sounds like something that might have been written in blood in the dark of the moon by a character in *Treasure Island*.'" Rabin laughed. "But just because it was embarrassing does not mean it was not *true*. Of course it was not prudent to advertise the scroll too much—we had to avoid a gold rush. But a lot of what was said at the time by the scholars involved—Milik, Mowinckel, Silberman, even de Vaux—was off the mark. I think I can say that I was successful in putting them right," he murmured with mild, scholarly satisfaction. "*Their* idea was that this was a kind of *joke* perpetrated by a semiliterate scribe—a crank. Now, a sort of hoax about a fabulous but nonexistent Temple treasure clumsily scratched on a copper plate by a dirt-poor ascetic in a filthy goat-ridden cave in the desert would have been potentially amusing, would it not? But I fear my Israelite ancestors were not noted for their sense of humor! No?

"No, I believe that the Copper Scroll is what it appears to be—a verbatim protocol of the priests' evidence. It is a priestly document from Jerusalem, I am sure of it. A listing of the secret hiding places of the Temple treasure. That's all it is—a list—there is no colorful prose, not even any verbs. It is dry as a bone! Problem is," he continued, "that the descriptions of the hiding places are meaningless. Take these clues for instance."

He looked up a passage in the book he had taken down from his shelves and started to read. "One of the hoards consisting of sixty-five bars of gold was hidden in 'the cavity of the Old House of Tribute in the Platform of the Chain.'"

He looked at me with a quizzical expression on his face.

"And how about this? This pile of goodies is listed as being 'in the gutter which is in the bottom of the water tank.' Or this treasure trove carefully concealed 'in the Second Enclosure, in the underground passage that looks east.' Or this priceless collection 'in the water conduit of the northern reservoir.' I ask you! Jerusalem postmen are noted for their skill at tracking down addresses written in all the languages and scripts of the world," he said, chuckling, "but with addresses like this, even they would have to give up! For our generation they are quite meaningless. As for the specific treasure of the sanctuary, I fear the information is no less vague."

"Do you think that these phrases could be codes?"

"It has occurred to me. But, on balance, my sense of the document is that it is prosaically what it seems to be. A list of addresses that sadly, are no longer meaningful."

Again, he read from the book. "'In the desolation of the Valley of Achur, in the opening under the ascent, which is a mountain facing eastward, covered by forty placed boulders, here is a tabernacle and all the golden fixtures.' This may well refer to the Ark," he added, rubbing his chin with unnecessary vigor.

I had a sudden flashback to the night I spent walking over to the cave of Dumghe with my police bodyguard, Tagaruze: Dumghe was a mountain facing eastward and it was indeed covered with great round boulders. I had been told that the *ngoma lungundu* was hidden beneath it. Was it possible that there was a connection?

"The valley of Achur?" I interrupted. "Does that resonate with you at all? Does Achur mean anything? Do you have any idea where it is?"

"No, unfortunately not," he replied. "The anonymous author of the Copper Scroll as you may realize gave no map references. It has been posited that it refers to an area around Mount Nebo in Jordan. This is what the apocryphal book of Maccabees says. He took a book down from the shelves and read aloud.

The prophet [Jeremiah], being warned of God, commanded the taber-
nacle and the Ark to go with him, as he went forth into the mountain,

where Moses climbed up [Mount Nebo], and saw the heritage of God.
And when Jeremy came thither, he found a hollow cave, wherein he laid
the tabernacle, and the Ark, and the altar of incense, and so stopped the
door. And some of those that followed him came to mark the way, but
they could not find it. Which when Jeremy perceived, he blamed them,
saying, as for that place, it shall be unknown until the time that God
gather His people again together, and receive them unto mercy.

"Another thing," he said, "is that there are a number of indications that there may have been two or more Arks. The first Ark was built to house the two tablets of the law that had been engraved by 'the finger of God.' When the people of Israel started worshiping the golden calf rather than the One God, Moses broke the tablets and was commanded to create a new set himself with the identical text. Jewish tradition suggests that there was one Ark intended to house the broken tablets of the Law and another for the tablets carved by Moses."

Rabin smiled at me in a boyish way, and for a second I could see the Berlin schoolboy of decades before.

"The sages of blessed memory drew a moral from the idea that even the old broken tablets had a place of honor in the Ark—the moral was that even an old scholar like me who has forgotten most of his learning still deserves respect. And he still deserves his *rest*."

The old man, who suddenly looked very frail, ushered me to the door and explained that it was time for his afternoon sleep. He faltered as we reached the entrance to his study and his face seemed to go blank. Gathering himself he murmured gently, "My mother made me learn a long poem in English when I was a little boy. Let's see if I can remember some of it:

Maybe 'tis true that in a far-off land
The Ark of God in exile dwelleth still,
It resteth ever with the pure of hand,
Who do his will.

He recited it in the fluting voice of a prepubescent boy. Smiling, he let me out.

Again the Jerusalem sirens were letting the world know that all was not well in the City of Peace. Wondering if the "pure of hand" were still guarding the Ark in some remote corner of the world I walked back to the Old City with a good deal on my mind.

A couple of days later I arranged to meet Reuven at Finks' Bar, on the corner of King George and Histadrut Streets in western Jerusalem. There were troops everywhere and the city was tense.

True to his word, Rabin had sent me through the mail a bibliography with several dozen entries. He also sent me a brief and courteous letter apologizing for breaking off before we had really finished our conversation. He wanted to define his thoughts more clearly.

When I was a boy in Germany, [he wrote] all those years ago, during the Weimar Republic, who would have imagined that the Dead Sea Scrolls would be discovered? The scrolls, written on parchment, are much more fragile, after all, than gold or silver objects or even the Ark made of shittim wood. And if they were rediscovered in the caves of Qumran after two thousand years, why not the Ark and the Temple treasure!

Reuven read the letter, nodding in agreement. I told him that Rabin had said that the Copper Scroll seemed to offer the best way forward if it were ever possible to decode the clues. As I ordered a whisky for both of us, he skimmed through the bibliography and brought me up to date on recent searches for the Ark. He had been making enquiries for the previous few weeks.

As Rabin had suggested, a lot of people were after it.

There was a young American eccentric who hung around the Petra Hotel just inside the Jaffa Gate. He drank a lot of vodka and had more girlfriends than he could handle, but he had a degree in Semitic languages from Stanford and a good mind. He had made friends with an Arab family who owned a house not far from the Temple Mount and had allegedly been burrowing enthusiastically in their courtyard. Reuven said there were others like him and distractedly gave me an account of recent claims.

He spoke at length about three Americans who had been hot on the trail of the Ark. There was the Ron Wyatt from Tennessee that Rabin had mentioned who had actually claimed to have found the Ark in a cave near Jerusalem. He told me of a research physicist in the Radio Physics Laboratory of SRI International in Menlo Park, California—who had flown over the Temple Mount to x-ray its foundations with caesium-beam magnetometers but had failed to locate the Ark. And there was a Tom Crotser, who had announced in 1981 that he had unearthed the Ark near Mount Nebo in Jordan. Photographs had been taken but only one had been released to the public and that appeared to show a recent-looking brass chest with a decidedly modern-looking nail sticking out of it.

Finks' was full of writers, poets, and some quite well-known politicians. As usual it was dimly lit. All of the seven tables were taken—people were eating goulash soup or *tafelspitz* with *khren*—horseradish and beetroot sauce—Austro-Hungarian house specialities pandering to the diaspora traditions and nostalgia for elsewhere that permeates every aspect of Israeli life.

A dark-suited politician came over to our table and in a low voice told us that there had been some alarming discussions of opening up an entrance under the Temple Mount. The *Shin Bet*—Israel's internal security service—was studying likely Muslim reactions. The politician explained: "There were some un-authorized excavations done by Ateret Cohanim a year or so back looking for the Ark, which caused a good deal of resentment on the part of the Muslim population. In October 1991, a group called the Temple Mount Faithful marched on the compound carrying provocative banners. It was rumored that they were planning to lay the foundation stones for a new Temple. As you know, twenty-two Palestinians were killed in the ensuing riots. If any major excavation was done down there now, blood would be spilt throughout the Muslim world from Casablanca to Karachi! And Jews would not be spared."

A few minutes later, my oldest Jerusalem friend, Shula Eisner, who worked with the mayor of Jerusalem, Teddy Kollek, sashayed into the bar with the mayor and a group of overdressed American guests of the city. Shula came over for a moment. I had told her about Reuven and his interest in the Ark, and I took this opportunity to introduce them. As she was leaving, I asked her if the municipality had been involved in closing down the Temple Mount excavations. And whether they were involved in discussions to open them up again.

"Guys," she said, laying on her Bronx accent, "don't even ask the question! Jerusalem is quiet at the moment. Let's keep it that way. Anything to do with Temple Mount is a tinderbox! As for the Ark of the Covenant—just leave the poor old thing in peace!" and she floated off to join Kollek and his guests.

The bar emptied, and around midnight we made our way out onto King George Street. Just before we made our separate ways, Reuven asked, "Do you have any spare time?"

"I suppose I could have," I replied grudgingly.

Reuven's driver was waiting for him on King George Street just a few yards from Finks'. When we got to the car, Reuven opened the door and pushed me in. I got out at Jaffa Gate. Reuven wished me goodnight in a preoccupied sort of way and promised he would soon be in touch.

The streets were still full of soldiers. There seemed to be some kind of security alert and I did not feel at ease walking through the dark alleys of the Old City, even though there were checkpoints at just about every corner. I was glad when I got home.

A fresh desert breeze wafted in from the Judean hills as I stood on my roof terrace looking over toward the Dome of the Rock. I could not look at the Temple Mount without thinking of the Ark. I decided to do some reading myself.

For the next couple of weeks I buried myself in the Judaica Reading Room at the Hebrew University and National Library in Jerusalem. The shelves were full of dusty, disintegrating tomes, many of which had been gathered after the Second World War from destroyed Jewish libraries and seminaries throughout Europe. The old library and synagogue stamps from Pressburg, Lodz, and Odessa spoke of hundreds of years of destroyed intellectual endeavor. Many of the Library readers were black-coated orthodox Jews poring over rare rabbinic treatises. Pale-skinned young men with close-cropped hair and thick glasses, they swayed backward and forward as they read.

After my weeks in the library, I passed several days seeing no one and barely leaving the house. This new interest of mine was becoming an obsession and I spent hours poring over my notes trying to make some sense of the Ark. The telephone rang, I did not answer.

As they had not seen me for a while, my Arab friends from the *suq* assumed I was ill and brought me *hubiz*—flat Arab bread—glistening black olives, and hard-boiled eggs. I drank their *qahehweh*, thick muddy Arab coffee, and pondered the mystery of the Ark.

Over the previous years I had visited Jewish communities throughout the world. I recalled an evening I had spent with the chief rabbi of Djerba, an island off the coast of Tunisia. It was around the time of Passover. The rabbi invited me to dinner in a small whitewashed house in the heart of the ancient Jewish quarter called Hara Seghirah. Over dinner the conversation turned to the destruction of the Temple.

He described in graphic detail the sack of Jerusalem, the ruination of the Holy of Holies, the tramp of jackboots over the marble paving stones of the dwelling of the Most High. And as he described this national disaster, he wept. The tears flowed down his haggard cheeks and onto his straggly white beard.

Rabin, I thought, was right about one thing. If the Ark had been destroyed either by the Babylonians or by the Romans, Jews would indeed still be lamenting it.

And the idea that Jews would have done anything and every-thing to save precious pieces of their heritage was also confirmed by what I learned in Djerba. The venerable rabbi told me that a group of priests had fled to the North African coast after the destruction of Jerusalem by the Babylonians, founding the Djerba community and bringing with them a door and a stone rescued from the Holy of Holies. The stone can be seen to this day. There was no tradition of the Ark going to Djerba, but priests had taken what they could salvage of their spiritual heritage.

"*Follow the priests,*" Rabin had said.

It was February 1993 and Jerusalem was beginning to enjoy an early spring. I sat one morning in my small courtyard, under the lemon tree, surrounded by pots of cyclamen and small-leafed basil and tried to summarize in my mind what was historically known about the Ark up until its disappearance from King Solomon's Temple in Jerusalem.

Once the Israelites under Moses's command had escaped slavery under Pharaoh and crossed the Red Sea, they made their way into the Sinai Desert. On the first new moon after their escape they camped in front of Mount Sinai. God commanded Moses to climb the mountain to receive the Law.

Having received the Law in the form of the Ten Command-ments engraved upon stone tablets "by the finger of God," he descended the mountain to discover that the Israelites were worshiping a statue of a golden calf. In fury, Moses smashed the tablets, and was commanded by God to create a new identical set himself.

The Ten Commandments formed an essential part of the ongoing agreement, or covenant, between God and the Israelites. Moses was given instructions by God to build the Ark of this covenant, in which the stone tablets incorporating the covenant would be placed.

There are two quite different biblical descriptions of the construction of the Ark.

The first description has the Ark constructed by Bezalel, the artist, upon the orders of Moses. The box was covered all over with the purest gold. Its lid (the *kapporet*) known in English as the "mercy seat," was surrounded with a rim of gold. On its lid were golden cherubim whose outstretched wings formed an arch above the lid. There were two gold rings on each side through which carrying poles could be inserted.

The second version of the construction of the Ark is simpler. According to the book of Deuteronomy, it was Moses himself who made the Ark, and the Ark was a totally different kind of object. It was just a regular wooden container. There is no mention of nails, or of joints, or of glue. So perhaps it was simply a kind of recipient hollowed out of the trunk of a tree with a knife or chisel.

The Ark, in both forms, was made of acacia wood—*shittim* wood in Hebrew. In many arid zones in Africa, the acacia is the archetypal tree. In the Sinai desert—the land bridge between Africa and Asia—the acacia species rules supreme. It would have been just about the only building material available in the wilderness.

The wood of the acacia is exceptionally hard, very heavy, very dense, and will last for a long time. In desert conditions, it would not perish. In Egypt there are acacia panels that have survived for well over 3,000 years.

Under the right conditions the Ark could virtually last forever.

The Ark was 2.5 cubits long, 1.5 cubits wide, and 1.5 cubits high, which translates as about two feet wide, two feet tall, and just under three feet long.

It was about the size of a large suitcase.

It was easily transportable, easy to hide.

But what was it for? The Ark's first purpose was to serve as a receptacle for the stone tablets. The second was to serve as the throne of God, who was visualized as sitting just above the outstretched wings of the cherubim. The lower part of the Ark was seen as the footstool of God.

In whichever form the Ark was made, it was placed in a tent shrine called the Tabernacle. Soon after, Aaron, Moses's brother, brought sacrifices for the Lord. He prepared his sacrifices according to the letter of the law, but the sacrifices were consumed by a fire, but not by a fire that had been prepared by *him*.

The fire just happened.

And later his sons Avihu and Nadav made *improper* offerings *not* done according to the letter of the law. They brought the wrong sort of fire before the Ark, and its fire killed them.

The fire went out of the Ark.

The Ark had something of the quality of a flame thrower. It could and did kill.

"Two fiery jets issued from between the cherubim above the Ark," goes the account in the Jewish legendary literature called the Midrash, "burning up snakes, scorpions, and thorns in its path and destroying Israel's enemies."

The Rabbinic sages called this the fire of God.

Like a secret missile covered with camouflage sheets on its military transporter, the Ark was always covered with blue cloth and animal skins. Even the priests were not allowed to look at it.

In the Bible there is a prayer of great antiquity that seems like a prayer you'd say over a weapon.

> *When the Ark traveled, Moses said: "Arise! Scatter your enemies, and let those who hate you flee from in front of you." And when the Ark rested, he would say, "Return ..."*

In every Hebrew Torah scroll these two menacing verses are enclosed by two letters—the letter *nun*—the Hebrew N—written upside down on either side. What does it mean? The rabbis explained that this unique code signified that the verses were not in their proper place.

They said that the verses celebrating the military nature of the Ark constituted a separate book of the Bible.

The Ark was carried on its poles in front of the advancing army by the priests. During the conquest of Canaan it was the Ark that caused the waters of the River Jordan to open up, allowing the Israelites to cross over safely. It was the Ark, carried as part of a military band behind the seven priestly trumpeters as they famously marched around the walls of Jericho, that caused the impregnable double-walled fortifications of the city to collapse.

As the Israelites streamed into Canaan, the Ark was placed first in Gilgal and then in Shiloh, twelve miles north of Jerusalem. Here it stayed for 300–400 years, occasionally being taken out at times of war. Once it fell into the hands of the enemy and was placed in the temple of the Philistine god Dagon in Ashdod. The Ark soon finished off Dagon, whose statue was discovered in bits on the floor.

The Philistine population was not spared either. The people were afflicted with bleeding hemorrhoids and the land was cursed with an infestation of mice.

The Ark then spent twenty years in Kiryat Yearim, a hill village close to Jerusalem, until King David decided to take it to his new capital. He built a special cart, put the Ark in it, and started off, accompanied by a great crowd of people singing and rejoicing. Then the cart hit a rut in the road. For a moment it looked as if the Ark would fall to the ground. There was no priest standing by to steady it, so a man named Uzzah reached out his hand.

The Ark blasted him to death.

The rejoicing stopped and the Ark was deposited in the nearby house of one Obed-Edom the Gittite. Three months later King David came back to fetch it. This time he did things better. Before setting off for Jerusalem, the king made special sacrifices and then supposedly danced naked before the Ark. He was also carrying an *ephod*—a mysterious and undecipherable object never satisfactorily explained—which had also been created in the Sinai at the same time as the Ark.

After a period of peace, King David observed to the prophet Nathan that while he, David, was living in a fine house of cedar, the poor old Ark was still languishing in the tabernacle tent. Should something not be done about it? The Ark was not keen to move and let it be known that it would stay where it was for the time being, thank you very much. It would not be until the time of King Solomon, the future king, that the Ark would move into a proper house—the magnificent new Temple of Jerusalem—which would be built to house it.

* * *

By now, I believed, as Rabin did, that the Ark once *existed*. The historical account surrounding it was too complex and nuanced for the whole thing to have simply been made up. What it actually *was* was another thing altogether. The more I pondered its function, the less I understood it. In the wilderness of Sinai, Moses was attempting to transform his ex-slaves into a viable military force. Would these men have been emboldened as they advanced upon enemy lines by following a simple box or coffin carried on poles by the priests? Even if the box or coffin was construed as the dwelling place of the invisible God. It apparently had destructive powers too, but how these powers worked, if they can be credited, was anybody's guess.

Whatever its true function or meaning, it once existed. That being the case, it could theoretically be hidden somewhere. There were numerous clues in the ancient texts. Some of them suggested that the Ark was in Jerusalem, others that it had been taken far away from Jerusalem. Whoever hid it would certainly have been a priest. *But how would it be possible for anyone to follow the passage of priests two and a half thousand years later?*

The next morning I woke up to find strong sunlight pouring into my bedroom, revealing untidy piles of books and papers, unwashed clothes, empty bottles of wine and whisky, and copper trays covered with the debris of meals brought up from the *suq*. I had overslept.

On the other side of the small courtyard there was a metal door leading out onto the street. There was an electric bell mounted to one side of it. As I gazed blearily at the mess, the bell sounded, jolting me out of my morning reverie. I went out with a towel wrapped round my middle and saw my friend Shula. She had been giving some American guests of Teddy Kollek a tour of the Old City and had come to see me.

"What's all this business of the Ark of the Covenant?" she chided me. "I thought you were the sanest person in Jerusalem. Why don't you leave crazy stuff to the crazies? Teddy's not happy about it. We've got plenty of crazies in Jerusalem and we don't need any more. Get on with your translations of Hebrew poetry. Write your book on the Jews and Islam. Go back to London to see your girlfriend. But do me a personal favor. A *personal* favor. Leave the Ark alone!" She gave me a great hug and said that she would have to go back to join her group.

She was heading to the *kotel*—the Western Wall. I washed and dressed quickly and went with her some of the way through the Jewish Quarter and then we parted. I continued down through Dung Gate and struck out across the open land toward the seven golden onion-shaped cupolas of the Russian Orthodox Church of Mary Magdalene at Gethsemane, on the lower reaches of the Mount of Olives.

I knocked on the heavy wooden gate and waited in the shadow of the great wall, which protected the convent. After a while, the bolts were drawn and Luba, a short, stern-faced Palestinian convent servant I had known for many years, let me in.

We walked through the fragrant shade of the garden, heavy with the intoxicating scent of sun-warmed pine trees, to a little building among the copse that the nuns used to receive people from the outside world.

As Luba offered me some mint tea, she welcomed me: "*Marhabah! Ahlan! Ahlan wasahlan hawajah.* Welcome back sir! What can we do for you? Who would you like to see, *hawajah?*" she asked, using the honorific *hawajah* in a charming, teasing way.

I explained that I had ordered an icon from the nuns who made them and it should be ready for collection. She went off to fetch it.

There was a pile of papers and church magazines in Russian and English on the table next to where I was sitting. I picked up an old copy of the *Jerusalem Post*. There I found a short article on Ron Wyatt.

According to the *Post*, he first came to Israel in 1978. His plan, which struck me as being utterly absurd, was to go scuba diving in the Red Sea to look for Egyptian chariot parts, as a way of proving that Pharaoh's army really had been swallowed up and that the Biblical account of the exodus from Egypt was true.

He soon claimed to have discovered the original site of the Red Sea crossing, the original sites of the biblical cities of Sodom and Gomorrah, and the genuine original site of the crucifixion of Christ, which has never been satisfactorily located.

He first claimed to have discovered the Ark of the Covenant in about 1982 during secret excavations just outside the walls of the Old City. According to him, the Ark was hidden here before the arrival of the Babylonians in an underground chamber above which he located the original site of the crucifixion. No less.

He had a sizeable following in the United States, which included a number of powerful if gullible televangelists, and indeed there was a research institute in Tennessee dedicated to his findings.

As I finished the article, a handsome, longhaired Russian orthodox priest from New York, a friend of Shula's, whom I had met once or twice, wandered into the vestibule. We chatted for a while about people we knew in common in Jerusalem. As he was turning to go, I asked him, "Have you seen this article about Ron Wyatt?"

"You mean the guy who discovered the lost Ark?"

"That's the one."

"Yes," he laughed. "I've heard a lot about him. He found what he said was an 'earthquake crack' just below the site of what he claimed was the crucifixion, which extended down to the hiding place of the Ark. According to him, the actual blood of Jesus flowed down through this crack onto the Mercy Seat—the lid of the Ark. What Wyatt took this to mean was that the traditions of Old Testament animal sacrifice reached their most sublime point with the sacrifice of Jesus, whom he sees as the new High Priest. When the blood of Jesus dripped onto the Mercy Seat, the great and final act in the cult of sacrifice was consummated. It's a pretty gripping thought."

"Wonderful, but why didn't he reveal any evidence?"

"He claimed that the Israeli antiquities department had made secrecy a condition of his permit. So the access tunnel to the chamber was sealed with reinforced concrete. He refuses to say where it is situated and the Ark will remain where it is. The Israelis, he claims, want to keep it that way. Wyatt believes that more than a dozen people have died because they have since tried to locate the Ark! He has held back the documents, video, and photographs he alleges to have in his possession, but one day, he says, he will show them. He says traces of Christ's blood are clearly visible. Shula told me that the CIA guy in Jerusalem, who is famously dim, says the Israelis don't want the connection between the Ark and the crucifixion revealed as it would lead to the mass conversion of Jews to Christianity."

"Oh, dear. What I don't understand is how, without a shred of evidence, a story like this can possibly have the status of anything more than an old wives' tale?"

"Quite. But it sure keeps chins wagging in Jerusalem. Oh, I forgot the best bit. Wyatt claims to have had a DNA analysis done of Christ's blood, which proves he was born of a virgin! If he had no father I guess that means he had no Y-chromosome!"

The priest grinned irreverently, waved at me, and left, just as my old friend, Luba, returned with the icon. I gave her the amount that had been agreed, plus a few shekels for the work of the church.

"People have been talking about you, *Hawaja*," she scolded. "*Haram*. Poor fellow! They say you are working with the Jews. Is this true? Do the Jews not have friends enough already? I've heard them say you are looking for the Ark of the Covenant. Is this really so? How is the Ark going to help the Palestinians? Will it save us from the Jews? Or will the Jews use it against us? It was a dangerous thing—I read about it in the Bible—and people are scared of it. Both here and in my village I see many more people than you think. Some of them are violent men. Take my advice. Be careful!"

She took both my hands in hers and squeezed hard.

Before I walked back to the Old City I sat under the ancient cedars and gazed down at the Temple Mount, listening to the distant noises of the city and the nearby rustlings and crepitations of this most sacred garden of Gethsemane. Clearly Wyatt was one of the enthusiasts Rabin had warned me about. Jerusalem was full of cranks looking for the Ark in soil that had been raked over for thousands of years by Assyrians, Romans, Crusaders, and assorted modern investigators of varying degrees of seriousness. I was beginning to feel that Jerusalem was the least likely of places in which the Ark would turn up. I felt anyway that I could put Wyatt and Co. out of my mind. Luba's warning was more worrying.

A few weeks later I was walking in the Old City of Jerusalem carrying a supply of the world's best humus from Abu Shukri's famous establishment near the Via Dolorosa. To my surprise I saw Reuven rushing down the street toward me, his coat flapping wildly about him. Every vestige of his vaguely orthodox look had disappeared. He was dressed in a conventional navy blazer and a Hermes tie. This was not his orthodox uniform. His luxuriant beard had been transformed into a small, stiff affair, and he had shaved his moustache.

He looked scared. His suntanned face was red with exertion and he was breathing with difficulty.

"Quick," he said, looking over his shoulder. "Let's have a coffee, I have something urgent to tell you."

I led him to a small Arab café I sometimes used in the Muslim Quarter. It was lost in a maze of little alleys and had a second-floor room reached by a metal spiral staircase, which was hardly ever used except by young courting couples.

If Reuven was in sudden need of a secure refuge, this was the place.

I ordered two cardamom-flavored coffees and jerked my thumb in an upward movement toward the upper room. Reuven went ahead, breathing with some difficulty, and I followed. There was no one else there. It was a good place to talk. We sat on low, perfumed sofas upholstered in elaborate woven Damascus cloth. The coffee, served in small glass cups, arrived almost immediately.

"*Shukran*," I thanked the waiter, and asked him not to allow anyone up there while we were there. "What on earth is the matter?" I asked Reuven. "You look awful."

"So do you," he said. "Have you stopped eating or what?"

I explained that I had spent some time in solitary, scholarly confinement.

He smiled thinly and said, "You have been industrious, but *I've* been a fool."

"What do you mean?"

"You remember Anis, that dealer who sold me the Yemenite document about Muhammad?"

"Yes, I remember very well."

"When you told me it was a forgery I stopped the check. I gave him back the manuscript, of course, but he was not pleased. The problem is that I had already told him all about my mission. I was absolutely convinced that the document was genuine and really would change the religious and political situation in the Middle East. Of course I told him to keep quiet about it. At the time, Anis was quite sympathetic, or at least he seemed to be. As you know, he is a Muslim, but a rather unobservant one. We often used to have a whisky together in the American Colony Hotel bar. Since we had this financial disagreement he has turned against me, and I believe he has spread the word that I am trying to subvert Islam. With everything that's going on in Israel at the moment, I need that like a hole in the head."

He looked away for a moment.

"He's also apparently told some fundamentalist Muslim friends of his that I am looking for the Ark and that I am connected with Ateret Cohanim. The problem is that he has let people believe that I somehow want to use the power of the Ark against the Palestinians and Muslims in general. I told him how the Bible describes the Ark and the awesome power it was supposed to have. Some of these people are very superstitious and believe Jews have superhuman powers anyway. The message has got round that I am plotting against Islam."

He lowered his voice to a whisper. "Word in the street has it that Hamas has been showing an interest in me. You know the Hamas flag features the Dome of the Rock? They've been saying I want to dig up the foundations of the mosque to find the Ark!" He giggled helplessly. "You see, it could hardly be worse!"

Hamas is the Arabic acronym for the Islamic Resistance Movement (Harakat al-Muqawamah al-Islamiyya). It had been founded some years before by Sheikh Ahmed Yassin at the beginning of the First Intifada—the Palestinian uprising against Israeli rule, which lasted from 1987 to 1993. The charter of Hamas calls for the destruction of the state of Israel and its replacement with a Palestinian Islamic state in the whole of historical Palestine. Hamas was not very keen on Jews in general and Reuven had every reason to be afraid.

Reuven told me that he and Clara had moved to a rented flat in Tel Aviv for security reasons, and today he had just come back to his Jerusalem place to get some books. Clara had telephoned and pleaded with him to go straight back. However, inveterate collector that he was, he had taken the opportunity to nose round some antique dealers in the Christian Quarter.

When he left one store, with a couple of manuscripts and books under his arm, a couple of Arab-looking men had snatched the books from him and pushed him around a bit.

"It was the books they were after. They wanted to see what I am up to. I think I was very lucky."

"I doubt they're Hamas," I said. "If they had been, and if Hamas has anything on you, you wouldn't be sitting here enjoying a cup of excellent coffee! But strangely enough I just heard from a Palestinian friend that rumors are going round about me too. I guess people saw you coming to my place in the Old City. Or did you mention my name to Anis?"

Reuven shook his head distractedly and got heavily to his feet. We walked to Jaffa Gate where Reuven's driver was waiting to drive him back to Tel Aviv. At the last minute, he suggested I go with him.

I love Jerusalem like no other place on earth. But sometimes it makes you feel claustrophobic. Tel Aviv is the best antidote to too much Jerusalem. Having nothing better to do and feeling like a break, I climbed into his comfortable dark blue Mercedes 500SE.

His encounter in the Christian Quarter seemed to have taken a lot out of Reuven. The headache he frequently had as a result of his slight wound in the Yom Kippur War was troubling him. He rubbed the side of his head, took a handful of pills, and in a few minutes was fast asleep. I sank into the luxurious leather seats and enjoyed the ride down through the forests of Judea.

I reflected that the Ark had passed this way more than once thousands of years ago during earlier Jewish conflicts with local populations. As I was wondering what its impact on the current conflict was likely to be, I dozed off as well and woke up only when the engine was switched off in front of the elegant apartment block where Reuven lived, near Dizengoff Street. Clara was out for the evening, it was the maid's evening off, and we had their place to ourselves.

Reuven showered and changed into a pair of jeans and a white T-shirt.

"What happened to your orthodox clothes?" I asked.

"With the security situation everywhere in the world being as it is, I do not feel like sticking out like a sore thumb. With a *shnoz* like mine," he said, tapping his nose, "anyone can tell I'm a Jew, but I do not need to advertise it any more than God intended. Clara has persuaded me to dress in a more discreet manner, at least for the time being."

"And your quest, Reuven?" I asked softly.

"This is what I wanted to talk about. I want you to help. I've been reading all I can and a number of people have been assisting me. Some progress is being made. However I can now see that the whole thing might be a little more complicated than I first imagined. I am losing my sense of what the Ark really was. I don't really know what it is I am *looking* for.

"On the one hand it appears to be some kind of a weapon. On the other it often formed part of a kind of procession along with tambourines and trumpets. And in addition it was both the footstool and throne of the Almighty. All very good, but what *was* it? There's a big question mark over what it actually *was*."

My friend looked worried and driven. It was obvious that the whole issue of the Ark was beginning to frustrate him. The more he studied it, the less he understood what it was all about.

uncircumcised *goy*, and downed his glass. He ate silently for a

It would therefore be very difficult to find it. But with a massive investment of money, he kept saying, and with a proper businessman's organization, it should be possible. He rambled on, talking of special investments to finance the long-term search for the Ark and then plunging back into its intricate and ambiguous history.

He rubbed his head in his characteristic gesture and I supposed that his "Yom Kippur headache" had returned.

With a strange look on his face he left the room, moving like a sleepwalker, leaving me alone for about half an hour. In the distance I could hear him on the phone to someone, speaking volubly in Hebrew.

When he came back he was carrying a tray full of bread, olives, salted and pickled herring, dill pickles, soft goat's cheese—*jibneh* in Arabic—the humus I had bought from Abu Shukri's that I had put in the fridge, and a bottle of white Golan wine. He opened it, served us both, muttering under his breath that he should not be drinking wine with a bloody, uncircumcised *goy*, and downed his glass. He ate silently for a few moments and seemed to regain his composure.

It was a warm, unbearably humid Tel Aviv night and I was dressed for Jerusalem, not for Tel Aviv. I had taken a shower but I felt sticky and could feel the sweat trickle down my back.

"Come outside, there's a bit of a breeze," Reuven said, leading me onto a covered terrace from where I could see the lights of the esplanade and, beyond that, the inky darkness of the sea.

"I have been speaking to Rabbi Getz at Ateret Cohanim," he continued. "He doesn't actually claim to have seen the Ark or to have found its hiding place, but he believes in his heart it

e

might be down there under the Temple Mount in some secret place although he knows as well as we do that the area has been excavated constantly at least since Roman times. I am beginning to doubt it's there at all. If it had been, why did the knights Templar, who had full access, unlimited man power and who spent years looking, not find it?

"For the moment, anyway, the government has forbidden any more digging. The last time Getz and his friends burrowed into the foundations, Muslims up on top heard the noise coming up through a cistern and rushed down to see what was happening. You know about the unrest that followed. The entrance has now been sealed up by ten yards of reinforced concrete. I've decided I do not want to be involved in any digging around in Jerusalem. Especially after what I heard about Hamas."

"That I understand," I said, nodding in agreement. "In any case, people looking for the Ark in Jerusalem are tripping over each other. In addition, there's not the slightest proof at all that it is there."

"Quite so," said Reuven gloomily. "Getz said that they had weeks down there before they were discovered. They found traces of many earlier excavations but little else. I think that I am at a dead end.

"A couple of days ago I was reading the Talmud and came across the passage in Masekhet Shekalim about the Temple priest who noticed that a flagstone on the floor of the Temple wood store was shaped differently from the others. The assumption was that this marked the hiding place of the Ark. He went to tell a colleague about it and was struck dead on the spot. That passage spoke to my heart!" He laughed. "I'm not really afraid of being struck dead, but I'm just beginning to wonder if we should not be looking elsewhere. We were talking the other day about the possibility that the Ark had been taken to Egypt. Maybe that's where we should be looking? Maybe that's where *you* should be looking?"

He looked at me questioningly. I had been dreaming of getting more actively involved in the search for some time. His obsession was becoming my obsession. Now that we had both more or less concluded that the Ark was not in Jerusalem, I was keen to look elsewhere. The thought of setting out on a mission to Egypt was very tempting. But as I stared out at the distant seashore I wondered if I really should embark on what some people would see as a wild goose chase. Did I—a British gentile—really want to go sleuthing round the Eastern Desert in Egypt in search of a Jewish Holy Grail?

"I'm not sure, Reuven," I said. "Go to Egypt in search of the Ark? I'll have to decide first what I want to be, a scholar or an adventurer."

"You could, of course, be both," he said. "Anyway, from what you said and from what I have been hearing, there are many traditions that seem to lead to Egypt. But as you're thinking it over, perhaps you could bear these in mind."

He went back into the apartment and returned with a small velvet-covered box, which he placed gently on the table.

"Open it," he said

There were three very plump diamonds inside.

"These are for the first stages of the work if you need them," he said. "Our war chest! And this is just for starters."

I slid the little box back across the table. I did not want Reuven's money. Over the following years it was good to know it was there for emergencies but I stubbornly refused to take anything for myself.

"I am afraid you are not a practical man," he replied sighing. "And I wonder if you will ever really get anywhere without changing your attitude toward money. Anyway if this does not tempt you, maybe this will."

He took out a piece of paper, which had been tucked under one of the old leather-bound Hebrew books on the table and passed it to me with a very formal, slightly ironic gesture.

It was just a few lines, written in Hebrew, from a poem by the twelfth-century Spanish Jewish poet Yehuda ha-Levi:

> And I shall walk in the paths of the Ark of the Covenant,
> Until I taste the dust of its hiding place,
> Which is sweeter than honey.

Reuven knew how to touch my Celtic heart. There was an inspiring beauty in these few lines. And what, indeed, could be sweeter than finding something that for millennia had never ceased to excite the imagination of men?

THE CITY
OF THE DEAD

"*Wallah*, this is the hiding place, *effendi*! *This* is where the Ark was put."

I had no idea what on earth my somewhat dippy and excitable friend Daud Labib was talking about. For the preceding few minutes I had been reflecting on the fact that over the previous year my interest in the Ark had started to take over my life. Indeed it was principally because of the Ark that I now found myself in the spring of 1994 in Cairo, Egypt, having finally succumbed to Reuven's entreaties to try to find out more about the world's most sought after artifact. Whatever reservations had constrained me before had been put aside.

There were two main reasons for coming to Egypt. In the first place I wanted to investigate ancient traditions that maintained that the Ark had been brought here long before the destruction of the First Temple. Second, I had wanted to try to understand the background of the exodus of the Hebrew slaves from Egypt. Over the previous week I had stood in the shade of the Pyramids the Hebrews had helped construct, walked in the fields where they would have collected straw and mud to make their bricks. Whatever the Ark was, and I was still deeply unclear about this, it had started life, at least conceptually, here in the land of the pharaohs. I had wanted to *feel* and *see* and *smell* the reasons that led to the creation of the Ark.

So far enlightenment had evaded me.

The following day I was going back to England for a stint of library work but when I returned to Egypt I planned to examine various Ark-like artifacts from ancient Egypt in Cairo's museums.

My undersized friend was walking in front of me. Gazing down at him I started wondering inconsequentially how it was that his particularly small head could possibly have produced such a disproportionate mass of dandruff: it had settled on the shoulders of his black, synthetic shirt like an ermine stole.

This morning Daud had dragged me out of the archive where I spent most of my time to take me on a tour of his favorite places in Cairo. He was a Copt—a member of the Egyptian Coptic Christian minority—who lived in a suburb of Cairo but who was originally from the southern Egyptian town of Qift, which had played an important role in the history of the Copts.

The word "Copt," deriving from the Greek word for Egypt (*Egyptos*), simply means "Egyptian," a point that Copts are not slow to bring to your attention. Their liturgical language, Coptic, is the descendant of the ancient Egyptian language. But no one speaks Coptic anymore—Arabic is the spoken language of the Coptic minority as it is for the rest of the predominantly Muslim populations. The Copts see themselves as the true heirs of the great civilization of ancient Egypt.

Daud was pointing proudly at a nondescript building set back from the dusty road down which we were walking. His dark eyes radiated enthusiasm. "The Ark was put here," he repeated, making a stabbing gesture with his right hand.

Daud was unlike anyone I had ever met in Egypt. A brilliant and scholarly man who was working on a doctorate on ancient Coptic manuscripts, he carried his irritating eccentricity and individuality before him like silken banners.

"*This* is where the Ark was put!" Daud bellowed, pointing to a plaque on the wall that proclaimed that this was the Ben Ezra synagogue.

I knew of nothing that connected the Ark with the Ben Ezra synagogue. This synagogue is world-famous because of the discovery in one of its storerooms of the world's most important collections of medieval documents. I was planning to see what this archive—the Cairo Genizah—had to say about the Ark, if anything. But that would not be here or now, as the documents had been removed to Western university libraries in the nineteenth century. But there was absolutely nothing as far as I knew to suggest that the Ark had ever been hidden here.

"What are you going on about, you excitable little Copt? How do you mean the Ark? Nobody's ever said the Ark had anything to do with this place."

In fact I was more than a little mystified. I'd certainly not mentioned my interest in the Ark to Daud. We were close friends and in the past had shared confidences but once, in an unguarded and inebriated moment, he had boasted about carrying out jobs for the Egyptian Mubahath al-Dawla (the General Directorate of State Security Investigations), and since then I had been a little careful about what I told him. In Egypt, the Ark, with all its political and religious ramifications, was not a subject to bandy around with the likes of Daud. How could he possibly know about my involvement? I felt an unpleasant clamminess at the base of my spine. I looked at him questioningly.

"You know, *ya achi*, Musa's *basket* when he was hidden in the reeds: 'the Ark of bulrushes.'"

He began to recite by heart in a monotonous chant, which he accompanied with a rhythmic movement of his hand as if he were swinging a censer:

> And Pharaoh charged all his people, saying, every son that is born ye shall cast into the river, and every daughter ye shall save alive. And there went a man of the house of Levi, and took to wife a daughter of Levi. And the woman conceived, and bare a son: and when she saw that he was a goodly child, she hid him three months. And when she could no longer hide him, she took for him an ark of bulrushes, and daubed it with slime and with pitch, and put the child therein; and she laid it in the reeds by the river's brink.

In the Hebrew of the original Biblical account, the word used for the humble basket in which the baby Moses was hidden by his mother was *teva*. But the *English* translation was "ark." I breathed a sigh of relief. Daud knew nothing about my true reason for being in Egypt. Of course I knew about the ancient tradition that Moses of the house of Levi was hidden on this very site among the rushes in a floating basket, a miniature coracle. The rushes were the feathery papyrus reeds that still line the banks of the Nile and that have been used for making paper for around 5,000 years.

His recitation over, my friend made the sign of the cross, bowing and mumbling to himself. Turning his bony, mottled face toward me, he smiled and fingered the large gold cross he wore over his shirt. Daud had crossed himself in a stagey, ironical way, like some corrupt Italian prelate. And like some corrupt Italian prelate I knew it did not mean much. He had begun to lose his faith while he was studying at an American theological college. He had lost it completely by the time he had finished another undergraduate degree and an MA in an English university. He was fond of quoting Gabriel Garcia Marquez: "Disbelief is more resistant than faith because it is sustained by the senses." Daud was no longer religious but he was proud of his remarkable knowledge of the Bible, great swathes of which he knew by heart and could quote in Coptic, Arabic, or English. And for reasons I did not at first understand, he always wore sacerdotal black shirts with a large gold cross swinging from a metal chain around his neck.

Notwithstanding his overall eccentricity, in one respect he conformed to Egyptian norms: he was opposed to all the doings of the Israeli state (he refused to use the term "Israel" and persisted in calling it "the Zionist entity") and extended this animosity to the Jews of recent times with the exception of Einstein and the Marx Brothers. He had reservations about me too, as I was a frequent visitor to Israel, but had substantially overcome them as I had done some work on an illustrious ancestor of his called Labib who had played the leading role in the (failed) revival of Coptic as a spoken language. It was my interest in the Coptic language revival that had led me to contact his family, and thus meet up with him.

Daud was anxious to show me this ancient but much restored Cairo synagogue as part of the tour of the city he had planned for me. This was not, however, out of love for the ancient Jewish heritage in Egypt, but because it was the site of an ancient Coptic church. The church, he told me, had been bought by the Jews for the paltry sum of 20,000 dinars over a thousand years before, in AD 882.

"Only 20,000 dinars—they had it for nothing, *effendi*. You can't imagine the price of land in Cairo," he said. Once they had purchased the church, the Jews turned it into a synagogue. "Damned cheek, *ya achi*," he said indignantly. "They tricked us out of our birthright, same as they are doing with the Palestinians."

His anger caused his face to break out in small pink blotches. For Daud it was as if the purchase of the church had taken place the day before—yet another reminder of the vividness of historical memory in the Middle East.

"Come on, you ineffably daft Copt," I said. "The Jews would not have much use for a bloody church, now would they? Anyway I read somewhere that the Copts couldn't afford to pay their taxes and were *forced* to sell the church. You *could* say the Jews helped them out."

"*Wallah*, another Jewish lie!" he snorted, shaking his head violently and causing another layer of his shedding derma to explode over his shirt. "The Copts were rich in those days. They could afford their taxes. They were the intellectual and commercial elite of Egypt—always were, still are. No, the rubbish Jews cheated us."

The day was oppressively hot. We were standing in the shade of the synagogue. "*That was the hiding place*," he repeated, stabbing his finger at a point to one side of the building. "That's where the bulrushes used to be. That's where the prophet Musa was hidden and that's why we built a church there—one of the finest churches in the whole of the Middle East."

He put his arm round my shoulder and opined piously: "*Wallah*, Musa was a great man! He had horns, it is true, like quite a few Jews, so they say. But he was a very great man. A great prophet." He smiled crookedly. "He managed to rid Egypt of all its rubbish Jews when they escaped from slavery under the pharaohs."

His face became somber again. "Problem is, they came back. And desecrated our damned church."

Again he fingered his cross, a troubled look on his face.

After a brief look around the synagogue, we walked through *medinat al-mawta*, the City of the Dead, Cairo's ancient cemetery, which has given shelter to the living as well as the dead for over a thousand years. Thieves, outlaws, pilgrims, professional reciters of the Quran, and guardians of graves have often made their homes here in the tombs and, over the last many decades, their numbers have been swollen by hundreds of thousands of homeless people. The cemetery used to be in the desert, far outside the city, but the city has grown around it and this vast area is now right in the center of the great noisy metropolis that is Cairo.

The City of the Dead was an island of relative calm. In its alleys there were bands of black goats and dirty, ragged children. Today the whole area was covered by veils of smoke and mist that formed and dissolved around the shapes of the tombs, leaving one to guess what was real and what was imagined. The few spring flowers were dulled with a coating of fine white dust.

Daud obviously knew the cemetery well. Walking at breakneck speed, despite his pronounced limp, he led me on a tour that took in most of the important shrines and mausoleums.

He gave me a hurried explanation of the main sites and then pushed on restlessly to the next one. Finally he came to something that really interested him. Just next to a stone-built marvel of high medieval Islamic architecture, crowned with a dome, the tomb of some long-dead poet or saint, a group of men were constructing an ugly concrete breezeblock wall around what appeared to be a small vegetable patch.

After our long walk in the heat of the day, the normally indefatigable Daud now complained of tiredness and wanted to stop for a while to smoke a cigarette. We walked over and sat close to them on slabs of masonry from another age fringed with red and yellow lichen. A cold tainted draft seemed to be coming out of the tomb itself.

From the proprietary way he had walked around the tomb, Daud gave the impression that he knew the place.

From the color of their skin I guessed that the builders were from the south of Egypt or perhaps from farther south still, from the Sudan. They were black, emaciated men with faces devoid of any semblance of hope. They appeared so crushed by the burden of their lives that they did not greet us or even acknowledge us.

A woman walked out of a squat aperture set into the side of the tomb. She greeted Daud with a knowing smile. On her shapely hip she was resting an aluminum tray on which I could make out some small gold-rimmed glasses and a number of home-rolled cigarettes. She placed the tray on the ground and poured out thick black tea, the color of ink, which is typical of Upper Egypt, from a charred pot sitting on the ashes of a cooking fire, and served the men: each one received a glass of tea and a cigarette. The men squatted on the ground, arms resting on their thin knees, in the lengthening shadow of the wall they were building, and lit up. The fragrant smell of hashish mingled with the smoke of the fire.

"This is a drug den," sneered Daud, showing his blackened teeth. "They are building the widow a wall, and she pays them with tea, drugs, and I don't know what else. Egypt is a strange place. Our wonderful law bans the growing of tobacco—nobody knows why—so we have to import millions of tons of it every year; but every delinquent grows hashish in his back garden. This widow, this Maryam, grows it and sells it."

One of the men picked up a drum and started playing an intricate, pulsating African rhythm. Daud had forgotten his tiredness and started performing a kind of lopsided disco dance. Ricky Gervais has serious competition. It was the strangest dance I had ever seen: he would leap in the air, eyes rolling, cross himself fervently and then bow deeply in the direction of the setting sun. No one paid much attention.

After a while Maryam went back into her tomb and came out wearing a colorful sequined shawl over her long shabby cotton dress. She walked over and stood squarely in front of me. Smiling, she too started to dance, her movements sinuous and sexy. Daud eyed her anxiously.

To the widow's evident annoyance, the drummer stopped playing, put his drum on the ground beside him, and shot me a truculent look, a glimmer of interest in his eyes. I guessed he was wondering if there were any chance that I would pay him something to continue.

The widow faltered in her dance and tossed her head. The dust rose up around her fine ankles like a small cloud as she descended on the drummer. A victorious look on her face, she lifted the drum above her head and started playing it herself. Dancing and playing. Triumph in her eyes.

I was sitting in the shadow of the tomb watching this pantomime. I had wanted to imagine the days before the appearance of the Ark in the world, to understand what may have led to its construction. Bizarrely what was happening here had given me more enlightenment than all my walks around the pyramids and building sites of ancient Egypt. The scene before my eyes reminded me of something I had almost forgotten, something I had read without paying much attention years before when I was a student. I was reminded of the victory dance of Miriam, the prophetess and sister of Moses and Aaron.

Once the Israelite slaves had managed to evade Pharaoh's army, which was dramatically engulfed by the waves of the Red Sea, Moses recited a poem of triumph—known to be one of the most ancient passages in the Bible: "I will sing unto the Lord, for he hath triumphed gloriously: the horse and his rider hath he thrown into the sea ..." Then his elderly sister Miriam takes the stage. Like Maryam here in the City of the Dead, she had a drum (*tof*) in her hand—an instrument that the Israelites had encountered and adopted for their own purposes in Egypt— and started to dance, no doubt triumphantly.

As the woman strutted in front of the emancipated slaves, one can imagine the gestures she made in the direction of Egypt.

But the unfragrant widow was no longer dancing triumphantly; she was dancing sexily. Too sexily for my taste, and far too close. I imagined that she was a prostitute of some sort. She was rather handsome and had a lithe, curvaceous body. But this was not for me. Predictably she was holding her hand out for money.

"She invites you to rest your weary body in her humble tomb. Or do I mean womb?" whispered Daud, giggling.

"Er, no thanks," I said.

"If the widow is not your style," said Daud huffily, "I can assure you that she is mine. Very much mine. Perhaps you could lend *me* a few pounds?"

He was swinging his cross with a circular movement of his hand, one of his eyebrows raised expectantly.

"You loathsome little Copt," I muttered.

Dusk was turning to night and the fruit bats were starting to swoop and circle in the half-light, making their typical high-pitched buzzing sound. I had a flight to London the following morning and I was looking forward to an early night. I had little desire to walk back through the City of the Dead alone, nor did I wish to wait around here while Daud had his way with the widow. Shaking my head I stood up to leave and gave the woman a few well-worn Egyptian notes.

Triumphantly she tossed the drum back to the man, who was now lying on the ground, smoking another joint, looking at the darkening evening sky. He started to play again, this time with greater inspiration. The hard pounding seemed to shake the very bones in my body. Dim figures crawled out of apertures in the walls and tombs and made their way to the circle around the drummer, their faces lit up by the flickering fire that had been blown into life by a malodorous gust of wind. They all appeared to be under the spell of the drum.

My mind flashed back to the scene that had been enacted following the Israelites' deliverance. Did the tired, brutalized slaves sit round like this as they prepared to flee into the wilderness of the Sinai? Did the drum have the same magnetic appeal for those desperate men as it had for these desperate tomb-dwellers of the City of the Dead?

As I tried to visualize this scene, I saw the Israelites crowding together, placing the few personal effects they had brought with them on the ground. I found it remarkable that the first object unpacked by the fugitives as they fled slavery and oppression, under their charismatic, flawed leader, was an African drum. Or perhaps Miriam had not unpacked it at all but had carried it perhaps by a chain or cord around her neck as a symbol of impending liberation as she crossed through the path miraculously opened up in the Red Sea. Once they were safely on the Sinai side, the drum was used to sound out a rhythm of deliverance, victory, and hope.

And miraculously it was hope that I now saw etched on the faces of the Sudanese builders. They had forgotten their weariness and poverty. The hashish had hit, and they were under the spell of the drum. It seemed to me that in some way I could not define I had been given a glimpse into the past.

I gave the drummer ten U.S. dollars and his friends laughed and shouted, rose to their feet, shook my hand, and accompanied us to the lane on the other side of their newly built wall.

On the long walk back, the tombs threw dark shadows cast by cooking fires and the distant beams of car headlights. Daud spoke briefly and then fell silent. He had wanted to stay with the widow and was annoyed I had not given him any money. He had a fiancée whom I had met a few times. She was a plain, thin girl from a middle-class Coptic family from Alexandria. Daud fantasized endlessly about her breasts, which he claimed to have glimpsed on one or two occasions. He could not hope to sleep with her or have a more extended inspection of her bosom until they were married, and it would take him years to save up enough money for the wedding. So he consoled himself, as he now explained, with visits to the widow when he could afford the small sum she demanded.

"None of my business, I know, you dirty-minded Copt, but do you think going to the widow is the right thing to do?"

Daud spun toward me, his eyes flaming, dull red patches disfiguring his face. He was furious.

"Where there is no law, there is no transgression," he barked. "That's from the book of Romans in the New Testament. You tell me what the law is, *effendi*, and I'll tell you if I have done anything wrong. You'll say it's adultery—well, it's not—I'm not married and nor is she. And, Mr. Rubbish Puritan, you might like to consider that Egyptian genius poet—Edmond Jabès. What did Jabès write? He wrote what I consider to be my creed, my Lord's Prayer: 'The laws of light are inspired by the laws of dark. What is good for one is also good for the other. We have studied the dark and the day through their common voice and conclude that opposites are one.'"

He glared defiantly at me, and I had to admit that with this quotation—adapted by Jabès, as I later discovered, from a kabbalistic rabbi—my very erudite friend had defended himself rather neatly. As I listened to his words I thought of the Ark. Without meaning to, Jabès had summed up its mystical significance, its dualism. It seemed indeed to incorporate the law of light and dark.

Whatever elation Daud felt by his victory was soon replaced by a characteristic mood swing. He told me he was depressed by the poverty of *medinat al-mawta*, depressed by his own poverty, which forced him to take whatever work he could find and which stood in the way both of finishing his doctorate and of his marital bliss, and he told me he felt ashamed for his people, who might have been rich a thousand years before but who were now, for the most part, impoverished.

He started to sob uncontrollably, cursing his fiancée, cursing his fate, and cursing me.

Earlier we had seen a white stork gliding high over the tombs, riding a thermal current as it wondered what to do next. Daud told me that for the ancient Egyptians the stork had represented the *ba*—the characteristic essence of each human being.

"And my *ba*," he sobbed, "my *ba* must be poverty and rubbish sexual deprivation. I should have been someone like the great Copt Saint Anthony, who was from Fayyum, like my uncle. My uncle had sex every day of his life. Poor Anthony never had sex at all and spent twenty years not seeing anyone and living off crusts thrown over a high wall. And that's my fate. I don't know when I'll be able to afford to have a proper session with the widow."

"Oh, shut up, Daud" I said.

As we walked in silence through the darkness of the tomb city, I crept back into my scholar's shell. The Sudanese rhythm was still pounding in my brain and I started thinking about the strange etymology of the Arabic word for "drum." Both the ancient Hebrew *tof* and the Arabic *tuf* probably derive from ancient Egyptian and may be associated with the Greco-Egyptian demon Typhon (the origin of the word "typhoon") who became the counterpoint to the benign Osiris, lord of the underworld, whom Typhon had incarcerated in a wooden Ark and thrown into the Nile. Perhaps originally the drum was smitten to keep Typhon away. In many parts of the Middle East and Africa drums were symbols of authority. Perhaps by beating the drum, Miriam was making a very specific political point: the Egyptian gods had been overcome; the God of the Israelites would lead them to salvation and redemption.

I could still just hear the muffled sound of the distant drum through the cacophony of wails and moans of the Tomb city. I thought of the lines of T. S. Eliot: "Inside my brain a dull tom-tom begins, absurdly hammering a prelude of its own, capricious monotone that is at least one definite 'false note.'"

For a while I wondered what the "false note" was. I just knew that there was one. Somewhere in the conceptualization of my mission there was something missing, something I was over-looking.

Our path took us down a narrow gap between a series of stone sepulchers. It was now pitch black. A bat flew so close it brushed against my hair. I began to feel ill at ease but found reassurance in the distant sound of the drum. The insistent African rhythm was calming. It took me back to Mposi, the small Lemba village in central Africa I had lived in years before.

"You can forget that Egypt is in Africa," I murmured to Daud.

"Not if you live here," he said sourly. "The place is full of black refugees. These fellows come from over the border. They've taken all the building jobs in Egypt and they're not as poor as they look. These low people have no idea of our great Egyptian Christian civilization."

"Oh, come on, Daud. Don't you ever tire of being a Copt chauvinist. Don't you mean Muslim civilization?"

"*Wallah* no, *effendi*, Egypt was a Christian country for hundreds of years before the Arabs came. If you read the Coptic Gnostic gospels from Nag Hammadi that I study you will see that everything started in Egypt. Sometimes things that started here would spread farther—to the Middle East or to Greece—but they would always *return*. The people from my town of Qift practically invented civilization. Qift is Koptus in Greek—the essence of Coptness is in Qift. We Egyptians—I mean us Coptic people— were the first people in the world to sit on proper chairs at table and eat food with forks and knives like human beings. The rubbish Arabs are tent-dwellers—they crouched in the sand and ate their horrible food with their hands.

"The real Egypt is Coptic. You go into the Eastern Desert and all you see is Coptic monasteries and the tombs of Christian Coptic saints. The basis of the modern culture of the world is the history and civilization of us Copts. These horrible black Muslim people you just saw don't know about this, they only know these African things, primitive things: AIDS, prostitution, drugs."

"I guess the Hebrew slaves lived like that," I reflected. "I can't imagine that the pharaohs treated them particularly well. They were in Egypt for a couple of hundred years at least, working on construction sites, just like these people, and the culture they developed, as slaves, would probably have been similar to this: an African culture of the oppressed."

"These rubbish Africans are oppressed because they deserve to be oppressed," he said, swinging his cross and looking as if he had cheered up a bit.

I would be leaving early the following day so once we had got out of the City of the Dead I said good night to Daud and made my way back to where I was staying.

That night, in my simple whitewashed hotel room overlooking the Nile on Abd ul-Aziz al-Saud Street, I dreamed of the City of the Dead. Israelite slaves were sitting around smouldering fires, eating a potage of Egyptian *ful* beans with their fingers. Their womenfolk were moving sullenly to the sound of an African drum.

A bellicose Moses was dreaming of bloody revolt and war.

He was already dreaming of making the Ark.

5

A KEY
TO THE PAST

The Spencer-Churchill family, which counts among its
more illustrious offspring the late Diana, Princess of Wales,
and Sir Winston Churchill, once owned a lovely seventeenth-
century Jacobean manor house in Yarnton, a small, sleepy
village a few miles north of Oxford. Today the manor is the
unlikely home of the Oxford Centre for Hebrew and Jewish
Studies—an internationally renowned center of scholarly
activity that includes an important forum for research into the
Dead Sea Scrolls.

It was the Oxford Centre's founder president, Dr. David
Patterson, who had put me in touch with Chaim Rabin in
Jerusalem the year before, and who had invited me to spend
a week or so at the manor to enable me to consult Oxford
University's Bodleian Library prior to returning to Egypt.
There were a number of rare books and articles on the Ark that
could be found only here.

The River Thames is situated a few hundred yards away
from the manor, down a rough track, and as I meandered out
from the Great Hall into the formal gardens, the fragrant river

mist was still clinging to the warm, damp earth. I bumped into Patterson in front of the old tithe barn and we went for a stroll across the fields toward the river and returned via the pleached-lime walk that shields the back of the ancient estate. For a few moments we sat outside on a bench in the sunken formal garden to one side of the great house, chatting about mutual friends, listening to the birdsong and enjoying the sight of the honey-colored walls, the spring blossom and daffodils on the far side of the lawn. It was a far cry from the cacophony of Cairo.

Patterson ushered me back into the house where we took refuge in his dark, oak-paneled study. He wanted to know what I would be doing in the Bodleian. I told him something of my recent research and of the intriguing conversations about the Ark I had had in Jerusalem with Rabin the previous year.

"I'm glad you met up with Chaim," he said. "He is undoubtedly one of the finest scholars in the field." I gave Patterson a brief summary of my thinking about the Ark. He listened attentively, stopping me once to bring in some coffee from the dining room next door. Initially he saw my interest in the Ark as being in the long and hallowed tradition of the history of ideas, and therefore perfectly valid. However, once I had told him a little about Reuven and his utopian schemes, his face fell. "Listen, for heaven's sake, the Ark disappeared from history two and a half thousand years ago. I doubt it will ever turn up now."

"Other things have turned up," I replied. "The Dead Sea Scrolls, the documents from Nag Hammadi, the treasures of Tutankhamen."

Patterson frowned as he gazed over the front lawns of the house. Taking a sip of his coffee he sighed: "Perhaps—but would it be desirable? It's the most God-ridden object of the world's most God-ridden people. Some things are better left unfound. The consequences for the world if the Ark were ever found could be far greater than you imagine."

Patterson's face softened and he smiled at me. "This Reuven ben Arieh, whoever he is, wants you to help him. I can see that his passion for the subject is taking you over. I would very strongly advise you to resist. His reasons for wanting to find the Ark will never be your reasons. You have quite different agendas. Reflect very carefully before you go any further down this dangerous road. I would also suggest you speak to Naki Doniach while you are here. He's an old man but he has a wise head on his shoulders and he happens to love you. If you decide to ignore my advice, that, of course, is your affair. I'll not try to persuade you. A true teacher defends his students against his own personal influences. At the very least you'll have something to tell your grandchildren. In any event I'll keep this rather unsatisfactory *démarche* under my hat."

Feeling chastened by his words, I hastily gathered up my books and got up to go. I had to catch the bus that would take me to Oxford and the Bodleian library. As I was opening the great oak door of his study, Patterson murmured: "Oh, and good luck!"

Later that day I was having a solitary early lunch in the old parlor of the King's Arms, just opposite the Bodleian's Oriental Reading Room. A few elderly theologians, one of whom was brandishing an old-fashioned ear trumpet, were sitting at the bar loudly discussing the death of God. Looking up from my Ploughman's and Guinness, I saw a familiar figure filling the door. Dressed, as he always was, not in elegant tweeds like the theologians but in a stained brown corduroy jacket, Nikodemon Doniach, OBE, looked like a benevolent and somewhat battered thrush. Head cocked on one side, he beamed, nodded in a friendly way at the dons, and asked if he could join me.

I had met Naki a good number of years before when I was just starting my postgraduate studies at Oxford. One particular morning, I was happily trying to discover the meaning of an Arabic word, which I could not find in any of the standard Arabic dictionaries in the Oriental Institute Library. I recalled that on the second floor of the Institute there was a room marked "Arabic Dictionary." Assuming that inside it there would be some great multivolume lexicon, I walked up the stairs, found the room, and knocked. A voice called: "Come in!"

I walked in and found Doniach sitting stoutly at a table with a writing pad open in front of him. There were no dictionaries in sight.

"I'm looking for the Arabic dictionary," I faltered.

"I *am* the Arabic dictionary!" he replied.

After a suitable pause he explained that this room was the office of the Oxford English–Arabic dictionary of which he was the editor. Once he had finished the English–Arabic, he went on to edit the Oxford English–Hebrew dictionary. He had a good command of at least a dozen other languages: he knew a number of Semitic languages, most western European languages, and for years he had worked for British Intelligence as a Russian expert. He was now well over eighty but neither his intelligence nor his appetite for work had dimmed.

Naki knew Reuven quite well. Reuven had close links with various intelligence agencies, and perhaps this is how they first met; or perhaps it was something to do with their experiences during the Second World War. Neither of them would ever say. What I did know was that they had a common friend, a Jewish bookseller—also with intelligence links, according to Reuven—whose shop was off the Rue St. André des Arts in the Latin Quarter in Paris, and they often met in the book-filled *salon* he reserved for favored guests, clients, and occasionally hard-faced men in suits who spoke French with a strong Israeli accent and who had no obvious interest in books. It was here that Reuven, whose sumptuous eighteenth-century apartment was only a few streets away, bought many of his oriental manuscripts.

In the bar of the King's Arms, Naki ordered a sandwich and a glass of wine and sat at my table.

"Bloody Reuven," I said. "I've become just about as obsessive as he is. He's got me involved in one of his schemes and I can't think of anything else." I told him that Reuven had reignited my interest in the history of the Ark of the Covenant.

"Oh, the Ark. That *is* fun," he said with a moment's hesitation. No doubt Reuven had already discussed the matter with him. A certain unaccustomed watchfulness came over him.

"I heard from someone that Reuven got into some kind of *trouble* in Jerusalem last year," said Naki. "Was it not something to do with the Third Temple and blowing up the Dome of the Rock? Something to do with the Hamas organization, I think—but anyway, with one of those Palestinian groups."

"That's right," I said. "He thought Hamas had got wind of his activities. Apparently they suspected he was planning to dig under the Dome of the Rock in the hope of finding the Ark. He was afraid he was about to get into trouble. He was pushed around a bit."

"*Splendid* fellow, our Reuven, but I *do* sometimes wonder if he is not mixed up in *too* many things. Not things that you as a scholar and gentleman should *necessarily* want to be involved with yourself. Now, how are you getting on with this Ark business?"

"I'm having difficulties with the overall concept of the Ark and also of the man who made it," I said. "Ever since I read Freud's *Moses and Monotheism* I've been fascinated by the figure of Moses, and now I feel I need to understand him better to have a sense of what the Ark was really all about."

"I remember *so* well Freud's other *marvelous* article on Michelangelo's Moses in the Church of San Pietro in Vincoli in Rome," Naki cut in. "Freud sees the incredible *negative* force in the statue as a depiction of Moses's attempt to suppress his fury at the *ghastly* behavior of the Israelites."

Knowing that Naki was not entirely immune to flattery, I added, "What I find very interesting, Naki, is that Michelangelo's horned Moses, based on the mistranslation in the Latin Vulgate translation of the Bible, is the most concrete example we have of the need for good lexicographers, like you."

The horns sprouting from the head of the Moses are the result of the mistranslation of the Hebrew root KRN, which can mean either "to shine" or "to grow horns." Jerome, who translated the Bible into Latin, got it hopelessly wrong.

"Yes, it wasn't Jerome's best effort. He should have got the correct meaning from the context without too much difficulty." And with a wry grin Naki quoted the Hebrew of the biblical text, which describes how Moses looked when he came down from Mount Sinai with the tablets of the law: "And when Aaron and all the children of Israel saw Moses, behold, the skin of his face shone; and they were afraid to come nigh him."

I paused to get Naki another glass of wine from the bar, and when I returned asked him what he thought of Freud's rather more controversial *Moses and Monotheism*.

"Freud started writing it in about 1934," said Naki, "just when the world I had known and grown up in was beginning to crumble. The Nazis were coming to power and were burning not only Freud's works but entire Jewish libraries and private collections. As a bibliophile, that hurt me particularly. For me that was the point when the lights started to go out all over Europe. I remember Freud saying, 'The world is making some progress: in the Middle Ages they would have burned me, now they are just burning my books.'"

"They would have burned him too if they had had the chance," I said, "but nobody realized that in 1934."

"No," Naki agreed, taking an understandably tentative sip of the King's Arms claret. "It is a very strange article. Let's just set the scene. Freud was an old man of 78 in 1934, suffering agonies with mouth cancer, and for some reason at this horribly difficult time he turned his mind to Moses—the national hero of the Jews, and the creator of the Jews' most sacred object, the Ark. Freud had a strange, utterly un-Jewish vision of Moses. He saw him as an Egyptian prince of the blood who believed in the kind of heretical Egyptian monotheism introduced by the pharaoh Akhenaten, which his followers—the Israelites—with their stubbornly engrained *polytheism*, did not believe in at all.

"Finally the Jews killed Moses, according to Freud, and it was only then, in remorse, that they turned to his Egyptian religion. And by the way, Freud might have something, because the origin of the name Moses (*Mosheh*) is not Hebrew at all—it comes from *mesu*, the Egyptian word for child."

"You know," Naki continued reflectively, "*Freud* really saw Moses as *Freud*. As Moses gave the Law to mold human behavior, so Freud gave the Law to understand it. The Nazis who were burning Freud's books were the Israelites who would not accept Moses's teaching. Or something like that," he laughed self-deprecatingly. "How do *you* see him?"

"As a tough, resilient, competent Jew. More Ariel Sharon than Freud. A rough, military leader who started life on the wrong side of the tracks, a bit of a hard man. I am sure that at court he would have had a pretty difficult childhood, which perhaps could explain why, according to Jewish tradition, he stammered. He liked black African women and didn't mind upsetting his brother and sister when he decided to marry one—a Cushite. Freud's idea of Moses as an Egyptian prince who spent his time at court is quite interesting. It suggests that the Ark might have been similar to some of the elaborate coffers that were found in the tomb of Tutankhamen. But how courtly was he? He's described as being a mild man, but at the same time he was very violent.

"After all, he was so enraged when he saw an Egyptian overseer beating a Hebrew slave that he killed him on the spot. He was a man with an uncontrollable temper. He even broke the tablets of the Law when he saw the Israelites worshiping the golden calf. I'm not saying the Israelites were not a mighty pain in the neck. They never stopped grumbling. Their constant refrain was that they were better off as slaves in the fleshpots of Egypt than as liberated Bedouin schlepping across an empty desert. And they come up with the great line: You bring us *here* to die? In Egypt there were no graves?"

"*Exquisitely* Jewish, that," said Naki, sighing. "You know, your sense of Moses," he continued, "is close to that of the first-century Jewish historian Josephus Flavius. Of course, dear old Josephus started off as a Jewish military commander against the Romans. Then he changed sides. But in the same way that Freud sees Moses as Freud, Josephus sees Moses as Josephus. In his *Antiquities of the Jews*, Moses is referred to as 'general' more than a dozen times, if I remember correctly, and on a few occasions "supreme military commander."

"For Josephus he is a warrior much more than a sage. As he lies dying, according to Josephus, Moses addresses the Israelites as 'comrades in arms,' and when he *does* die, it is his *military* qualities that are most sorely missed by his people. None of this is in the Bible, of course. But Josephus was two thousand years closer to the time of Moses than we are, and he may well have had sources about his military character that are lost to us. Yes, I think you've got it. Ariel Sharon sounds about right! But what's it got to do with the Ark?"

I took a pull at my Guinness and noticed that the theologians, God safely interred, were trooping out after the don with the ear trumpet and gaily heading to their various colleges for lunch.

"Obviously, Naki, I do not know where the Ark is," I started.

"Obviously," he replied rather more drily than was absolutely necessary.

"But equally I do not know *what* it is. Or what it was. This is what I have been trying to get to grips with in Egypt. I shall not be able to help Reuven find it if I do not know what it is! At one level the Ark was a work of art. Bezalel the artist built it according to one biblical passage, but Moses was ultimately responsible for it. In another passage Moses himself created it. I know it was eventually supposed to be some sort of mysterious, magic object with incomprehensible power. If it really was some sort of weapon we could understand why Moses the field commander, Moses the general, thought that it was worth putting in front of the troops. But was it? The Bible is absolutely silent about the Ark's properties—we just know something of its allegedly deadly effects.

"All we actually know of its *properties* is that it was a small wooden container about the size of a suitcase. The Israelites were made to follow it through the desert and then into battle. For me it is difficult to see how a wooden container could inspire them to great acts of military heroism. It was like following a coffin!"

"I believe the Ark is likely to be an imitation of some Egyptian or Near Eastern cultic phenomenon," said Naki seriously. "I think I read somewhere that Tutankhamen's treasure included something very like the Ark. If Freud was right and Moses was indeed of royal blood, what would have been more natural for him than to have followed a royal Egyptian cult object? You should go to see the Tutankhamen artifacts when you return to Egypt."

"I still don't understand why Moses would want God to communicate with man from a wooden container," I murmured stubbornly, shaking my head. "And I don't understand why a military commander would have selected a wooden container—even an allegedly magic wooden container—to lead his troops into battle. And I *particularly* don't understand why they would follow a coffin—the word *aron* is used for sarcophagus or mummy-case in Genesis."

It was true, since I had started thinking about the Ark the various contradictions in the narrative had begun to plague me.

I simply could not think of the Ark as a container or a coffin. All my senses screamed out that there was something else, something beneath the surface, not far from the surface, but something that perhaps had not been seen before.

"Very interesting, that whole business," said Naki. "You know in the Babylonian Talmud there is a commentary on the verse 'And Moses took the bones of Joseph with him,' and there is a description of how the bones of the patriarch were placed in *one* Ark, and the living God was in the *other* Ark, and the two of them—one symbolizing death, I suppose, and the other symbolizing life—were carried in front of the Israelite armies. That could be a solution: two Arks loaded with symbolic significance. Life and Death. Bit Freudian, I suppose," he said shrugging.

"That's a clever idea," I said. "It does seem like a plausible scenario: a reminder to the troops, if they needed reminding, that there were only two outcomes in the case of battle. Life or death. But they are still *wooden containers*. Two bloody wooden containers."

"All right," said Naki. "Let's try to think less conventionally for a moment. Let us at least for *once* in our short lives try to be original. Let's have a hard look at this word. In the first place in Hebrew, I think you will agree, that the word *aron* comes from the root ARN or ARH."

"Yes, it's a bit unclear," I said. "It could be either ARN or ARH."

"OK, we are agreed on that. If we look at other Semitic languages to try to get a deeper sense of what the word might mean, what do we see? The most obvious thing I can think of is that in Akkadian there is an apparently clear cognate in the form of *aranu*—which means coffin, which of course can also be a wooden container. Which takes us precisely back to the point that you find difficult!"

"Exactly," I said. "And there's an Arabic cognate with the same meaning as the Hebrew as well: *iran*—it also means box."

"That's news to me. I don't know any word in Arabic meaning box or coffin and consisting of the same root letters," said Naki, knitting his brows in concentration. "In Akkadian, anyway, *aranu* means coffin or sarcophagus, and in the first millennium it also means plain domestic chest. But we also have to beware the etymological fallacy. The fact that there are cognates apparently from the same root does not necessarily mean that they mean the same thing."

"But could you see *aron* making *more* sense in the context of all we know about the Ark, deriving from *another* root?" I asked.

"I don't know about their making more *sense*," he replied, "but there are certainly a couple of *perfectly* respectable Hebrew roots that could help." He took a notebook from his pocket and started writing down appropriate Hebrew roots. "Let's look. RWN means something like 'overcome.' In the *qal* form, *aron*, or something close, taken from the RWN root, *could* theoretically mean 'I overcome' or 'I lay to waste.' And then there is the root RNN, which in Hebrew means making 'making a ringing sound,' or in Arabic, 'making a twanging sound.' *Aron* could come from these, theoretically. In which case, theoretically again, something like *aron* could mean: 'I make a ringing sound'—or 'I am the one that makes a ringing sound' or 'the layer to waste.'"

He sipped his wine and looked wryly at me. "You're not trying to retranslate the Bible are you?"

"No. I'm just really thinking aloud. Seriously. Which of those roots would you say works best?"

"'Only connect,' my young friend, as Forster said. 'Only connect,'" he replied with a chuckle. "You'll have to decide. You pays your penny, you takes your choice."

Something stirred inside me. I thought back to the impoverished black men in the City of the Dead, the swooping bats, the dancing widow, the mesmerizing drum, and my nocturnal walk with Daud. I had a vaguely uncomfortable memory of that evening. It was the shadow of a memory, which provoked a thought that seemed relevant to what Naki was saying; but it dissolved before I could grasp it, like a fleeting dream.

I was soon brought back to the present by the smoky hubbub of the King's Arms, which by now was filled with first-year university undergraduates shyly trying to place drinks orders. For a while we talked about the way in which words in other Semitic languages composed of the same letters or root could be used to elucidate the meaning of obscure Hebrew words. By and large, words in Semitic languages are derived from a three-letter root. Thus the word *shalom* (peace) in Hebrew is derived from the root SLM. If the meaning of this word happened to be obscure it could be found through the Arabic root SLM, which has a similar sense.

"This approach is not as popular as it used to be," said Naki, "but what do you do when you are confronted with a *hapax*?" A *hapax legomenon* is a word that occurs only *once* in the written record of a language. "You get an unknown word that occurs only once, and often the ancient translators had not the *vaguest* idea what it meant. They just guessed. And if understanding a text means more to you than life itself—and this was often the case—not understanding a word was terrible. There are about 150 *hapax legomena* in the Hebrew Bible, and context alone does not always help to get the meaning. You *have* to rely on words in other Semitic languages formed from the same root. Sometimes they work, sometimes they don't. Sometimes you find a cognate but it does not help you."

"'Leaving one,' as T.S. Eliot put it, 'still with the *intolerable* wrestle with words and meaning,'" I said, completing Naki's thought.

He peered gloomily into his claret.

I told him something about Daud, and we spoke for an hour or so about Coptic and the issue of language revival. He was fascinated by everything I had to tell him about Egypt, and particularly about the various eccentricities of Daud. Immediately he came up with one or two dictionary questions concerned with Coptic loan words, with which he thought Daud could help him. I passed on Daud's address and telephone number in Cairo so he could call him if necessary.

As I left the King's Arms and headed down the Broad toward St. Giles I thought to myself that the history of words could be a key to the past. In the layered meanings and etymologies of the simplest word were arcane codes that could reveal long-lost secrets. My conversation with Naki had given me further food for thought. The Ark's regular association with trumpets, noise, and musical processions, plus the variant etymology suggested by Naki, indicated that it was entirely possible that the Hebrew word for Ark actually meant something to do with a musical instrument.

* * *

Further clues on where the Ark was and what it was might be found in the Oxford libraries. One of the sources that seemed most likely to contain some clues was the so-called aforementioned Cairo Geniza—a rich hoard of documents that had been discovered in the nineteenth century in the Ben Ezra synagogue in Cairo where Daud had taken me.

The Cairo Geniza consists of almost 200,000 Hebrew manuscript fragments, written over a period of a thousand years between the ninth and nineteenth centuries that are the world's best source of information on the medieval world of the Mediterranean and much else besides. A *geniza* was a special storehouse where Hebrew texts no longer in use could be deposited: it was against Jewish law for Jews to actually destroy a document in the sacred Hebrew language, which was considered to be the language that God himself spoke. Hebrew documents were too holy to be burned or binned. They had to be stored indefinitely. Or until they turned into dust.

The remarkable thing is that the documents of the Geniza survived their storage more or less unharmed in the dry conditions of Egypt. For the most part the Geniza fragments are today housed either in Cambridge University Library or in the Jewish Theological Seminary in New York. Hundreds of scholars have written about the light cast by the Geniza documents upon the past. Would they have anything to say about the Ark?

Over coffee one morning Naki mentioned that there were one or two small fragments in the Geniza that appeared to have come from a tenth-century manuscript that dealt with the hiding places of the Temple treasure including the Ark. This seemed like a promising lead. Naki had recently found the complete text of this tenth-century document, which had been inexplicably included in the introduction to a rare Hebrew book called *Emek ha-Melekh* (Valley of the King), which had been published in Amsterdam in 1648. This odd insertion was called the *Tractate of the Temple Vessels*.

What the *Tractate* had to say was that the Temple treasure, along with the Ark, was located on a mountain. It was not absolutely clear where the mountain was, but from the context it might be possible to infer that it was Mount Nebo in present-day Jordan or farther into Arabia proper.

The night after Naki told me about this, I could not sleep. It seemed to me that I had stumbled on something critical. Even though this was a medieval and therefore relatively late source, it could be, I thought, that it contained ancient material that could provide genuine clues to the hiding place of the Ark. I spent a few days in the dark recesses of the Bodleian reading Naki's copy of *Emek ha-Melekh* and wondering whether the apparent clues here were ones worth following up.

According to the *Tractate*, the Ark had been removed prior to the conquest of Jerusalem by the Babylonians in 587 BC. The Ark and the other treasure were hidden in the same place, on the western side of a high mountain—and would be discovered with the coming of the Messiah. What was of particular interest was that the *Tractate* included an internal reference to its text having also been inscribed onto a copper plaque by a scribe called Limur. This immediately suggested some sort of link with the famous Copper Scroll from Qumran—part of the Dead Sea Scrolls—which also dealt with lost Temple treasure. But was there really a link?

As I soon discovered, the differences between the *Tractate* and the Copper Scroll from Qumran are significant. In the Copper Scroll from Qumran the treasure is said to be hidden in *sixty-four* different places. In the *Tractate* it was hidden in *one*.

In the Copper Scroll the treasure is said to have come from the *Herodian* Temple, and was hidden therefore just before the arrival of the invading Romans in AD 70. In the *Tractate* the treasure came from the First Temple and was hidden before 587 BC.

The amounts of gold and silver mentioned in the Copper Scroll are rather modest, whereas the treasure in the *Tractate* is counted in the millions of bars of gold.

One afternoon Naki and I were sitting in a room in the Bodleian, the slanting sun picking out motes of dust hovering over the ancient tomes like hosts of gnats. As I talked about the Ark, Naki gazed out at the lovely cupola of Sir Christopher Wren's seventeenth-century Sheldonian Theatre and the spires of Oxford beyond as if he were perceiving this famous view from an angle that was utterly novel to him. It began to be clear to us both that all that had been said about the Copper Scroll, attributing it to the ravings of some mystical crank, could better be said about the medieval writer of the *Tractate of the Temple Vessels*, whoever he was.

"I would scarcely have been surprised if they'd discovered a message written in invisible ink at the end of the *Tractate*: 'Eat this after reading,'" said Naki chuckling.

The *Tractate*'s description of fabulous hoards of treasure seemed to be utterly exaggerated. In addition, it had been written nearly 2,000 years after the disappearance of the Ark. The clues, such as they were, were pretty vague and were little different from some of the clues in other ancient texts. What I could take from it was that the *Tractate* seemed to suggest that the Ark had been taken to Arabia and it could be that this was based on some earlier tradition. This was certainly one of the ancient Jewish traditions and it had been embroidered by Muslim writers who had been rather fascinated by the Ark. As it stood, however, it was not, as far as I could see, a practical guide to help us on our way. It pointed in a general direction but that was all.

On the other hand, the more prosaic Copper Scroll, as Rabin had said, perhaps could still be considered a potential code for the discovery of real treasure. Over the next few days I read and reread the Hebrew text of the Copper Scroll. I tried to get some sense of what the clues might mean. Hours and hours and hours of hard application revealed precisely nothing. If it was a code, it was a code I didn't understand, although I spent many hours trying to crack it. Finally I came to the conclusion that it was not a code but simply a straightforward description of hiding places in a world that had disappeared and about which we know almost nothing and about which we will never know very much.

In any event the Copper Scroll related to the period of the Second Temple. I was pretty sure that the Ark had been removed from the Temple six hundred years before. With some regret, I began to feel that the Copper Scroll, fascinating and seductive though it was, could be eliminated from the list of usable, useful, and relevant texts. In any case, the clues in the Copper Scroll, such as they are, were pretty assiduously followed up by John Allegro, the controversial English scholar who had the distinction of unfurling the corroded copper scroll in a lab in Manchester and first glimpsing its astounding contents. He had led a series of digs in Jordan and the West Bank, bankrolled by the London *Daily Mail*, but found nothing. The Copper Scroll, as far as I was concerned, could be checked off.

The day of my departure from Oxford was a gray, mackerel day, misty with the promise of rain. I packed my bag and left Yarnton for the Oxford railway station. Before taking the train into Paddington I called in on Naki who lived a few minutes' walk from the station. He had written a short letter with a number of further queries for Daud, and had found one or two articles on the Ark of the Covenant that he had photocopied for me.

As I bade him farewell, Naki gripped my arm.

"Don't give in to orthodoxy," he said. "Try to think originally. And by the way, do give my best regards to Reuven should you see him. But please don't believe *everything* he says. And don't do *everything* he tells you to do. He's had a very different sort of life to yours, and plays by *very* different rules."

I thought of my own sheltered British childhood and Reuven's wartime nightmare, and had to agree that he was probably right.

When I got into London I went straight to see my girlfriend. I used my key to let myself into her flat. It was not a long visit.

"*Imbecil!*"

The shoe flew across the room. It was a red stiletto-heeled number from the workshops of Salvatore Ferragamo. It had been flung by Maria, my Latin American *amorata*. It seemed to be a farewell of sorts.

I held out my arms in a gesture of reconciliation.

"What do you take me for, a chicken?" she asked. "It's time you understood that I am an eagle."

"Maria, you're a goose!" I said, trying to make her smile.

"No, you're goose. What's more important, me or Reuven? Me or that stupid imbecile Ark?"

"*Bébé!*" I implored.

She raised her slim, unimaginably beautiful arm again. The second shoe hit me. Nonetheless I moved toward her. We had spent a few memorable nights together immediately after my arrival from Egypt but most of the days had consisted of arguments about my protracted absences and my quest for the Ark. She reiterated her position. She wanted me to stop chasing my dreams and come down to earth. With her. Anyway, now that I had decided to return to Egypt, she had had enough. She insisted that I leave and suggested I give due attention to her words.

I crossed London to my flat in St. John's Wood. I thought to myself that Maria was like the Ark for me. I didn't ask myself why I loved her, I just did. It was beyond reason. I didn't really know why I was so determined to find the Ark. That too was beyond reason. Dejectedly I poured myself a stiffish drink and attended to the answering machine. There were a number of increasingly volatile messages in Spanish from Maria; a message in Brooklyn English from my Jerusalem friend Shula and one in what could best be termed Russo-English from an old friend at the School of Oriental and African Studies where I taught. He had summoned me this very evening for supper. I first telephoned Shula. She told me what was happening in Jerusalem and I told her what was happening in my life.

"A choice between Maria and the Ark?" she hooted. "That's no choice. Dump them both."

Once I had prepared my bag for the following day, I took the Bakerloo line from Maida Vale to Piccadilly and then changed to the Piccadilly line, which took me to Russell Square. Morosely I headed out to see my friend Alexander Piatigorsky, novelist, philosopher, and expert on Buddhism. He sat me down in a battered old armchair and laid a low table with smoked salmon and sturgeon, pickled cucumbers, black bread, cheeses from Latvia, and a bottle of Stolichnaya, which he insisted on serving at room temperature. Sasha had been my confidant for many years, and my first need was to tell him about Maria.

"Beauty, sex appeal, intelligence, and money are not *everything*," he said, his extraordinary voice resonating lugubriously in the small sitting room.

"They're not?"

"She is a wild, passionate woman but what, philosophically speaking, you need is a period without women. A period with *serious* men."

As I digested this bleak assessment, I told him about the other dilemma in which I found myself. Should I fully succumb to Reuven's entreaties or not? I told him about Patterson's warnings and the muted encouragement I had had from Naki. I told him how I was irresistibly drawn to this enterprise. But was this the path I should be taking?

He poured two small glasses of vodka, dipped a finger in his, flicking the vodka in all directions as he muttered a Buddhist prayer, and in his heavily accented English, fixing me with his one good eye, said, "The Buddhists say, 'If you are facing in the right direction all you have to do is keep on walking.' But," he added ironically, "you *do* have to be facing in the right direction." He walked backward and forward across the room, his hands behind his back, occasionally muttering something. Then he stopped and looked at me.

"Come on my friend!" he said. "My *dear* fellow. You will *never* find the Ark. Of that you can be, let us say, philosophically speaking, *absolutely* sure. But perhaps, just perhaps, the Ark will find *you!*"

OPPOSITES
ARE ONE

The heat hit like a wall as I left the terminal. It was the following day and I was standing outside Cairo International Airport in Heliopolis—the ancient Egyptian center of the cult of the sun god Ra—queuing sweatily for a taxi to take me into the center of town, my stained old canvas traveling bag slung over my shoulder.

A much-polished black Mercedes with tinted windows drew up a few yards away. The rear window opened and I saw Reuven beckoning with an impossibly well-manicured finger for me to join him.

"*Shalom uverukha,*" he said grinning, pulling me into the air-conditioned car beside him and giving me a hug. Unlike most of the European Jews I have known, Reuven was not usually one for much physical contact so I was slightly taken aback. I hugged him back quite naturally—I was delighted to see him.

He told me that he was in Cairo on business and that Naki had told him I was arriving today. I had spoken to Naki only the day before and he had said nothing at all about Reuven's being in Cairo.

We chatted for a few minutes and Reuven suggested I come over to his hotel and that we dine together. In the couple of days since he arrived, he told me, he had seen the U.S. ambassador, magnates, and ministers. He knew everyone.

He was staying at the Mena House, a famous old hotel that had once been the luxurious hunting lodge of Ismail, the nineteenth-century Khedive, or ruler of Egypt. The hotel nestled in a fine garden in the shadow of the Pyramids and when I had stayed there ten years before, the food had been excellent and I had a surprisingly vivid memory of a particular Egyptian wine I had been served. I was more than happy to renew my acquaintance with the Mena House, and even happier to catch up with Reuven's news.

He was dressed in an off-white linen suit, wore a pristine Panama hat, and had had his beard trimmed in a sort of modern Islamic style. There was no sign of his orthodox dress in any sense. Indeed, on his lap he held a string of thirty-three turquoise prayer beads of the sort sported by Egyptian gentlemen of a certain age, and he was wearing a pair of luridly colored crocodile shoes.

"*Very* Levantine, Reuven," I murmured nodding in the direction of his unfortunately clad feet.

"I thought I'd better make a tiny little effort at camouflage. Today, before I picked you up, I was talking to some of the most important Islamic scholars at the al-Azhar Islamic University about some manuscripts I bought last week in London. So I dressed up like a wealthy collector. Well, I *am* a wealthy collector. I'm traveling on a Dutch passport and am trying to give the impression of being something other than an Israeli Jew with plans to blow up the foundations of the

Dome of the Rock. Wouldn't play well at al-Azhar. Probably."
He laughed out loud.

During the twenty-mile drive from the airport to the Mena
House, Reuven told me about a conversation he had recently
had with an Israeli extremist called Yehuda Etzion who in 1980
had planned to blow up the Dome of the Rock as a way of sabo-
taging the Camp David Accords. Etzion knew that if he had
succeeded he would have brought about a Middle East war. But
he was convinced that Israel would win and the Arabs would be
crushed. He was planning to force the rebuilding of the
Temple, which he was convinced would bring forward the
coming of the Messiah.

"I heard about it," I said. "The guy's nuts."

"Of course. But the discovery of the Ark would make such
acts unnecessary. Even mainstream Jewish opinion, which
always veers between rationality and religious sentimentality
would accept the idea of a new Temple if the Ark were found.
And so, I believe, would the Muslims. They would probably
revere the Temple just as much as we do."

I coughed dubiously.

He told me he had found some intriguing Arabic texts that
spoke of the centrality of Jerusalem, rather than Mecca, for
Islam. The scholars at the Al-Azhar had initially been a little
shocked, then somewhat noncommittal, he said, but overall, he
thought, quite interested.

"Dynamite," he said.

"Er, how do you mean dynamite?" I asked, startled.

"Oh, the effect will be dynamite when the news gets out. If
they change the *qibla*—the direction of prayer—toward
Jerusalem rather than Mecca, as it once was, early in the

Prophet's ministry, it would have the immediate effect of bringing together all three of the great monotheistic religions: Judaism, Christianity, and Islam. They would all be praying in the same direction. That's only a step away from *thinking* in the same direction."

Reuven was very excited by these documents, and from his descriptions and the photocopies he showed me in the back of the Mercedes, they seemed to be quite early and genuine. However, I was pretty sure they were written by some early Jewish convert to Islam hankering after his former traditions, which would critically—indeed fatally—undermine their usefulness. I needed to see the originals before I could be sure, so I displayed an appropriate measure of enthusiasm and decided to say nothing more.

As we sat down to dinner I told him about my conversations with Naki and particularly about the *Tractate of the Temple Vessels,* which seemed to suggest that the Ark had once been taken, along with a fabulous hoard of treasure, to somewhere in Arabia. We ordered some oriental salads, a Nile perch, and, at my suggestion, a bottle of white Obelisk wine. He had the *sommelier* open the wine, then, as soon as his back was turned, and somewhat to my alarm, he put the Obelisk in his briefcase and extracted an unappealing, unlabeled bottle of something red.

"This is kosher wine," he hissed. "I steamed the label off just in case anyone noticed." He took out a French waiter's corkscrew and, with a grimace, pulled the cork.

"Good. Now I can drink with a clear conscience. Take the other bottle back to your hotel if you like."

It wasn't necessary in the event. With some satisfaction I drank most of the golden-colored Obelisk with its characteristic hints of straw and gooseberry, and Reuven sipped at the sweet, red kosher wine he sometimes pretended to like.

We talked until very late. I told him in detail about the *Tractate of the Temple Vessels* and the high hopes I had entertained in Oxford that this document could be the key to our quest. Reuven told me that he had already been given an account of the contents of the *Tractate* by one of the people he paid to research Jewish texts and that he had subsequently purchased a finely bound copy of the book from an Amsterdam antiquarian. He agreed that probably what Naki and I had concluded was correct.

Reuven's reasons for wanting to find the Ark were pretty compelling and some of them appealed to me. But my underlying reasons were different. Reuven was interested in national redemption for the Jewish people that, I suspected, included building the Third Temple. I was obsessed by the task of finding an object of immense historical importance that had eluded men for millennia. Finding it for the sake of finding it. While he spoke of celestial Jerusalem and the role of the Ark in the End of Days, I was concerned more with its remarkable history and the practical problems of locating it.

I told him about Vendyl Jones—an American researcher who claimed to be the inspiration for Steven Spielberg's *Raiders of the Lost Ark*. Jones had established the Vendyl Jones Research Center, had substantial funding, extremely good contacts in Israel and elsewhere, and, according to the American media, had already discovered a few years before, in 1989, the anointing oil used for the crowning and sanctification of the kings of Israel. He claimed to have come to the sacred oil by following the clues in the Copper Scroll.

"I know. He's well known in Israel. I've heard all about Vendyl Jones," said Reuven gloomily. "If what he claims is true, it's not bad. He appears to have used the Copper Scroll as his starting point but I think he makes things up as he goes along."

"I don't know about that. What I do know is that he has been on the trail of the Ark for at least twenty years and he has all the support and backup he can use. I must say it's not an entirely agreeable prospect to be in direct competition with the real-life Indiana Jones!"

All of a sudden we both felt overcome by the difficulty of the task. We sat in silence in the hopelessly grand restaurant, which was now empty except for us. Reuven looked tired and depressed. I took him by the arm and led him out into the garden where I hoped that the breeze coming in from the desert might freshen the atmosphere and lighten his mood. I ordered a Laphroaig for Reuven and a bottle of Stella—Egypt's best-known beer—for me. The garden was decked out with fairy lights. Some trick of the multicolored lighting allowed me to observe that Reuven's face was even more deeply furrowed than when I had seen him in his Tel Aviv flat about a year before. His hair was fading to a dull gray at the temples.

Without warning and looking out toward the desert, he announced: "Clara and I are going to spend some time in India. Partly business, partly mission." He shot me an apologetic smile.

"But how does *India* come into your quest?" I asked laughing. "You're not going to find the blessed Ark in *India!*"

"It's not just the Ark. It's the Islamic thing. My real quest. There are great Islamic libraries all over India and Pakistan—in places like Lucknow, Lahore, Aligarh. I've decided to invest a good deal more money in the project and I'm employing people to scour the Middle East to look for documents. For a while Clara and I shall be doing the job in the subcontinent. She's very excited. She's in London at the moment getting stuff for the trip. For some reason she's terrified of Jerusalem and the West Bank but will go anywhere in India. She feels safe there."

I felt I was losing touch fast.

"You're giving up on the Ark, Reuven?" I asked, stupefied. "This makes no sense at all. You're not honestly telling me that after all you have told me you are giving up on the Ark because Clara is afraid of her shadow?"

He looked away from me for a moment and then tried to meet my eyes. For the first time I perceived a look of guilt or shame on his face.

The year before in Jerusalem, he had told me quite a lot about Clara's early life. Now he told me a little more. She had had wartime experiences in Europe even more traumatic than his. He mentioned a few horrific details of her time in the camps as a little girl. She had survived, but at a price. According to the New York analyst she had been with for years she was deeply insecure and like all insecure people needed to dominate her immediate environment totally. But she was also genuinely afraid for him.

"She was terrified when she heard of the Hamas involvement last year," said Reuven. "And she received some sort of threat over the telephone last week in Tel Aviv. Someone speaking Hebrew with an Arab accent. She just can't understand how anyone got the number. She said it was someone from Hamas. She told me that if I didn't get out of the Ark business, she'd leave me. She doesn't mind me carrying on with my Islamic research, but since the Hamas threat, for her the Ark is *out*. She has put herself between me and the Ark and I shall find it difficult to forgive her. But I could not bear her to leave me. After my quest, she is my life."

"After your quest ... that's the problem, Reuven," I said gently with Maria very much on my mind. "Women always need to think that they are the transcendent fact of a man's existence."

He waved his hand dismissively. "Nonsense. Come up to my room. I have something to show you."

In the corner of his luxurious suite there was a mahogany stand bearing a gleaming Louis Vuitton suitcase. He opened it and inside there were a dozen or so books, a number of past issues of *al-Ahram*, the Egyptian newspaper, and a number of maps. Reuven took the contents and piled them on a table close to the French windows. He spread out a map of Africa and the Middle East.

He started talking about something that had been close to my heart for a long time: the connections between Africa and ancient Israel. He pointed out unlikely routes by sea and by the Nile, the direction of prevailing winds, desert tracks used by smugglers and slavers. He showed me an article in *al-Ahram* describing how the Red Sea might well have opened up a passage with the right wind and climatic conditions. He knew more than I had imaged he would on this topic. Folding up the map, he looked at me intently, his face showing signs of exhaustion. The brightly bound books spread out on the table were all about Ethiopia.

They were very far from the sober, difficult Hebrew and Aramaic texts that I used to find Reuven buried in the year before.

"There are a lot of current theories suggesting quite plausibly that the Ark was taken to Ethiopia." Pointing enthusiastically at the pile of books he said, "These books are full of it. It's something we simply have to look into." Glancing at his gold Cartier watch, he yawned and smiled apologetically, rubbing the side of his head—he had one of his terrible headaches and would have to closet himself in a darkened room until it passed. Proposing that we meet again the following evening, he accompanied me to the forecourt of the hotel where his driver was waiting to take me into town.

We shook hands. "I can't believe you are renouncing your great passion," I said.

"Well, I am," he said roughly. "I'm personally giving up the search. But that's the way things go. As you ought to know, people do what they can in their lifetime, in their own area, and then pass on the flame to the next generation. That's what I am doing. I'm passing it on. I'm passing it on to you."

Dirty dawn light was seeping into my whitewashed bedroom. It was very early in the morning and the city was only just beginning to stir. I had had only a few hours' sleep, but to confirm to myself that I really was back in Egypt I forced myself out of bed for a glimpse of the Nile in the early-morning light. From the small balcony I could see the great river and a good deal of the busy road that runs along its banks. A couple of hundred yards down the road I could see a couple walking along in deep conversation: a black-shirted man with a limp who looked somewhat like Daud, and a taller man wearing a light suit. I thought nothing of it, went back to bed, and dozed comfortably off. Several hours later something woke me. Through the communicating door I could see Daud creeping around in my sitting room, doing something furtive with a brass tray.

"What the hell are you doing here and who let you in, you creepy, debased little Copt?" I asked drowsily, rubbing the sleep out of my eyes.

"*Sabah al-kheyr*. Good morning! Your breakfast is ready, *effendi*," Daud announced cheerfully. "The guy on the front desk is a Copt, as you know, and when I told him I had bought breakfast for the distinguished British *effendi* in Room 6, he was only too happy to provide me with a key." He struck the key rhythmically against his gold cross.

I pulled myself out of bed and sat down on the sitting room sofa. After a few moments' conversation it became clear that it *had* been Daud I'd seen on Abdul-Aziz al-Saud Street earlier that morning. He'd been in a meeting, he told me, and had now decided to wake me up in style. Fingering his cross, his shoulders hunched, he told me how embarrassed he had been about our last conversation and his miserable state as we walked back from the City of the Dead.

"Forget all those things I said," he murmured. "'Let the light of the day efface the word of the night,' as we say in Arabic."

He'd brought me the standard Egyptian fava bean breakfast dish called *ful medames*. We ate the *ful* out on the balcony and enjoyed a good Egyptian coffee in the hot, late morning sun. Daud was in excellent spirits—the mood of quiet desperation that had characterized him for some time had completely disappeared.

"I'm told you were at the Mena House last night," he said. "That's not a place for someone like you. It's just for rich tourists."

I did not bother to ask him how he knew. Daud always had strangely reliable sources of information about most things. But it did occur to me that if the Mena House were not for me, what would a friend of his be doing there? To change the subject I told him about Naki and presented him with the letter and the various lexicographical queries he had had. He smiled enigmatically and put them into the pocket of his black shirt.

That afternoon I had asked Daud to arrange for me to have a private viewing of some of the holdings of the Egyptian Museum of Antiquities in Tahrir Square, close to the east bank of the Nile. For some time I had wanted to see the artifacts that were the closest in conception to the description of the Ark in the Bible. Freud's suggestion that Moses was an Egyptian prince influenced by the heretical monotheism of the pharaoh Akhenaten interested me and I was eager to see the artifacts from this period. I had also read that some of the coffers and chests found in the tomb of Tutankhamen were extremely close to the more elaborate descriptions of the Ark in the Bible. Perhaps the museum holdings would help me to understand better the nature of what I was looking for.

"Now you'll see what Coptic civilization is all about," said Daud.

"You're mad, Daud. You are obsessed by bloody Copts. For God's sake, it's a museum of ancient Egyptian antiquities!"

"Same thing, *effendi*," said Daud stubbornly.

For Daud this was the great repository of the true pre-Islamic heritage of Egypt: the heritage of his people. Without doubt it is the finest collection of treasures from the time of the pharaohs in the world. We walked smugly past the queue of harassed-looking tourists and were ushered in to the cool, high-ceilinged office of one of the curators, where we were served more thick black Egyptian coffee. Daud chatted for a while with his curator friend, who then conducted us around the exhibits.

We first visited the remarkable collection of artifacts from the reign of the heretical pharaoh Akhenaten (1364–1347 BC). During the New Kingdom, the cult of the sun god Ra turned gradually into the uncompromising monotheism of Akhenaten. Ra was not only the god of the sun, he was also the god of the universe. He *was* the universe. He created himself out of himself. Ra was visualized as Aten, or the Great Disc that gave light to both the world of the living and the world of the dead.

What impact, I wondered, did the monotheism of the heretical pharaoh have on the imagination of Moses? If Freud was right and Moses was not a Jew but an Egyptian—not a slave baby found by an Egyptian princess in a basket, but an Egyptian prince—Moses could indeed have absorbed his belief in the One God from this Egyptian source.

With these thoughts on my mind, I followed Daud and his friend upstairs to see the treasures of Tutankhamen. Naki was not the only one to have suggested that there was some similarity between some of the objects found by the British archaeologist Howard Carter in the tomb of Tutankhamen in 1922 and the Ark of the Covenant, and I was anxious to see if the similarities were real. Whoever the historical Moses was, he would surely have been aware of some of the artifacts of the period of Tutankhamen.

Among the funeral objects there was a small wooden shrine overlaid with gold, which was close to the Biblical description of the Ark but not exactly the same. However, the principle of construction was identical—wood covered with fine sheets of gold. The canopic chest was also similar and seemed to have an arrangement for carrying it on poles; in addition, there was a small and very heavy solid alabaster chest with two ibexes at either end of a boat, with their horns forming a kind of canopy somewhat similar in conception to the cherubim on the lid of the Ark. When these objects were first discovered by Carter, they were in a sort of storeroom to one side of the burial chamber, which is now referred to as the treasury.

The treasury was filled with ornate boxes and model boats: many of the boxes were Ark-like and some had carrying poles. One particularly ornate chest along with carrying poles was almost exactly what one imagines when one reads the biblical description of the Ark. Another striking item in this room was a large gilded canopic shrine, inside which was a chest made out of a single block of calcite. Inside this chest were the canopic jars, each in the shape of a highly decorated coffin holding the pharaoh's embalmed organs—liver, lungs, stomach, and intestines.

I stared at these displays and could see that in many ways the Ark was really very similar to a number of these objects. The more ornate of the two biblical descriptions of the Ark was similar to that of an Egyptian chest. It was also striking that the images in beaten gold on the doors and sides of the shrines contained two terrifying winged women, which were reminiscent of the cherubim in solid gold superimposed upon either side of the Ark, according to the biblical account.

I gazed at these stunning objects for a long time. Everything here formed part of an ancient Middle Eastern religious system in which gods were presented in a very specific way, often seated and flanked on both sides by winged creatures.

A couple of days before in Oxford I had bumped into my old friend David Hawkins, one of the world's leading scholars of the language and culture of the ancient Hittites, who were one of the great powers of the ancient Near East. He was a colleague of mine at the School of Oriental and African Studies. Over a pint of beer in the King's Arms, he had explained to me that even as far north as Anatolia, modern-day Turkey, the standard way for gods to be presented was sitting on some kind of a seat with winged creatures on either side. And the same was true of Babylon and ancient Egypt. Exactly like the Ark.

A critical difference between the Ark and the usual statues of ancient Near Eastern deities, though, was that Middle Eastern gods were usually big and very visible whereas the God on the Ark, Jehovah, was eerily invisible. There were statues of Middle Eastern gods, but the Jews were not allowed to try to depict their god. So between the conventional winged creatures there was a gap.

He was there, one supposes, but you could not see him.

"In the context of the ancient world," said David, "this was a difficult one to pull off. It might have seemed like a cheap con trick."

"Possibly," I agreed, "or else it might have been just a tiny bit unnerving."

"Or not," he replied tartly.

It did look to me as if the more elaborate account of the making of the Ark in Exodus was simply an attempt to bring the central object in the Israelite cult into line with other great Middle Eastern religions. Looking at the chests of Tutankhamen

I realized that these were works of consummate craftsmanship that would have taken many skilled workers a very, very long time to achieve. A well-equipped workshop, fine tools, the best materials would have been required. None of these things could have been available in the Sinai desert.

And why would the text have stressed the importance of the Ark being constructed in acacia wood? The wood here on these chests was completely covered by gold. The wood was secondary, unimportant. Which of the two accounts in the Bible was likely to be more accurate? The one in Deuteronomy where the humble Ark is presented in all simplicity and modesty, or the one in Exodus where the Ark is dressed up to make it look like any other Middle Eastern God-shrine? I mumbled to myself the first-person passage in Deuteronomy where Moses gives his account of what happened when he went back up the mountain after breaking the first tablets of the law in anger when he saw the Israelites worshiping the golden calf. I considered this version to be the "simple" account:

> At that time God said unto me, "Hew two tables of stone like unto the first and come up unto me into the mount and make an Ark of wood. And I will write on the tablets the words that were in the first tablets which you broke, and you shall put them in the Ark." And I made an Ark of shittim wood, and hewed two tablets of stone like unto the first, and went up into the mount, having the two tablets in my hand.

Looking at the fabulous chests of Tutankhamen, I realized in a flash that the Ark was not like that. The Ark was something like the *ngoma*—simple, rustic, homemade, using available wood from the desert. Its meaning was utterly different too.

"Why are you mumbling to yourself, *effendi*?" asked Daud.

"I was just trying to remember a quotation. Nothing important. I was just looking at those chests."

"They look very much like the Ark of the Covenant, don't they?" he said with a strangely malicious smile that I found a little unsettling.

"I don't quite remember. They possibly look a bit like *one* of the biblical descriptions of the Ark as I recall," I said cagily.

"There's a sort of elaborate model," said Daud, "and the simple model. One is very fancy, all gold and cherubim, and one is a simple wooden container."

"How is the widow?" I said, trying to change the direction of the conversation.

He ignored that completely and, scratching his head, said, "The Egyptians certainly had things that looked quite a bit like the elaborate model and the idea of priests carrying cultic things round on poles was very common."

He looked at his watch and indicated that we should make our way out of the museum. As we walked through the great halls he continued, "If you go to Luxor you'll find reliefs on the walls of a colonnade in the Great Temple that tell the story of an important feast in ancient Egypt called the Festival of Apet. The relief was made during the reign of Tutankhamen at the pharaoh's command. This means it was constructed just a few decades before the exodus of the Israelites from Egypt.

"The festival of Apet included the spectacle of Arks being carried aloft on poles by priests in the full sight of the adoring masses. There were times of the day when you'd have difficulty avoiding bumping into priests carrying around Arks on poles. They were everywhere. The nasty, evil-smelling Hebrew slaves were presumably kept well away from fragrant cultic areas, but nonetheless they must have seen objects like this all the time. The Arks of Apet have the form of little wooden boats, probably covered with gold."

Daud was positively bursting with pride at the achievements of his ancestors. He told me about the incredible discovery, two years earlier, of fourteen ships dating from the period of the first dynasty (2950–2775 BC). Almost 5,000 years old, the ships were found buried side by side in the desert, about eight miles from the Nile. The vessels may have been intended for the afterlife use of Aha, the first ruler of Egypt. Their wooden hulls and decks were intact and even the woven straps that were used to hold the planks together and the compacted reeds that were used to fill the gaps between the planks were preserved. Similar boats for the afterlife had also been found at the Great Pyramid at Giza.

"First proper boats in the world were built by the Copts," Daud concluded smugly.

The thought that immediately occurred to me was that if these wooden boats could survive for 5,000 years in the right conditions, the idea of the wooden Ark of the Covenant surviving for a paltry 3,000 years did not seem so fantastic.

Even though I wanted to steer the conversation away from the Ark, I couldn't help asking Daud a final question.

"Daud, do you yourself think that the Arks of Apet could have had the same form as the Ark of Moses? Do you think that the wooden coffer of the Bible was actually just a kind of model boat?"

"It might have been. It's actually a bit confusing. I know that there are two words in Hebrew for what you call in English

'Ark.' There's the word *aron*—that's right, isn't it?—and the word *teva*. *Aron* is the Ark of the Covenant and *teva* is Noah's Ark and the thing the prophet Moses was found in next to the Coptic church. The thing is, they are all translated into the Greek with the word *kíbotos*. There is room for some confusion here. I mean I daresay one could justify an ancient tradition that the sense was 'boat.'"

"Seems a bit unlikely," I said. "The idea of carrying a little boat in front of troops crossing a desert makes approximately zero sense."

"You're right, *effendi*. At least it makes no sense to *us*. Might have done to *them*, but unfortunately we don't know anything about the way their mind worked. In Arabic as well, the word for Ark is *tabut* and this is also the word for the ark that concealed the baby Moses—and in the Muslim tradition this ark is also in the form of a wooden container. But anyway, probably, the Jews' Ark was just a *chest*—like one of the elaborate chests in the treasure room of Tutankhamen."

"Perhaps," I said grudgingly. "Anyway, the Tutankhamen chests are strikingly similar to the more elaborate of the two biblical descriptions of the Ark."

"It makes you think," said Daud who bizarrely did not seem to be tiring of this endless Ark conversation. "You know if Tutankhamen's boxes could survive in such perfect shape for over 3,000 years, I believe the Ark could have survived as well."

There was something about his bony, ill-shaped face, and a teasing lilt to his voice as he said this, that made me suspect he knew far more about my interests than he was letting on, and far more than I wanted him to know.

"Sounds a bit far-fetched to me," I muttered, lengthening my stride and pushing ahead into the frenetic evening crowd. I wanted to walk away from this conversation as fast as I could.

Daud soon caught up with me. His limp never prevented him from achieving impressive bursts of speed when required.

He gripped me firmly by the arm, swung me around, and looked me straight in the face.

"I think we need to talk," he said.

Dodging the cars, we made our way through the din and pollution of the grimy downtown district, which stretches out from Tahrir Square to the Ramses and Ataba Squares. On al-Alfi Street, Daud ducked down a little alley and into a small hotel that had seen much better days.

I had heard that the Windsor was a good place to go for a drink, but I had never been here before. However, there was something strangely familiar about the place.

Daud steered me through a dimly lit, antiques-lined corridor to the not uncongenial Barrel Bar. The Windsor had originally been built as a bathing annex for the Egyptian royal family, which gave it a certain bizarre chic. It was subsequently demoted to a British officers' club. It still had an agreeable dingy, clubby atmosphere. Today there were half a dozen Egyptian men drinking whisky and beer and speaking three or four languages at the same time. I bought a couple of Stellas and we sat down at a corner table.

Lighting one of his repellent Egyptian cigarettes, Daud took a pull at his beer and gave me a penetrating look. "I thought this particular bar would be as appropriate a place as any to have this conversation, perfidious Albion," he said with a rather foolish grin on his face.

"Why? Who are you calling perfidious, you corrupt little Copt? What's special about this bar? What conversation?" I looked round the bar nervously.

"Well, part of *Raiders of the Lost Ark* was filmed here, *effendi*. Our good friend Indiana Jones slept under this very roof. No doubt drank at this very table. Told outrageous stories and profitable lies on the very rubbish chairs we are sitting on. And I thought that this evening we could have a very, very interesting conversation. We *could* be talking about *your* quest to find the Jews' ultimate weapon—the Ark of the Covenant, my perfidious Mr. British Indiana Jones."

He was looking at me with a serious expression on his face which harbored just the slightest suggestion of a rather disagreeable smirk.

He obviously knew something, so I decided to own up. I took a pull at the ice-cold Stella, eyed him coldly, and, in as neutral a tone as I could manage, asked, "How do you know?"

"Ah, so it's true!" Daud's face expressed the liveliest gratification. "How do I know? It's not very complicated. Your friend Doniach telephoned me a day or so back to put me in touch with Reuven, thinking I could help him find ancient Arabic and Coptic manuscripts. I gave him a call. He had just got into town. And I met him face-to-face this morning, which is when he told me all about your interest in the Ark."

"Reuven?" I asked.

"The Dutch collector. You know. You had dinner with him at the Mena House."

"Ah, so *Reuven* told you," I muttered. "It's true, academically speaking of course, that I have a growing interest in the topic. You know, sort of history-of-ideas stuff."

"Reuven is an amazing man," Daud interrupted. "I didn't think Jews were like that. You remember that weird short story of Kafka where the mouse is about to be caught in a trap and the cat is looming behind it and the mouse says, 'Alas ... the world is growing narrower every day.' Reuven has had an awful life and his beloved people are in a perilous situation. But what does he do? He makes the world *expand* every day! I have never met anyone like him. He told me about his mission to try to bring peace to the world by finding some ancient document that would reconcile Muslims and Jews. It is a remarkable idea. It touches my scholar's heart. The man is a true visionary! The only thing I don't understand is why he is so driven. It's a kind of madness. He talks only of his mission.

"I think he feels that he let his father down when he was a little boy. Reuven has spent his life making up for the fact that when he was a kid of five he didn't want to learn Hebrew or go to synagogue. Ultimately we all do what our parents wanted us to do at some point or another. I've often thought that my own affection for Jews and Israel is part of the hard-wiring of my own childhood."

Daud fingered his cross nervously. "Yes—*my* father wanted me to be a priest. But I'm not about to oblige him—my only real ambition is to finish my doctorate. The other great thing about Reuven is that he has a fascination for all things Coptic. I told him about the Nag Hammadi collection and he can't wait to see it. He has asked me to help him. I know he's a Jew, I believe he's even an Israeli, but who cares? He is paying me incredibly, I mean *incredibly* well. *Wallah!* Do you know what it means? I'll be able to get married, *in sha-allah*. The sublime widow will be a thing of the past!"

To toast this much desired outcome, I called for a couple more Stellas.

"To a widowless future," I said, raising my glass.

Daud smiled his crooked black-tooth smile. "Listen—the money is good. But that's not really the point. You won't understand this but I really do *believe* in what he's doing to reconcile the peoples of this region."

"Come on. Don't give me that. You hate Jews and you couldn't give a stuff about the region. All you're interested in is your bloody Gnostic gospels!"

"Not true, *effendi*," he said, trying to look hurt. "I can see now that Middle East Christians have been abandoned by rubbish America and Europe. Reuven has persuaded me that the best ally the Coptic Christians in Egypt and the Maronite Christians in Lebanon and the Assyrians in Iraq and the Christians in the Sudan and in the rest of the Middle East have is the Jews." He lit another noxious cigarette.

I could hear Daud echoing Reuven's phrases and even intonation. Daud, I concluded glumly, was under the spell.

"But does he know that you fornicate with whores in cemeteries, are a pitiful, small-time police informer, and work for Egyptian intelligence?"

"Oh, yes, I told him that," he said gaily. "I mean I told him about my work. He was rather pleased. I know *he* works for somebody too. I dare say their wonderful rubbish Mossad will pass me the odd shekel from time to time." He giggled and whirled his cross around like a propeller.

"But Daud," I repeated, "you *hate* Jews and Israel. This is the issue where you show yourself at your vile worst. You never stop going on about the Zionist menace."

"It is true, *ya achi*, as you say. I have spent my life hating Jews—with a few honorable exceptions. Reuven has made me understand that in some ways Muslims and Jews and Christians are essentially the same. There are some differences but he is right—the differences are minimal. *Wallah*. Each of the three great faiths is the jagged point of a triangle. At the center of the triangle there is a dark shadow, which is where we overlap. The shadow is our common voice. 'We have studied the dark and the day through their common voice and conclude that opposites are one.'"

It was barely credible that even Reuven could have turned Daud—the arch anti-Zionist—into a fervent supporter of a grand alliance of Jews and Middle East Christians, an apostle of coexistence between the peoples and faiths of the Middle East. It was also barely credible that Reuven had spoken to Daud, an alcoholic, small-time police informer about my interest in the Ark without telling me first. I had told Reuven about the warning I had received from my old friend Luba in Jerusalem that looking for the Ark could get me into trouble with Palestinian extremists. The Muslim brotherhood in Egypt could easily have been tipped off. I could not *begin* to fathom his reasons.

"My academic interests are my affair. I can't say that I'm delirious with pleasure at the thought of them being picked over on every street corner in Cairo. Did he ask *you* to get involved in anything to do with the Ark?" I asked.

"He mainly wants me to look for manuscripts. What he did say was that I could help you if you needed it. He did sort of suggest that you were actually looking for the Ark here in Egypt. You don't have to worry—I won't pass that on to Egyptian intelligence—although it's the sort of tidbit they would pay quite well for. Is there any reason to think that it is here?"

"As you ask—there's nothing very specific to suggest it's *anywhere*, let alone in Egypt. That's the whole problem," I said. "There's just a passage in the book of Kings somewhere that suggests it *might* have been taken to Egypt before the Babylonian invasion."

"Yes, that's what *Raiders of the Lost Ark* suggests," said Daud, the foolish grin still on his face. "It also suggests that Adolf Hitler tried to get the Ark in order to rule the world. But the bit in the book of Kings about Egypt is more historical."

He pushed a strand of jet black hair back from his forehead, creating the usual snowstorm effect, and started to swing his cross. Grinning demonically, he started to chant: "'In the fifth year of King Rehoboam, Shishak, the king of Egypt attacked Jerusalem. He carried off treasures of the temple of the Lord and the treasures of the royal palace. He took everything, including all the gold shields Solomon had made.'"

"Bravo," I said grudgingly. "Yes, that's the passage. It seems he did not actually sack Jerusalem in the end but was bought off with the Temple treasure. It is *possible* that the Ark was taken then. But at the same time there is no actual proof that it was. If it had been given to the Egyptians during the reign of Rehoboam, surely there would have been endless lamentation, wailing, and gnashing of teeth. There would have been special days of mourning devoted to this tragic event. All there is is silence."

"Probably the name Shishak in the Hebrew actually signifies the Egyptian pharaoh Sheshonq. Sheshonq I was the founder of the 22nd Dynasty," said Daud. "He is known to have conducted a remarkably successful campaign in Palestine and the Sinai. But there is no mention of the Ark being captured in any of the Egyptian records—if they had captured anything as important as that, it would surely have shown up on one of the wall inscriptions at Luxor."

I wasn't sure about that. It seemed to me that the idea that the Ark, whatever it was, had been taken to Egypt long before the Babylonian conquest was not one that we could dismiss quite yet.

Before leaving my room to go out that evening, I put a call through to Naki in Oxford. After a moment's conversation I was convinced that his actions were transparent and honorable. His great dictum after all was "only connect." He was simply facilitating contacts between people he liked or found interesting. Between me and Reuven, between Reuven and Daud. It's the sort of thing he did all the time. If he had any hidden agenda it was beyond me. I knew that there was some special bond between Reuven and Naki that went back many years but I had long ago stopped trying to get to the bottom of that. But I had no doubts at all about his friendship for me. He wanted me to pass on his regards to Reuven with whom I had agreed to dine that evening, and he repeated his warning. "Don't let him talk you into things!"

Reuven and I had an overly elaborate dinner in one of the fancy marble-clad modern hotels along the Nile. That evening he was the model of urbane geniality. But I was upset with him and felt that my relationship with academic Egyptian friends had been compromised.

"Why in God's name did you bring Daud into it? He's a good friend of mine and I know him well—well enough to know that he's half mad and he's a drunk. He's interested only in the money."

"I think you'll find that Daud will prove to be a good friend to us all and an able collaborator," said Reuven in his businessman's voice. "He knows how to multitask and has a sensible relationship with financial resources. Unlike you, he understands money. You could learn something from him yourself. Do you know how he got his limp?"

"No idea," I said huffily. "I never asked. None of my business."

"He got his limp where I got my headaches. He was wounded in the Sinai during the Yom Kippur War. We fought in the same place at the same time. On opposite sides of course. That brings you close to a man." Reuven paused for a moment, then continued ponderously. "I have some experience in these things and with Daud. I know that I am not wrong. The arrangement he has entered into with me will change his life and may contribute to the changing of many lives."

He told me more about the conversation he had with Daud and how Daud had undertaken to spend time, when he was not working on his doctorate, looking for ancient Islamic manuscripts on Reuven's behalf. Reuven was rather convincing. At the very least, Daud was energetic, passionate, and had an extraordinary knowledge of everything to do with Egypt.

But Reuven really wanted to talk about the Ark. Time, he feared, was running out for him. He was going to have to start taking it easy. His headaches were becoming increasingly frequent and increasingly intense and he had had some dispiriting results from tests he had had done at the London Clinic a month or two before. He did not spell it out, but he had serious health issues to resolve. This was certainly his last trip without Clara. He had promised her. Would I take on his quest? He looked at me with those diamond-cutter eyes of his.

"The time has come," he told me. "There are glittering prizes waiting—not just for us but for the whole of the Middle East. I have spent over a year trying, in my own way, as an individual, using my own money. Do you know what I did? I've employed a dozen PhD students in Israel for the last six months. Their job was to go through all the Jewish texts—biblical, Mishnaic, Rabbinic, Kabbalistic—and to look for useable clues for the continued existence of the Ark. They came up with nothing. I think I can say now that there is nothing in the Jewish traditional texts that is going to help us find the Ark. I have read everything pretty much that those guys came up with. I'm at a dead end. I guess I do not have what it takes. What is needed is someone with the right kind of *shnoz*."

I blinked uncertainly at him and said, "The right kind of nose? Do you mean a Jewish nose? Am I understanding you correctly? You mean someone Jewish?"

He fingered his own substantial nose and said, "No, that's not what I mean. No, what I mean is someone who is receptive to Jewish things but not necessarily a Jew. Jews don't make good detectives. In fact I can't think of a single great literary Jewish detective. Plenty of British ones though, from Sherlock Holmes to Lord Peter Wimsey. It needs someone with a nose for these things. What the French call *avoir du flair*. We think you have this quality."

"Who do you mean by we?" I asked.

"Oh some of my Israeli friends," he said evasively.

"I don't know if I would make a good detective. All I can say is that I quite enjoy a good puzzle I can get my teeth into."

Reuven's eyes were moist. It was a very hot night and he kept wiping his brow with a linen handkerchief. His handsome face, with its well-worn patina of wealth and power, was revealing more of its owner than it ever had before. He seemed to be short of breath, and spittle had formed into a tight bead on his upper lip. He was trying to persuade me to take over his quest completely. He moved from poetry, to global politics, to national redemption, and then back again to poetry.

Then he stopped and gave me a smile I had not seen before. It was only afterward that I realized that it was the smile of a man who knows exactly what will happen next.

Feeling the hand of history on my shoulder, I sighed.

"OK, Reuven," I said. "I'll take it on."

7

THE FIRST
CATARACT

When I woke up the next morning I felt a lightening of the spirit. The walls of the hotel room seemed whiter and the morning sky bluer. The frontiers of my life had significantly changed.

I still had no idea how I would proceed with the task of finding the Ark, but at least I had made a decision. I had taken over the quest from Reuven. My obsession had finally and irrevocably won out.

I dressed with particular care that morning. I put on a clean white shirt, a linen suit, and a pair of decently aged Church's brogues before I set off to the American University in Cairo where I needed to check a couple of things in their library. As I made my way down Abd ul-Aziz al-Saud Street I felt as if I were walking on air.

A few days later Daud and I went out to the airport to see Reuven off. He was flying directly to Paris to meet up with Clara. They would soon be leaving for India. His active involvement in looking for the Ark of the Covenant was apparently over.

The night before his departure, Reuven sent his driver to take me out to the Mena House. He was in a strange mood and drank a lot more than he usually did. In the stately restaurant where we had dined the evening I arrived back from London, he produced another bottle of the kosher wine from his briefcase. We ate some sort of a *mezzeh* with *baba ghanoug* and *humus bitehinnah* and chickpeas and some Nile catfish. Reuven ordered a bottle of Pouilly Fumé for me. We talked for an hour or so of various developments in Israel, centering on the increasingly desperate search for the Ark.

Over a couple of glasses of Laphroaig in the garden, he reiterated as he always did that if ever I had need of funds I should just call Ronit—his personal assistant in the Tel Aviv office—and money would be wired to me immediately. But he was anxious to know how I was planning to proceed with the quest. He wanted to help arrange transport, hotels, security. He wanted to give me introductions to ministers, ambassadors, tycoons. He wanted to be involved in my plans.

But I had no plans. I had given him my word that I would devote myself to studying the Ark, but Reuven clearly wanted more dramatic action out of me.

"Go somewhere else. Please go somewhere else!" he urged.

"Why should I go anywhere else? I'm already somewhere else. The Ark is as likely to be in Egypt as it is anywhere. A good deal more so."

"Well, go to some of those old Coptic monasteries in the Eastern Desert. Go to the southern mountains. Try looking for remote caves. Hire a Landrover and guides. Take a girl along. I'll get Ronit to come down. Mount an expedition. Hire guides. I'll cover all the costs. Just do it!"

I squirmed, yawned, adjusted my glasses, and smiled wearily at him, thinking that the Eastern Desert was a big place to search for something if you did not even have the slightest, faintest, wavering glimmer of an idea where it was. On the other hand the idea of mounting an expedition with the highly intelligent, beautiful, long-haired Ronit was not unappealing, as he knew very well, and for a second or so my resolve faltered. But only for a second. I told him that the best thing for me was to continue with my reading until I had some slightly firmer sense of where I was going. But I knew that sooner or later I would have to travel, perhaps to the ends of the earth.

We strolled around the gardens of the hotel, enjoying the evening air and the inspiring spectacle of the Great Pyramid. Reuven seemed a little irritated with me and I felt a cooling of his affection. He kept asking if I had reached any sort of conclusions.

"I'm sort of more at the introduction stage," I answered, smiling. "The conclusions, I fear, are some little way away!"

He suggested acidly that I might accelerate the process by reading some more up-to-date books.

"You do nothing but read the Bible and the rabbinic tests—the Mishnah, the Talmud. I've *done* that. My *assistants* have done that. It got me nowhere. It got *them* nowhere. It'll get you nowhere. Try thinking. For goodness' sake, change tack! Read something else!"

What he appeared to have in mind were the luridly colored volumes about Ethiopia I had seen in his suite on my previous visit to the Mena House and that to my mind compared poorly with the serious, difficult, leather-bound old books in a range of oriental languages with which I associated him, and that in many ways had formed the basis of our friendship.

The work that had most excited him recently, and with which he was now insistent that I engage, was a recently published book by Graham Hancock called *The Sign and the Seal: The Quest for the Lost Ark of the Covenant*.

As we got back to our table in a dimly lit corner of the garden, he pleaded with me to read it before he left Egypt. He wanted to know what I thought of it. It appeared, he said, to suggest that the Ark was to be found in Ethiopia, that Hancock had located it there.

"I do rather fear that a book of this sort isn't really going to help us all that much," I said tetchily, thrusting my hands into my baggy linen trousers. "It may be entertaining but it's obviously a book of popular journalism."

I reluctantly took my hands out of my pockets and picked up the book that Reuven was eagerly pushing toward me and read aloud from the cover.

"'This book shatters the greatest secret of the last 3,000 years.' Wow! That's quite a claim. Look, I think it's fairly obvious that there is no scholarship here, Reuven," I said, flicking through the pages. "The man does not even know any of the relevant languages. Edward Ullendorff who, as you know, is a very senior colleague of mine at SOAS, has frequently remarked that you can know nothing of Ethiopia without knowing its languages. Ullendorff knows all of them. Reading this will be a complete waste of my time. If I want to know anything about Ethiopia, all I have to do is pick up the telephone and talk to Ullendorff. He knows more about Ethiopia than a hundred Hancocks. Daud told me that he had read somewhere that Ullendorff rubbished Hancock's entire theory."

Reuven took my two hands in his and gazed at me with his diamond-cutter's eyes. "Please. Just read it," he said, "you'll see he's on to something. Maybe he stumbled on it inadvertently. Maybe he did not deserve to. Perhaps he was far too ignorant to get there deliberately. Maybe an angel whispered something into his ear. But he's onto something. I can feel it!"

Sitting in the Mercedes on the way back from the Mena House to Cairo, depressed by Reuven's impending departure, I thought of what he had said. And that night, sitting on my little balcony overlooking the darkened river, punctured by mosquitoes, I started to read Hancock's book. Reuven was not entirely wrong. Some parts of it did seem to make some sense.

One of the more sensible ideas was that the Ark had been removed from the Temple of Solomon during the reign of the infamous and sacrilegious King Manasseh (687–638 BC) and, some time prior to its arrival in Ethiopia where Hancock claimed to have found it, it had been spirited away by the priests to the tiny island of Elephantine in the Nile, near Aswan and just below the first cataract. The remarkable thing about Elephantine was that a Jewish temple had been built there, possibly during Manasseh's reign. The idea was worth looking at.

Huddled in a hotel blanket against the damp chill rising from the river, I read a few pages. Then I turned again to the relevant passages in the worn little Hebrew Bible, which had been given to me years before when I was a young volunteer in Jerusalem. I read and reread the texts. Rabin had given me two pieces of advice: *go to the text, follow the priests.* But there was simply no clue. I went again to the great Hebrew lexicon, Brown, Driver, and Briggs, which I had brought with me from London, and looked up the etymologies of some of the key words and concepts.

As I sat up that night, I allowed my mind to roam and I permitted myself a few moments of pure speculation. I recalled the Jewish legends that described the miraculous objects into which the Ark had breathed life in the Temple and the utter sanctity that surrounded it. If Manasseh had been half as bad as he was portrayed in the Bible, the priests would have *had* to get the Ark away. If they did remove the Ark beyond the reach of the sacrilegious king, where would they have taken it?

Had they gone west they would have reached the coast, which would have been patrolled by troops loyal to the king; had they gone north or east they may have strayed into territory controlled by the Assyrians. The route from Jerusalem, which would have presented the priests with the least risk of being discovered, was probably down through the craggy Judean hills to the barren that which lay beyond. Following little-frequented desert tracks they would have been well advised to head toward Egypt, the powerful neighboring state where they would be far enough away to be safe from pursuit.

Alternatively, perhaps Manasseh had been glad to be rid of his priestly archenemies and to be rid of an object that in the past had inflicted such harsh and unusual punishment on the enemies of the One God, such as him. Perhaps he thought of the plague of bleeding hemorrhoids meted upon the unfortunate citizens of Ashdod, Ekron, and Gath. Obviously the Ark was a potent weapon, a secret weapon, and as such it should not be allowed to fall into the hands of the enemy, but it had been known to turn on those who did not follow the law, and at this stage of his life Manassseh most certainly did not follow the law.

Perhaps he had patted the priests on the back, lent them his best mule to carry the troublesome Ark, and sent them on their way with humus sandwiches for the road and a keg of the best wine the royal vineyards could produce.

Dawn was breaking by the time I finally got to bed. I slept for an hour or so, breakfasted on *ful medames* on the sunny terrace, and telephoned Reuven at the Mena House.

"You read it?" he asked breathlessly. "Good. I am *convinced* he is onto something. He reckons the Jerusalem priests took it away from Jerusalem and brought it to Egypt. That's the way forward. Follow the path the priests took. That's what Rabin told you, isn't it? *Follow the priests.*"

Reuven had his driver take him to the airport and Daud and I took a taxi out to bid him farewell. The traffic was even worse than usual. A pall of pollution hung over Cairo. On the long drive out to Heliopolis I thought more about the Elephantine theory. Whether the Ark had been removed at the time of Manasseh's crimes against the religion of Israel or subsequently—perhaps prior to the destruction of Jerusalem in 587 BC—it was at least a reasonable hypothesis that the priests would have wanted to take it to a sacred Jewish site outside Israel. There was only one—and that was the Jewish temple of Elephantine. *If I had been a priest, I thought, that is what I would have done.*

Reuven had little desire to be leaving Egypt. His good-byes were protracted and sorrowful. Before he went through to passport control, he presented me with a couple of bottles of Laphroaig and a tearful smile and pressed a bulging, brown paper envelope into Daud's not entirely reluctant hand. He was going off to meet up with his beautiful wife but he did not look like a happy man.

I had some serious reading to do over the next couple of days as well as various things to do in a Cairo archive. Having read as much as I wanted to, I passed Hancock's book to Daud who was happy to add it to his library.

A couple of days later Daud reappeared. He was wearing a shiny new black suit. His cumbersome gold cross partly obscured a tie on which I observed an amply proportioned girl in a bikini squatting on a pyramid. He stormed into my room in the hotel, flung the book on the sofa, and said:

"*Wallah*! You take me for an idiot! This is not a scientific book. I may not have finished my PhD but I do like to think of myself as a scholar."

Daud was very cross. His bony malformed face was streaked with what looked like tears.

"This Hancock," he said, picking at a blackened tooth. "He knows no Coptic. I repeat: he knows no *Coptic*. He jumbles everything up and drags in every cliché from modern rubbish writing from the Freemasons to the Holy Grail, from the rubbish Great Pyramid to Atlantis and mystic energy sources and spacemen-built-the-pyramids fantasies, when everybody knows it was the Copts. And that's the worst thing. He knows *nothing* about the Copts."

"But Daud, he's not writing about the bloody Copts," I said reasonably. "Anyway, it's fairly readable and from the bit I have read, quite pacy. It resists orthodoxy, which is a good thing. I agree that you have a point in that he follows current fads. But I think it's OK in its way. I promise you that nobody's trying to diminish you as a scholar, Daud." I was concerned that I had hurt his feelings.

1. An Egyptian Ark-like object found among the treasures in the tomb of Tutankhamen.

2. Traditional representation of the Ark of the Covenant.

3. A 19th-century depiction by Jacques Tissot of the Ark being carried around the walls of Jericho by the Israelites.

4. The Dome of the Rock, one of the finest Islamic buildings in the world, built in the 7th century on the site of the Temple Mount in Jerusalem, under which the Ark has been said to be hidden.

5. The Shetiyyah—the foundation stone of the temple that according to the tradition preserved in the Jewish text, the Mishnah (Yoma 53b), was the stone upon which the Ark of the Covenant rested in the Holy of Holies in the Jerusalem temple.

6. Sevias' *kraal* in the Mposi chieftainship, Zimbabwe.

7. Dumghe, the sacred mountain of the Lemba, where Sevias suggested the *ngoma* was concealed.

8. Chief Mposi of the Lemba tribe, in 1987, shortly before his death.

9. Mposi, 1987. Receiving tribal authorization to undertake my research into the Lemba's tribal secrets.

10. One of Chief Mposi's wives kneels in reverence before him during the ancestor party in 1987. This was the night my search for the Ark began.

11. Lemba women traditional drummers.

12. Lemba men drinking home-brewed
chibuku beer, at the ancestor party.

13. In Mposi, 1987.

14. Professor M.E.R. Mathivha.

15. Talking with Professor Mathivha in 2002.

16. The Lemba "witchdoctor" who presided over the ancestor party.

17. Elephantine Island on the Nile. This ancient entrepôt once housed a Jewish temple where the Ark of the Covenant was purported to have spent some time in its journey from Israel.

18. St Mary of Zion Church in Aksum. There is a popular theory that the Ark is secreted in this church in Ethiopia and is guarded by a priest of the Ethiopian Coptic church.

19 & 20. Sailing in the Arab *dhow*, which took me up the coast of Africa, north of Zanzibar, in search of the Lemba's lost city of Senna.

21. The ruined castle of the *Mukhtar* of Senna in the Hadhramaut, Yemen.

22. The *Mukhtar* (headman) of the Lemba's
lost city, Senna.

23. The Gogodala at Port Moresby airport welcoming me to Papua New Guinea. The Gogodala hoped I could help them prove they were one of the lost tribes of Israel.

24. Arriving with Tony Waisa in Balimo, Papua New Guinea, in 2003, and met by the Gogodala guard of honor.

25. With Gogodala tribesmen in traditional dress, receiving me as their long expected redeemer, "Bogale."

26. Being rowed by Gogodala tribesmen on the Fly Estuary lagoon.

27. Sister Bibiato, the tribeswoman "chosen" to find the "Covenant Box," points to the place where she thinks the Ark is hidden.

28. Looking for the Ark in the snake-infested lagoon of the Fly Estuary, Papua New Guinea. Would I finally find the Ark here? (And would I survive the snakes?)

29. Writing up my notes on the banks of the Gogodala lagoon.

30. Gogodala tribesman, showing the "Jewish" Star of David body markings.

31. A meeting called by the Lemba Cultural Association to hear about my discovery of their long lost Senna.

32. Discussing tribal matters with the Lemba when I returned to Mposi in the 1990s.

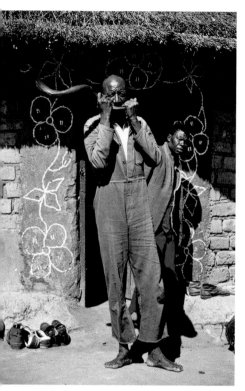

33. A member of the Lemba tribe playing a traditional antelope horn, which intriguingly resembles a Jewish *shofar*.

34. The youthful King of Venda authorizes our search for the *ngoma* in February 2007.

35. Norbert Hahn, an expert on the Soutpansberg, and Netshiendeulu, guardian of the burial place of the Venda kings, during the quest to find the elusive *ngoma* in February 2007.

36 & 37. The *ngoma* showing its astonishing interwoven pattern on the side and burn damage from the time it "exploded."

He took off his new jacket and hung it on the back of a chair. "You're condescending to me, *effendi*," he said. "Of course it's a rubbish book and you know it. Another thing. Why are you always dressed in that creased suit? No one in Egypt wears rubbish clothes like that. Why don't you wear a tie? Why can't you get a nice black suit so people will take you seriously? I'm ashamed to be seen with you."

He sat down on the sofa, his small, bony head between his hands, and started to weep.

"I feel so miserable," he howled.

"Come on, Daud, pull yourself together. I thought you were in good shape. You've got money now. You're about to get married."

"It's all off. I got drunk and made the mistake of telling that rubbish Copt whore about Reuven. When she discovered that it was Jewish gold that was going to finance her wedding, she said she wanted nothing more to do with it. She told her rubbish parents and they have decided she's to marry some rubbish in the Port Said tax office."

"A Copt?"

"Of course, *in sha-allah*, a bloody, rubbish Copt!" he shrieked. "What do you think? A camel-shagging Muslim?"

He stood up and took the jacket from the chair, brushed off snowflake-sized lumps of dandruff, puffed out his skinny scholar's chest, and admired himself in the wardrobe mirror in the sitting room. He had applied a good deal of aftershave. Taking a new crocodile-skin wallet from the back pocket of his well-pressed trousers, he examined the contents with gloomy satisfaction.

He sat down and then promptly stood up again. Then, engulfed by one of his characteristic mood swings, he twirled his cross furiously and limped round the small room with uneven steps. Pushing the door open, he started to sing.

"I'm off to see the widow," he bawled, "the wonderful widow of Oz."

And off he went.

I did not see him for several days. I spent my time in the archive with my books, my classical Hebrew lexicon, and the battered old Hebrew Bible. I tried to be as methodical as I could, to eliminate the theories that were obviously daft and to mesh together in a coherent way the various pieces of information that seemed to have some relationship with historical probability.

I was pretty sure that the place where most people had been looking for the Ark—namely Jerusalem—was not where it was. Jerusalem had been raked over for millennia. I believed that the priests would have taken it far away—perhaps to some remote hiding place in Egypt, perhaps farther afield.

Reuven phoned once or twice wanting to know what action I had taken and was disappointed when I confessed that I had hardly strayed from the hotel on Abd ul-Aziz al-Saud Street.

"Why are you so loathsomely indolent?" he wanted to know, only half in jest. There was something rather irksome about his attitude, as if I were an employee of his who had somehow failed on a business mission. Ronit telephoned from Tel Aviv to see if I needed tickets, a Landrover, or some company.

"Have you got the scent? Are you close on the trail?" she wanted to know.

"Ronit, I'm not a bloody beagle," I replied.

"What's a beagle?"

"It's a hunting dog with a particularly fine sense of smell."

"What I mean is," she continued stolidly, "do you think you are going to find it? Do you think they'll make a film? Do you want me to come down and help? Reuven said he'd give me time off. I've never been to Egypt. We could spend a night or two in one of those fancy Red Sea resorts."

"I'd love to see you, Ronit," I said quite sincerely. "But all I'm doing is trying to get my head around what is increasingly a complicated problem. I'm better off just spending a bit of time alone doing it."

And that's what I did.

I read and made notes every morning, stubbornly remaining on my balcony until the sun forced me inside.

I would spend the afternoon in a hot, suffocating Cairo library, reading anything relevant I could lay my hands on.

I tried to put myself inside the head of a priest fleeing the land of Israel with the precious Ark and heading south. Had he gone to Elephantine, would he have taken a boat up the Nile from about this point here—somewhere in modern Cairo? Or would he have crossed the Red Sea to somewhere like Qusayr and then traversed the desert to the point on the Nile closest to the sea—ancient Qift, which was Daud's hometown—before taking some sort of a riverboat to Aswan? Is there anywhere between these points where the Ark could reasonably have been taken?

* * *

Exactly a week after Reuven's departure, I received a call from Maria. Her voice was a remarkably flexible instrument that could express those harsh tones which seem to be a specialty of Spanish women and also the gentlest and sweetest. Today the tone was soft, insistent, and melodious. She was prepared to forgive me my past misdeeds, she announced soothingly, if I would simply come back to London and get on with translating poetry or finish my book on the Jews of the Yemen. Things would be as they were before. I had to leave this wretched Ark nonsense, as she called it.

I thought of her long, slim legs and small, utterly exquisite hands, I thought of her incomparable ankles, I thought of her dancing salsa in her kitchen as I drank the wine she was sent from a relative's estates in Chile.

And then I thought of Moses's sister Miriam, dancing and playing the drum on the Sinai side of the Red Sea and the momentous times prior to the construction of the Ark. I saw her feet stamping the ground, sand billowing around her sand-soiled ankles, her eyes flashing as she looked imperiously around. I saw the oppressed faces of the ex-slaves looking on with admiration, I saw her elderly brother glowering in the direction of the land of the pharaohs.

I told Maria that I was not ready to go back to London yet. Her voice grew harsh. I was self-indulgent, selfish, an *imbecil*. And that's how we left it.

Daud came round to the hotel later that day, grinning his lop-sided grin, looking happy and relaxed. He had spent a night or two with Maryam, the widow, in the dank tomb in the City of the Dead and had then gone to Alexandria to see a dealer who had a large collection of early Islamic manuscripts. Having spent a few days going through it, he saw that there was nothing that could help Reuven's cause, but the Alexandria dealer had told him of someone in Aswan, an ancient city in the far south of Egypt, on the Nile, who might possibly have something. He was thinking of going up the next day.

For a few days I had been trying to get in touch with an old friend—an Egyptian academic—and had discovered that he was on a research trip to Aswan, a town I wanted to visit anyway because of various potential associations it had with the story of the Ark. I decided to go to Aswan and told Daud I would join him. He had someone from the hotel pick up tickets for the night train. I telephoned Ronit and told her what we had planned and a few minutes later an ecstatic Reuven called me back to say that his office would make hotel arrangements for us. He was delighted that I was going somewhere, doing something.

The following evening at about ten o'clock we pushed our way through the dense crowds at Cairo's central station and boarded the rather luxurious night sleeper for the five-hundred-mile journey to Aswan. For most of the journey the train followed the course of the Nile. I slept badly as we bumped southward. On the bunk above my head Daud grunted and snored. Once or twice I heard the name of his erstwhile fiancée. Once he murmured the name Maryam. He snored again, louder than I could ever have imagined possible. A little later he appeared to be sobbing. Eventually he fell sound asleep.

Once, sitting up in bed and peering through the window, I caught a glimpse of an eerily beautiful landscape bleached of color. Dominating it was some great monument from the time of the pharaohs, bathed in soft moonlight. I fell back into an uneasy sleep.

As dawn broke just south of Luxor, I woke again and saw a felucca plying the waterway, which ran parallel to the railway line. There was an old man at the prow and a boy in the stern. Between them, lashed to the wooden deck, was a box. Was this how the Ark had traveled to its hiding place, tied to the deck of some Egyptian river craft attended by a couple of fugitive priests?

Arriving in Aswan from Cairo is arriving in Africa. Clustered around the station were poor, black Nubians selling leather goods, modern papyri, bundles of African drums. The smells and sounds and heat were African. We took a taxi from the station to the very grand terracotta-pink Cataract Hotel, which Ronit had booked for us.

The Cataract has attracted crowned heads, statesmen, the rich, famous, and glamorous for most of its life. It is considered to be one of the very best hotels in Egypt. However, there had been a shooting of tourists in southern Egypt a month or so before: Islamic terrorists had fired on a tourist boat near Aswan and when we arrived at the hotel it was almost empty. Ronit had done us proud and had secured rooms in the old part of the Cataract. From the balcony of my grand room, beyond the shimmering palm trees, I could see straight over to the island of Elephantine and the desert beyond. It was perhaps to this island, gleaming like a jewel below me, that the Ark had once been dispatched in the company of priests, its guardians, to evade the sacrilegious activities of King Manasseh.

* * *

Daud popped his head around my door to say that he was going to see his dealer and then planned to visit some distant relatives. I sat for a while on my balcony, enjoyed a glass of fresh orange juice, and reread the biblical accounts to try to see if they gave any clue to the passage of the Ark to Egypt at the time of Manasseh.

It seemed that the ancient chroniclers of Israel loathed the polytheistic Manasseh. He had committed just about every crime in the book. The stone-paved streets of the holy city of Jerusalem were awash with the innocent blood of old believers murdered at his behest. He placed foreign idols in the Holy of Holies and practiced sorcery, divination, and witchcraft; "he sacrificed his sons in the fire in the Valley of Ben Hinnom." During his reign Israel was a dangerous place if you happened to be a believer in the One God.

If we can believe the biblical account, it may be assumed that not long before Manasseh's tyrannical reign the Ark had still been in the Jerusalem Temple. We know this from a passage in the book of Isaiah, which describes the siege of Jerusalem by Sennacherib, the king of Assyria, in 701 BC. According to this account, at this critical moment in his reign King Hezekiah went to the Temple, where he entreated God in prayer: "O Lord of Hosts, God of Israel, the One who dwells between the cherubim." This is a fairly specific reference to the dwelling place of God above the "mercy seat" on the Ark between the golden cherubim. Presumably, then, the Ark was still in the Holy of Holies in 701 BC.

The hated Manasseh came to the throne fourteen years after this incident. He was only twelve years old. He ruled until about 643–642. The question is: would the priests, obsessed as they were with issues of purity and defilement, have allowed by far the holiest and purest object in their world to be defiled by the idol-ridden Manasseh? Not if they had the chance to move it.

In the same way as priests are said to have taken one of the doors of the Holy of Holies to the Tunisian island of Djerba to prevent it from being defiled after the destruction of the Temple in 587 BC, so, perhaps, for the same reason, priests removed the Ark during the reign of the wicked Manasseh.

A clue that it might indeed have been removed at this time is to be found in the Bible in a passage in the second book of Chronicles, which gives us some information about the reign of King Josiah (637–607 BC). In Jewish tradition Josiah was perceived as a good king, as good as Manasseh was bad. He is revered not least because he repaired the Jerusalem Temple and undid a good deal of the work of Manasseh. Among other things, he commanded the priests to *put the Ark back* in the Temple.

The priests, then, had taken it somewhere—perhaps somewhere in Jerusalem—perhaps somewhere farther afield—we do not know. With more than a tinge of sarcasm he explained to the priests that he no longer wanted the Ark "to be a burden on your shoulders." In other words, he wanted the Ark back where it belonged, in the Holy of Holies, not being carried around from pillar to post by a bunch of interfering holier-than-thou priests.

I recalled that Rabin had mentioned that, according to rabbinic sources, the prophetess Huldah had instructed King Josiah to hide it—perhaps from the priests—and he concealed it somewhere in the Temple.

But if the sages a thousand years later believed this, there is nothing to this effect in the Bible. The Bible does not tell us *where* the Ark was taken. Or where it was hidden. Indeed, it is the infuriating silence of the scriptures on the ultimate fate of the Ark that has created around it such an enduring aura of mystery. All we know from the Bible is that the Ark was initially placed in the Temple of Solomon—the temple that had been constructed to house it. What happened to it during any of the subsequent misfortunes and calamities that befell the Holy City we simply do not know. Our basic text is silent. Strangely, no other ancient Near Eastern text refers to the Ark at all.

Looking over toward the desert I felt a growing sense of frustration. I thought to myself that the word *Arca* in Latin, from which the English word Ark is derived, is also the origin of the English word arcane: esoteric, mysterious. Is there anything that is not mysterious about the Ark?

I tried to gather my thoughts and think more constructively. I called room service for a pot of strong coffee and tried to restate the problematic. Almost certainly the Ark was taken away from the Jerusalem Temple before the Babylonian conquest in 587. It could have been much earlier, perhaps during the reign of Manasseh, perhaps even during the earlier reign of Rehoboam. Given the circumstances of the day, Egypt would have been one fairly obvious place to take it, and had it been taken to Egypt, the island of Elephantine would have been a very good option, perhaps the best option. Graham Hancock was not the only one to conclude that it might have come up-river to Elephantine—the magical island I could see from my balcony.

Having said that, there is not the slightest proof that it did make its way to the island but it *would* have been a perfectly sensible thing for the priests to do, not least because of the presence of a Jewish community. Furthermore, during the fifth and sixth centuries BC there was a near-replica of the Jerusalem Temple here. Oriented toward Jerusalem, this cedar-roofed temple was the center of a Jewish cult presided over by Jewish priests where animal and other sacrifices were carried out just as they were in Jerusalem. It was the closest thing to the Jerusalem Temple on the face of the earth.

To clear my mind I drank two cups of coffee and I went to have a good long swim in the hotel pool. Feeling refreshed, I crossed over to the island opposite the hotel. No more than a mile long and intensely beautiful, it contains ruins from the very beginning of Egyptian history. Often used throughout the ages as a well-fortified garrison, the fortress island defended Egypt's southern border with Nubia. It is today a place of exquisite, lush gardens and African bird life. Exactly when and why the Jewish temple was first built here we do not know.

However we *do* know quite a lot about the Elephantine temple because of a remarkable and ancient hoard of papyrus manuscripts.

These were discovered near Aswan in 1893 by Charles Edwin Wilbour, a strapping American journalist and amateur archaeologist, described by a contemporary as having "a wonderful white bib of a beard reaching down to the second button of his waistcoat." Wilbour liked to spend his winters in Egypt and sail the Nile in his very own *dahabiyeh*, called the *Seven Hathors* after the Egyptian goddess Hathor who sometimes took the form of seven goddesses devoted to luck. His own luck was mixed. On the one hand, he inadvertently made one of the greatest discoveries in recent times; on the other, he died six years later without knowing it.

His various finds were shipped back to New York along with his other effects and languished in a warehouse until the death of his daughter, when they were given to the Egyptian Department of the Brooklyn Museum. In 1947, fifty-four years after their first discovery, Wilbour's papyri were found in a biscuit box and in due course were published.

When I was a student, I had had the good fortune to study some of these documents, which were written in Aramaic—a Semitic language close to Hebrew that for hundreds of years served as a *lingua franca* throughout much of the Middle East. These and other papyri include domestic contracts and other personal items belonging to Elephantine Jews. Among other things they describe how in 410 BC the temple was destroyed and how soon after it was rebuilt.

We do not know when the temple was first built. We do know that Jewish troops were sent to Egypt in about 650 BC to help Pharaoh Psammetichus I (664–610 BC) throw off the yoke of the mighty Assyrian empire. The Jewish troops stayed on, perhaps, and in due course, no doubt with Egyptian approval, the temple was constructed. It appears that Manasseh sent troops to Egypt in return for horses and chariots to defend himself against the Assyrians and no doubt the better to persecute his own people. But they did not help.

According to the Bible, Manasseh eventually had his comeuppance: the Assyrians captured him and took him in chains to Babylon where, like all defeated sovereigns, he was humiliated and tortured. To hammer home the folly of resisting the might of Assyria, he was hauled before the king with a metal hook through his jaw.

Once he was safely out of the way, the priests might well have considered the remote island of Elephantine a safe and fitting place to deposit the Ark. It is worth noting, however, that the Wilbour papyri, which describe life on the island and which tell us a good deal about the Jewish temple, have nothing to say about the Ark.

Not too much can be deduced from silence. Nonetheless it is difficult to imagine a church, let us say in the Eastern Desert, that just happened to have the good fortune to possess in its vaults the Holy Grail, not mentioning that fact at some point or another. No doubt the church would be called the Church of the Holy Grail and when it was referred to casually it would be called "that church in the Eastern Desert where the Holy Grail is kept." There would have been pilgrimages, local festivals, travelers' tales, and, more recently, millions of tourists.

If anything, the contents of the documents suggest obliquely that the Ark was *not* there: it includes letters to the authorities in Israel begging for permission to carry out animal sacrifices, and permission to rebuild the Temple after its destruction. If the Ark truly resided on the island at this time, would the island's priests have needed to go, cap in hand, to their Jerusalem superiors? The priests who had the Ark of God in their possession would not have needed permission to do anything.

I had spent a few hours on the island trying to imagine how the Ark would have fitted in to the life of this Jewish garrison community. In the late afternoon I returned to the hotel and sat in the shade of a clump of dusty bougainvillea in the garden and tried to come up with a workable scenario. According to Hancock, the Ark was transported to Elephantine before moving on to Ethiopia. As I pondered the issue I made occasional notes in a small notebook. I concluded that at least on the issue of Elephantine, Hancock may possibly have been right, but his thesis was critically short on evidence. What convinced me of this was that his argument's central plank is the contention that in the papyri there were *repeated* references to YHWH—the Hebrew form of Jehovah—dwelling in the temple of Elephantine. He took this as the proof that the Ark—the *dwelling place* of God—was therefore indeed in the temple.

However, as I recalled and as I was subsequently able to verify, there was only *one* reference in the Elephantine papyri to God dwelling in the temple and the phrase, which is regularly used in the Bible in a context which does not involve the Ark, in no sense implies the necessary presence of the Ark.

In the garden of the Cataract Hotel, peering hopelessly through the palm trees and tangled shrubs at the island, I had one small insight. I realized that the island was not as remote as I had imagined. Thinking about it in Cairo or Jerusalem or Oxford, it had seemed infinitely distant. The end of the earth. But here it was different. The Nile coursing powerfully a few feet away had been the main highway as well as lifeline to one of the great powers of the ancient world. Elephantine—which takes its name perhaps from an ivory market that once flourished here—was in the middle of this great waterway, at a critical strategic junction, a place of trade, of encounter, the place where black Africa meets the world of the Mediterranean and the Near East.

From the feluccas gliding past, piled with sugar cane, pots, and bales of fodder, one could sense the purpose of the river in ancient times. Functioning as garrison town, entrepot, and crossroads, Elephantine would once have been a bawdy, noisy, bustling place, full of African traders, slaves, soldiers, prostitutes, priests, alive to all the currents of the ancient world. Trade routes led from here into the heart of Africa, to Ethiopia, to the lands of the Great Lakes, and perhaps even beyond. In this garrison town there had been a mingling of cultures, of religions, of people. I realized that the Nile was a super highway into the heart of Africa. If the Ark had come this way it could have been taken south with relative ease, perhaps to Ethiopia, perhaps to some point farther south still.

That morning I had left a message at the neighboring hotel where I knew the Egyptian friend I needed to see was staying. I suggested we meet for a drink. I now walked over to his hotel, my head still teeming with the various possibilities of the passage of the Ark through Egypt.

There were people milling around from every corner of the globe. Hawkers carried modern Egyptian papyri, trays of wrist-watches, cigarettes. Small tradesmen pushed barrows full of pearly fish from Lake Nasser and gleaming fruit and vegetables. Aswan had not changed all that much over the millennia.

I headed straight for the bar and sure enough I spotted the familiar and immaculately dressed figure of Professor Muhammad al-Hawari of the Semitics Department of Ayn Shams University in Cairo, glass in hand. Muhammad was an old and trusted friend: it was good to see him. After a glass or two we walked back to the Cataract.

"It's true, is it not, Muhammad that there was a Jewish temple in Aswan?"

"Yes, more or less—anyway, on the island of Elephantine."

I told him of my interest in the Jewish temple. Al-Hawari was an expert on Semitic languages and a papyrologist with a particular interest in Egypt. He told me that in fact there were some explicit references in the papyri found in and around Aswan to a degree of syncretistic mingling of polytheistic and monotheistic religious traditions on the island of Elephantine; a mingling of Jewish and Egyptian traditions. A number of Jewish scholars, wishing to imagine the Jewish Diaspora community of the island as strictly orthodox, had tried to airbrush out these references, but Muhammad was more forth-right. According to him the Jewish temple was not really unlike other Egyptian temples of the time—it simply had a strong Jewish flavor. When he told me this I wondered if a strong Jewish *flavor* would be sufficient inducement for the priestly guardians of the Ark to bring their precious charge here.

"As a matter of fact," he said, "there was an Egyptian goddess called Anat who was worshiped here alongside Jehovah. Some-what better looking too."

With his two hands he suggested the outline of a voluptuous woman.

Reaching into his briefcase he pulled out a book that included a black-and-white plate of an Egyptian relief of Anat. In her Egyptian manifestation she was a gorgeous, long-legged, slim-hipped, high-breasted goddess of war, usually shown carrying a dagger.

Anat was one of the most militant gods of the Middle East-ern pantheon. Her evocation would have been anathema to priests of the old tradition. Would priests, old believers, really have wanted to bring the Ark *here*? But was there any other link anywhere between the Ark and Egypt? I discussed the matter for a while with Muhammad. He was not very encouraging. Notwithstanding his vast knowledge of Egypt and its history, there was nothing he knew of, with the exception of the ambiguous story of the pharaoh Shishak, that linked the land of the Nile with the Ark.

Professor Chaim Rabin had mentioned Shishak during our conversation in Jerusalem and Daud had later quoted the famous passage from 1 Kings: 14 about his ransacking of the Temple: "In the fifth year of King Rehoboam, Shishak, the king of Egypt, attacked Jerusalem. He carried off treasures of the temple of the Lord and the treasures of the royal palace. He took everything, including all the gold shields Solomon had made." But there was no actual proof that Shishak had carried off the Ark.

Daud came back to the hotel at about seven. He was still wearing his new black suit, which was now encrusted with the white dust of the desert. We went down to the bar and ordered a couple of Stellas. Twirling his cross rather more languidly than was his wont, he told me that he had spent the day with his second cousin's first cousin's second husband, walking around a ruined sixth-century Coptic monastery called the monastery of Anba Hadra, after a hermit who was consecrated bishop of Aswan in the fourth century AD.

"You know what happened to Anba Hadra?" asked Daud gloomily. "The poor boy got married when he was eighteen but just after the wedding, as he was heading home for what was almost certainly his first joyous act of copulation, he came across a funeral procession. This sight persuaded him to make a vow of eternal celibacy. He then retreated into the desert and applied himself vigorously to ascetic practices of the most punishing sort and developed a fascination with the life of our heroic friend St. Anthony of Fayyum. I believe I once told you about the supreme renunciation of the life of the flesh practiced by that sublimely pious Copt, which contrasts so nobly with the life of sexual excess practiced by my uncle —"

"Daud, why are you telling me this?" I asked patiently.

"Because I'm thinking of following his example. Anthony's example, I mean, not my uncle's. Certainly not my uncle's. It was always my intention when I was a young Copt to be a monk. I feel my vocation, *insha-allah,* is beginning to return. Celibacy beckons me, if that's the right word, with a drooping finger."

"Sounds like you've got a touch of sunstroke," I said taking a pull at my beer.

Daud scratched his head violently and through the miniature snowstorm I encountered an almost embarrassingly penetrating look.

"I felt something speaking to me in the monastery," he whispered. "A voice wafting in from the desert murmured in my ear. Something from our distant Coptic past. A sort of Coptic news broadcast from ancient times. You know," he whispered, "the monastery of Anba Hadra was the nearest Egyptian Coptic church to Ethiopia and it is very, very old. It was the crossroads of many mystical currents. It is said that the Templars came here. The Holy Grail came here.

"If the Ark journeyed from Egypt to Ethiopia, as some people seem to think it did, at any point after the construction of the monastery, which is to say from about the fifth or sixth century on, it might well have gone that way ...

"Actually, today I spoke to an aged and most venerable—what do you call it—I mean anchorite, a sort of guardian of the place; his face was gnarled with age and Coptic piety. He whispered in my ear that he had heard that the Ark had passed this way."

"Are you serious?" I asked, my heart beating faster.

"When I heard his words, all of a sudden I knew that this is what happened. The Ark passed through Deir al Anba Hadra on the way to Aksum, on the way to Ethiopia. I *believe* it. I felt it in my bones —"

"Daud," I said. "Where's the bloody evidence?"

Twirling his cross, he grinned in his most charming way.

"I was just having you on. Bloody rubbish. Just testing."

I laughed. But my own intuition whispered into some dim inner ear of my own that in one respect Daud was not necessarily wrong. There was no real reason to believe that the Ark was in Egypt or that it had ever spent much if any time in Egypt. There was no evidence of any sort. In truth there was no real evidence either way. Mentally I checked off Egypt as being a very plausible site for a hidden Ark. But perhaps, just perhaps, Ethiopia was another story altogether.

Later that evening we were sitting in the hotel garden drinking a whisky. Daud had become serious again.

"Sometimes, *effendi*," he said, "you should loosen up, go with the flow. You shouldn't be too intellectual about all this. There is an innocence in the objective world that you have to respect and be receptive to. Intuitive people have built-in receivers. You fail at your peril. There's a French poem somewhere that goes: "*ou l'innocence périt c'est un crime de vivre*"—it's a crime to live in a place where innocence has perished.

"Let's put it like this. Let's start at the beginning. You see the Nile? The Gnostic texts explain that the reason Egypt is the cradle of humanity is because of the life-giving properties of this great river. Everything of value comes from Egypt, comes from Africa, and even if it travels the world it will always come back to roost in its spiritual home. You can be sure that the Ark started life in Egypt. And you can also be sure that at some point the Ark returned to its African roots. If the Ark was hidden outside Israel, Egypt was the most likely immediate destination. But there is nothing in our Coptic traditions, oral or written, that suggests that the Ark is still here. We simply do not have any traditions along those lines. But Ethiopia is quite another story." He started to twirl his chain, a curious look on his face.

"Our Coptic brothers in Ethiopia have more traditions about the Ark than they have bread in their bellies. They live, eat, and drink the Ark in Ethiopia. Now listen. This is my reasoning: the Ethiopian Copts are almost the same as the Egyptian Copts—very, very much more primitive of course, but almost the same. The Ethiopian Coptic Church has been ruled by the Coptic patriarch of Alexandria for over 1,600 years and Ethiopian bishops have always been appointed by the patriarch. But even though we are members of the *same* church and with very *similar* Coptic traditions, the legends of the Ark proliferate in Ethiopia and are almost completely absent in Egypt." He shot me a triumphant look.

"We have a kind of simple little altar thing called a *maqta'*, which is no more than a small wooden container that contains the chalice and the wine used for the communion. My priest used to explain it like this: the Jews' Ark contained the tablets of the Law—which was their covenant with God—whereas our symbolic *Christian* Ark contains Christ's blood of the new covenant between God and man. Our *maqta'* is the origin of the so-called Ark thing you find on Ethiopian altars. But there the comparison ends. The traditions of the Ark in Ethiopia—in the churches and in their history—are paramount. They are what I call innocent traditions embedded in the memory and love of the people and the church. There's never smoke without fire. If Ethiopia is where the legends are, that should be our next stop."

8

LEGENDS OF THE QUEEN OF SHEBA

Ethiopia to me meant mass starvation. I had had my first experience of Ethiopia and Ethiopians about ten years earlier, in November 1984. As I have discovered over my life, it's not always easy to discern the rustle of history's wings. Momentous events happen when you least expect them.

I had crossed into Ethiopia illegally, over the Sudanese border, to witness Jewish refugees, struggling to escape the famine, making their way to the Sudan border. I was accompanied by Dawit, a well-educated young Ethiopian Christian. He showed me the paths and tracks that the Ethiopian Jews—the Falashas—were likely to arrive on. The first day, I encountered dozens of refugees close to the border. They told me stories of how they had been attacked, wounded, or raped by *shiftas,* or bandits, shot at by government troops, as well as by anti-government rebels. They told me how their forefathers had come to Ethiopia from Israel thousands of years before, at the time of Solomon and the Queen of Sheba, bearing with them the Ark of the Covenant. They were now returning to Israel. Minus the Ark.

The second day, we walked about five miles without seeing any refugees. As evening was beginning to fall, an Ethiopian army helicopter passed overhead. Dawit threw me to the ground and pushed me under a bush. Once we were well concealed, he said, "They'll kill us if they see us. They'll think we are Falashas. They hate them in Ethiopia. They are in league with the Zionist enemy. They are *buda*—they bring bad luck. They are metalworkers—they say they made the nails that were used to crucify Christ."

Thereafter we traveled at night, and slept under the trees during the day. We came across a few stragglers making their way from the Ethiopian highlands to the Sudanese border, but they were all too terrified and traumatized to talk to us.

Once we got back to the Sudan I saw the beginning of the Israeli operation to get the Falashas out of the hopeless, stinking refugee camps along the border. This was the famous Operation Moses about which I later wrote a book. The secret Mossad-led operation took the Ethiopian Jews from starvation in the camps to safety and a new home in Israel.

After returning from Egypt to London to continue with my teaching responsibilities at SOAS, I gave further thought to Daud's suggestion that there might be reason to suppose that the Ark was taken to Ethiopia. There were legends about the Ark that had persuaded many people that the original Ark was still hidden away in this little-known African country for which the Ark was in many ways the underpinning foundation myth. It seemed to me that there was some possibility that the Falashas or some other similar group might also have played some role in the history of the Ark at some point in the past.

In spring 1994 I decided to return to Ethiopia. Since my first experience with the Ethiopian Jews, I had written quite a lot about the history of this community. Now I was eager to visit some of the places that had impacted that history. But at the same time I wanted to see for myself what the Ethiopian Ark story was all about. Reuven was pleased that I had finally agreed to follow his suggestion and, in view of his admiration for Daud, begged me to take Daud along—and after long thought I decided that, on balance, this made sense.

One of the pleasures of traveling is in the preparation: reading up on the place you're going to, pulling out a much-loved old canvas bag, repairing a mosquito net, and—in my case, anyway—getting hold of the right kind of leather-bound Italian notebook. H. D. Thoreau quite rightly said that traveling is not a pastime and that it needs a long probation, and serious preparation is part of all that. So before setting off for Ethiopia I made sure I was ready for the trip.

Daud and I met up in Ethiopia's uninspiring capital, Addis Ababa. I had flown in from London. Daud had arrived from Cairo a couple of weeks earlier and had been traveling around the country. After very few minutes with him I realized that in Ethiopia he had adopted a new persona. He was strutting around, with colonial airs, looking disparagingly at the people and things we encountered, rather like a nostalgic middle-aged Brit visiting some former outpost of empire. In preparation for the trip he had immersed himself in the study of Amharic, the main language of modern Ethiopia, and when I met him he was busy practising it on the Ethiopians, to general amusement.

"With my newly acquired language skills, *effendi*, and my sensitivity to all things Coptic," he said, "I'll soon track down the Ark if it's here in this backward and pathetic excuse for a rubbish country."

I decided we should start our investigation in the former imperial capital of Gondar—a historic town close to Lake Tana—the source of the Blue Nile. Daud was excited to be going to a place that had played such an important role in the history of the Egyptian Coptic Church of which he was so proud. And he was excited to be involved in some detective work in a foreign country.

We took a small decrepit plane that flew low over the great central plateau. Ethiopia is one of the few countries I know whose poverty is pathetically obvious even from the air. You can see that the earth is thin, that nothing grows, and that it has an impossibly large, dirt-poor population. As we crossed the Blue Nile we ran into severe turbulence.

Daud was terrified and grabbed hold of my arm. "If we crash here, *effendi*," he said, "my corpse will float all the way back to Cairo."

I told him that the chances of his getting back either intact or in small pieces were remote. The Nile was full of snakes, hippopotami, six-meter-long crocodiles, and hundreds of varieties of fish. If he got back to Cairo it would be as an element of one or more of the above. But in principle he was right—the river, the Blue Nile, that flowed out of Lake Tana would meet up with the White Nile and eventually lead to Cairo.

At the tiny airport at Gondar, once again he tried out his Amharic, and explained to the immaculately mannered and smartly dressed girl who was trying to find us a taxi that he was a visiting Copt from Egypt with a deep love and knowledge of the remarkable manifestations of his ancient Egyptian culture in her impoverished and grotesquely undeveloped home town. Swinging his cross, he raised one moth-eaten eyebrow and gave her a supercilious smile.

In perfect English she replied, "There is nothing Egyptian about it. Incidentally, you think you are speaking Amharic but in fact you are speaking a debased and only just recognizable form of Ge'ez. We don't have great admiration for Arabs here and our church is much, much older and more authentic than anything you have in your country."

So there.

Daud's face broke out in characteristic pink blotches and he was on the point of debating this sensitive issue. But I stopped him.

"Leave her alone, you insane little Copt. You're just appalling," I whispered, taking him by the sleeve of his by now somewhat shabby black suit and pulling him into the taxi.

We stayed at the Goha Hotel, which is built on a steep hill overlooking the churches and castles of the city and which boasts the best restaurant in town and a small swimming pool. Over a good Ethiopian Castel beer and an inedible dinner that we took on the terrace with its spectacular views, Daud filled me in on what he knew of the various connections between the Ark and Ethiopia. He had been working on this for months, generously supported by Reuven as he went through all the available Coptic, Arabic, Ge'ez, and Portuguese documents written over a period of about 800 years. He had brought with him a thick and well-organized file of his notes and another thick file of photocopies of relevant passages from books he had discovered in various Egyptian libraries.

According to the Ethiopians, when Menelik returned to Ethiopia from the court of his illustrious father, Solomon, round about the ninth century BC, his retinue were so over-wrought at having to leave Jerusalem and the proximity of the Holy Ark that they decided to steal it, leaving a replica Ark in its place. This would have been shortly after its arrival in the Temple. The Angel of the Lord appeared to Azarias, the son of Zadok, the high priest, and conspired in the theft of the Ark and in the manufacture of the replica Ark.

On the journey back to Ethiopia, Menelik and his support-ers, along with their stolen trophy, had the good fortune to be guided by the archangel Michael. The journey was less arduous than it might have been. According to the Ethiopian national epic, the *Kebra Negast*, the caravan floated along, camels and Ark raised above the ground to the height of a cubit.

The Ethiopians, Daud told me, were not alone in their conviction that the Ark had finished up in Ethiopia. Daud had brought with him one of his most treasured possessions—a beautiful edition of *Churches and Monasteries of Egypt*, published in Oxford in 1895. Based on a thirteenth-century manuscript from the National Library in Paris, this book is an edited translation of a work by Abu Salih, who was probably an Armenian Christ-ian living in Egypt. It also includes the original Arabic text.

The book is a treasure trove of information on the Copts but it also has some information about Ethiopia. Among other things, as Daud pointed out to me, opening the book at folio 105b of the original Arabic text, it had something to say about the Ark. Daud read it out loud:

The Abyssinians possess also the Ark of the Covenant, in which are the two tables of stone, inscribed by the finger of God with the commandments that he ordained the children of Israel. The Ark of the Covenant is placed upon the altar; but is not as high as the altar; it is as high as the knee of a man, and is overlaid with gold; and upon its lid there are crosses of gold; and there are five precious stones upon it; one at each of the four corners, and one in the middle. The liturgy is celebrated upon the Ark four times in the year, within the palace of the king; and a canopy is spread over it when it is taken out from the church to the church that is in the palace of the king ... the Ark is attended by a large number of Israelites descended from the family of the prophet David who are white and red in complexion, with red hair.

Daud looked at me quizzically. "What do you think of that?" he asked. "It looks like the Ark is attended by priests."

"Exciting stuff," I said. "Your friend Hancock mentions it and claims that Abu Salih actually saw the Ark with his own eyes."

"He didn't," snapped Daud, his dark eyes flashing. "He most certainly didn't. It's certain that he never visited Ethiopia. Abu Salih picked up this information probably from Ethiopian Copts who came to Cairo during an ugly episode to do with the deposition of Mikael, a thirteenth-century rubbish crook, who also happened to be bishop of Ethiopia. There's a contemporary Arabic account of the history of the patriarchs of the Alexandrian Church that gives an account of the rubbish Mikael but, very tellingly, there is no mention of the Ark.

"In any case I don't think that most of the information Abu Salih gives about the Ark is genuine. The Ethiopians who fed him this nonsense were so overwhelmed by the magnificence of what they saw of Egyptian Coptic civilization, that they had to make something up to make themselves feel good. Which you can understand."

A waiter brought us a couple more beers and Daud looked at him with distaste, as if he were directly responsible for the boastful lies told by his compatriots almost a thousand years earlier.

Daud told me that Abu Salih was a contemporary of one of the greatest kings of Ethiopia—Saint Lalibela—and in the Ethiopian account of the king-saint's life, there is no mention of the Ark. This chronicle, *Zena Lalibela,* was written a couple of hundred years later but in copious contemporary Coptic records dealing with the Coptic bishops of Ethiopia there is no mention of it at all. It is inconceivable that if the Ethiopians had, or even believed they had, the Ark of the Covenant in one of their churches, they would not have referred to it time and time again.

He also told me that in Coptic records there was a specific mention of the St. Mary of Zion Church in Aksum in around 1322 but again, no mention of the Ark. He told me that there was some sixteenth-century Arabic text that picked up the story of the Ark and the Queen of Sheba, and that thereafter all the evidence connecting the Ark with Ethiopia was loose and contradictory.

Abu Salih's description of the Ark and, even more, his description of its function did not ring many bells with me. I thought that the original Ark was much more likely to have been a roughly hewn acacia box of some sort, made by Moses, than the elaborate artifact created according to a contradictory text by Bezalel, the artisan. In any event the biblical texts describing the Ark were written hundreds of years after the event, when the Ark was already in the Temple.

It seemed obvious to me that the descriptions of the Ark—with its gold accoutrements and cherubim—were written long after the event and were intended to make the Ark fit the undoubted magnificence of the Temple and fit in with the conventional representations of Middle Eastern gods. The Ark described by Abu Salih was something else again. It seemed to me to have almost nothing in common either with the elaborate descriptions of the Ark of Bezalel the artisan in the book of Exodus or with the simple wooden Ark of Moses described in the book of Deuteronomy.

Leaning back on my chair, I sighed.

"Whether it was there or not, what Abu Salih described was some kind of Christian artifact, decked out as it is with crosses," I said. "It could not have much to do with the original Ark. And it is used in a completely different way. The mass is celebrated upon it—on top of it—but no one would ever have treated the Ark like that. The Ark as we know it would have literally exploded in fire, smoke, and terrible noise. The Ark was strictly untouchable. I don't see honestly how these kinds of altar pieces can really help us with our investigation."

"Their altar arrangements are quite simply debased versions of what we do in Egypt," said Daud, puckering his nose in distaste. "They have nothing to do with the Ark. And the thing described by Abu Salih has nothing to do with the Ark either. It was probably carried on the *shoulders* of the priests."

He swung his chain merrily and went on, "It was not carried on the poles, and it did not have carrying hoops. It did not have the mercy seat and it did not have cherubim. The Ark is called *tabot* in Ethiopic and the word *tabot* is also used for altar stones, which are wooden, stone, or marble replicas of the tablets of the law, which you find in every Ethiopian church and every Falasha prayer house, and which are based upon the more venerable and culturally more important Egyptian Coptic *maqta*.

"What Abu Salih described was a *manbara tabot*, a kind of portable altar that you can still find throughout Ethiopia. I saw one in Addis Ababa at the Institute of Ethiopian Studies. That's all it is. Whether there was really a *manbara tabot* at his time in Aksum is anybody's guess."

Daud opened up his file of photocopies and showed me a somewhat later account of the *tabot*, written at the beginning of the sixteenth century by Francisco Alvares, chaplain of the first Portuguese embassy to Ethiopia. He observed of the chapel where the Ark was supposed to have been that

> it is named St. Mary of Syon ... because its altar stone came from Zion. In this country (as they say) they have the custom always to name the churches by the altar stone, because on it is written the name of the patron saint. This stone which they have in this church, they say that the Apostles sent it from Mount Zion.

In this Portuguese account there is no mention of the Ark. The artifact described was clearly a Christian altar stone.

With a contemptuous look on his face, Daud plucked another page out of his file. This was a passage written about a hundred years later by the Jesuit Manoel de Almeida. "He describes a small casket that could be vaguely Ark-like. But just look what they found inside it!" Daud read out in ringing tones: "They found, guess what, a 'pagoda, or an Idol, which had the figure of a woman with very big breasts.' Big breasts! *Very* big breasts!" he screeched.

Daud continued relentlessly. He pulled out another page from his file. The yellowing photocopy reported that the Portuguese Balthezar Tellez recorded scathingly in 1660 that the Ethiopians

> added much Reputation to their Church of Auxum or Aczum, by saying that their Chest or Tabot, was the very Ark of the Old Testament that was in Solomon's Temple, and that God brought it so miraculously to Ethiopia ... The Abyssines to gain more respect to this little Chest of theirs, always kept it so close and conceal'd, that they would not show it even to their Emperors. They call it by way of excellency Sion, or Seon, as they pronounce it, and for the same Reason the Church, where they kept this to them so precious a Relick, being dedicated to the Virgin Mary, had the name S. Mary of Seon.

"Rubbish from beginning to end. It's obvious that Tellez thought they were making the whole thing up. They had a pretty little casket and were working it to death. No one has ever believed this rubbish until the last few years. There are stories. Yes. But these are Christian stories. Confused Christian stories. Only God knows what they mean. James Bruce, the great Scottish explorer who was here in Ethiopia in the eighteenth century, dismissed the idea of the Ark being here with utter contempt: there may have been a stone of some sort but he thought that even this stone relic had been destroyed by the Muslim army of Ahmed Grañ in the sixteenth century.

"In any case ancient wooden things simply do not survive in Aksum. Anything over a few hundred years old is incredibly rare. But most damaging, outside of Abu Salih, who certainly never saw it, there's no mention of the Ark in really ancient texts."

"But Hancock's contention that the Ark is located in the stone chapel of St. Mary of Zion Church in Aksum is rather difficult to prove wrong," I said. "Particularly as no one has ever seen it except the priestly guardians of the shrine."

"That's where I was before you came out from London."

"Where?"

"I went to see the St. Mary of Zion Church. Reuven insisted I go there to check out Hancock's story. I went there dressed up as an Egyptian Coptic priest. I spoke to the priests there in their own language. They were very complimentary about my Amharic and even more so about my Ge'ez. Unfortunately, the primitive illiterates would not let me see it. It seems absurd—no it seems bloody *scandalous*—that they would not let a genuine Copt, a real Egyptian Copt, a genuine Coptic priest, for God's sake, see a holy Coptic object."

"Daud, sorry, you are not a real Coptic priest. You are a creepy, police informer with a taste for dubious whores."

"Admittedly, *effendi*," he replied with his most charming smile. "But they did not know that. What they told me was that they were worried that the Jews would steal it. They seemed to think that Israel wants to rebuild the Temple and put the Ark back in it. Apparently there are lots of Israelis and Mossad agents in neighboring Eritrea helping them in their struggle against Ethiopia, and the priests believe that they are planning to kidnap the Ark from Aksum. A police guard has been put on to thwart them.

"I asked them if it was really the original Ark," he continued, "and they said yes it was. I then asked them why there was no mention of it in the ancient Coptic documents. They didn't have an answer to that. When I asked them if it was like the Arks you find in every Ethiopian church they said: 'Yes. No different. Just genuine. That's the only difference.'"

Daud scratched his scalp and pulled a comical face of disbelief.

"I happen to know," he continued, "that the climate of Aksum is such that nothing made of wood could have survived from the time of Moses. It's not like Egypt. Maybe we'll never find it but of one thing I am quite sure—it was never at Aksum. In addition I happen to know that your esteemed colleague at SOAS, Professor Edward Ullendorff, by far the greatest *éthiopisant* the world has ever known, as everyone agrees, went inside the chapel of St. Mary of Zion Church in 1941 and saw the famous Ark. All that there was to be seen was an empty box of no great antiquity. The whole thing's a fake. Rubbish."

I nodded. I had heard Ullendorff make some such remark in the Senior Common Room at SOAS.

"But if the Ark never came here, why is there such a wealth of tradition about it?" I asked.

"Exactly. That's what I thought. That's why I suggested that we come here. You never know, perhaps it did come here. Perhaps it moved on. Whatever you might say, I do know now, after all the reading that I have done, that the idea that the Ark of the Covenant is in Aksum is not supported by any serious evidence. I've been there. I've researched it. We have to look elsewhere."

* * *

Over the following days Daud and I traveled around the villages near Gondar where the Falashas had lived until their departure to Israel. There were a number still left, hoping to be able to get to Israel one day, but with ties to Ethiopia that were difficult to break. Wherever I went I asked the Ethiopian Jews about their Ark traditions. Some said they had brought the Ark from Egypt by way of Aswan and the Nile city of Sennar. Some said they were descended from the Israelites who had brought the Ark from Jerusalem at the time of King Solomon. I heard lots of similar stories but there was little in the way of factual information. No one had any idea as to where the Ark was today.

Although the Falashas have been identified as a lost tribe of Israel that arrived in Ethiopia millennia ago, perhaps by way of Egypt, perhaps by way of South Arabia, a number of contemporary scholars such as Steve Kaplan of the Hebrew University are of the opinion that the Falashas are an *Ethiopian* population, originally Christian, whose religion emerged from specific sociopolitical circumstances in medieval Ethiopia. In an attempt to create a usable distinction between their own Agau-speaking society and that of the dominant Amharic-speaking Amharas, they laid claim to an Israelite identity. They dropped the Christian parts of their faith and adopted a kind of Judaism.

There is no real proof of this hypothesis and other equally good scholars such as Emanuela Trevisan-Semi at the University of Venice take a quite different view and maintain that the Falashas did indeed come from the land of Israel at some point in their history. If the latter supposition is correct it could be that their claims to have been involved with the arrival of the Ark on African soil are correct.

The few Falashas I met in Ethiopia had little to tell me. It was possible that their forefathers *had* played some role in the history of the Ark but there was little evidence one way or another. I knew the secondary literature on the Falashas pretty well and there was nothing in the hundreds of articles and dozens of books I had consulted in the SOAS library, which has one of the best Ethiopian collections in the world, which could reasonably be expected to help me with my quest. The Falashas were a strong possibility but for the moment there was not sufficient evidence.

It was also clear that there were a number of other Ethiopian groups who held similar Judaic beliefs and who believed just as firmly as the Falashas that it was their ancestors who had brought the Ark into Ethiopia and protected it ever since. One of these was the little-known Qemant tribe, which is to be found mainly in the area west of Lake Tana in the territory falling from the Semien Mountains to the dusty plains of the Sudan and which had strange Jewish-looking religious customs all their own, and their own language. I decided to see for myself what their traditions had to say about the history of the Ark.

Ever since I arrived in Ethiopia I had suffered from a persistent and violent earache. One day along with Daud, who was again dressed as a Coptic priest with his big gold cross dangling on his chest, I went to consult a pharmacist in Gondar. As he was finishing the job of putting some drops in my ear, I mentioned that I was wanting to make contact with members of the Qemant tribe.

The pharmacist, Ato Nega Geta, carefully put down his eardrop dispenser and waving his arms about exitedly, embraced me with unexpected fervor. As he now explained, he was a visionary man. He had had powerful visions all his life. His chief vision now was to save his people from cultural, religious, and linguistic extinction. He planned to rescue the traditions, culture, religion, and language of his people from oblivion. His people were the Qemant.

According to him there are about 150,000 Qemant in Ethiopia today. However, the old Qemant language is dying out and today no more than one percent of the Qemant population practices the ancestral faith or speaks the language.

There was no chance of our being permitted to leave the pharmacy. It wasn't every day that Nega Geta had people along who were interested in the Qemant. He sat me and Daud down, and fixing us with his unusually protuberant eyes, invited us to take an Ethiopian coffee (*bun*) with him. His pretty female assistant prepared the coffee, grinding the beans then boiling the coffee on a little charcoal stove at the back of the shop. A piece of incense was put in with the charcoal and the smell of coffee and frankincense filled the room.

The coffee was served in small china cups and was accompanied by small plates of peanuts and cooked barley. The *bun* was flavored not with sugar but with salt. As we drank our regulation three cups of coffee (anything less would be considered egregiously rude) Nega Geta told us what he knew about the history of the Qemant. Like the Jews, the Qemant have extremely strict ideas about what they can and cannot eat; permitted animals have to be ritually slaughtered in the Jewish manner and animal sacrifices are offered up to God.

They also have sacred groves called *degegna* where their worship is generally conducted. Nega Geta explained that this was in the tradition of the passage from the book of Genesis that spoke of Abraham, the patriarch, planting a grove in Beer-sheba and calling thereupon the name of God. They have a high priest called the Wember who was once the secular as well as spiritual head of the tribe. According to the traditions of the Qemant, their founder was Anayer, a grandson of Canaan, son of Ham, son of Noah. Anayer came to Lake Tana, the great lake near Gondar, from the north and on the journey from the north he met the founder of the Falashas. Both groups claim to have originated in the land of Israel.

This was fascinating stuff that I felt could easily lead to some unexpected information about the Ark. Hundreds of people had studied the Falashas and their traditions, but hardly anyone had ever done any kind of research on the Qemant. This was practically virgin territory. Excitedly, I made an appointment to see Nega Geta the next day.

The following morning Daud and I arrived at his pharmacy. He put some more drops in my ears and offered us coffee.

"I don't want your coffee," said Daud. "The real *Coptic* coffee we get in Egypt is quite different. It's sweet and delicious." Nega Geta looked upset and went off to find his assistant. After a few minutes she arrived and Daud explained to her in Amharic how he liked his coffee. No incense. No salt. Much sugar. Very much sugar.

After we had drunk three cups of *bun,* Nega Geta ushered us outside. "I'd like to take you to see our *degegna,*" he whispered in my good ear, "but maybe Daud the priest should stay here in town. There are many churches here. He would be happy here."

I explained that Daud was as anxious as I was to see the sacred sites of the Qemant. Looking pained, he ushered us into his aged car and drove toward the Qemant heartlands. The hilly, wooded territory, which falls down westward from Lake Tana to the Sudanese border, is one of the most beautiful places in the world.

"Sacred land," Nega Geta explained, "the sacred land of the holy Qemant."

After about an hour he parked the car by the side of a track and explained that the most sacred part of this sacred land— the chief *degegna*—was to be found on top of a hill nearby.

In silence we walked across land that showed little sign of its sanctity but plenty of the Ethiopian civil war, which had raged here from 1974 to 1991. Nega Geta guided us up a very steep slope to what he said was the high place of his people, the sacred grove of the Qemant. We arrived at the top of the sacred hill and paused to take in the remarkable views in every direction. As we rested, panting, in the shade of the trees, I asked him what he knew about the Ark of the Covenant. He replied that the Qemant had brought it with them from Jerusalem many years before. I said nothing and waited excitedly for him to continue.

"The Amhara Christians say they brought it and the Falashas say *they* brought it. But *we* brought it. We Qemant brought it. We had *much* knowledge of it. I believe it is still here with us," he said vaguely, peering around him with his exophthalmic eyes, while patting the trunk of one of the trees.

"Here is the Ark!" he shouted out suddenly, thwacking the trunk of another tree.

Daud had a sudden and apparently uncontrollable fit of coughing, and moved away to some rocks on the other side of the copse, where I could observe him thrashing around on the ground in paroxysms of what appeared to be laughter.

Nega Geta asked me if Daud was all right. I raised my eyebrows and said nothing.

"He's a Coptic priest, isn't he? We think they are dirty and have bad smell. It's better if he keeps way from the holy ancestors." He pointed at the trees.

Nega Geta explained that the trees were many things. Of course they were the Hebrew patriarchs. But the one he was stroking was also the Ark of the Covenant.

"The essence of the Ark is to be found in the structure of the tree," he explained. "That is what the Ark is made of. Literally. Wood."

"Er, I'm not quite sure that I understand you. But anyway this is not acacia," I said, smiling at Nega Geta. "The Ark was made of acacia."

"In the Qemant religion," Nega Geta sighed, "trees and wood are easily transformed into something else. Like other things are easily turned into trees and wood. Water and cow dung, for instance. Both can be turned into their opposite. Like everything in life. Love turns to hate."

He gave me a wise little smile.

Daud had controlled himself and was limping back to join us. Hearing Nega Geta's last words he leaned on one of the trees and smiled conspiratorially at me.

"We have studied the dark and the day," he droned, adopting a rather offensive pseudo-African accent for the occasion, "through their common voice and conclude that opposites are one."

Ignoring Daud, I continued questioning the Qemant who looked as if he had had quite enough of my young Coptic friend.

"What exactly *was* the Qemants' role in the story of the Ark?" I asked hurriedly. "I know you brought it from Jerusalem. But what happened to it then? Do you have any traditions about where it might be hidden?"

"Our ancestor Anayer arrived at Lake Tana from the north, from Israel, and on the journey from the north he met the Falashas. They both carried the holy Ark. And then our ancestors came to this hill."

"But what about the Ark?" I asked.

"You can ask our ancestors yourself," he replied with a smile. "You don't have to ask me. Ask them directly. There they are!"

And he pointed at the swaying trees towering above us. "These are the patriarchs. This is Moses," he said, slapping the trunk of what looked like a giant mango tree. "Here is Aaron," he announced, giving another mighty thwack. "This one here is Noah. Speak to these old men, open your heart and open your soul, and listen carefully for their answers."

I closed my eyes and listened. There was a somewhat unhelpful drumming in my head, which I attributed to the steepness of the hill we had just climbed and perhaps to my infected ear. I thought I could hear Daud spluttering again. I tried to concentrate as hard as I could on the Ark. I thought of all I had read and all I had heard. I thought of my failure to unravel the mysteries surrounding it. But all I could hear was the cawing of crows and the rustling of leaves in the slight, warm breeze rising up from the arid plains of the Sudan.

On the way back to the car I asked Nega Geta which way his people had come, according to their oral traditions. He replied that they came first from the north, up the Nile from Egypt and that they came by way of Sennar. The Falashas for the last 200 years have also periodically claimed to have come from the land of Israel by way of Sennar.

The town of Sennar is on the Blue Nile, not very far from the Ethiopian border. On a very clear day I imagined it might even be possible to see it from where we were standing. Its hinterland, also called Sennar, is the triangular-shaped territory between the White and Blue Niles.

In the past it seems as if Christianity implanted itself here, followed by Islam, and a number of sophisticated medieval kingdoms, principally the Funj kingdom, established themselves in this territory. No doubt the curious amalgam of religious traditions to be found in the border regions of Ethiopia owed something to the rich religious mulch to be found in the Sudanese lowlands.

It occurred to me that it was a mighty coincidence that the Lemba tribe, at the other extremity of Africa, also claimed to have come to Africa from Israel by way of their lost city of Senna, phonetically almost the same as Sennar. I wondered if there was any connection. It seemed to me that the similarity of these two names might somehow contain a clue that could help my investigation.

I sat up late that night on the terrace of the Goha Hotel. Ethiopia was thick with legends and competing claims about the Ark of the Covenant. None of them was very helpful. I had spoken to the man who knew more about Qemant traditions than anyone and it was clear that Qemant traditions and beliefs would not help me. I could rule out the Qemant. The Falashas were perhaps another story and I thought that further research among this fascinating community might yet provide useful information.

The majority Amhara claimed that the Queen of Sheba, who was an Ethiopian queen, visited King Solomon in Jerusalem, where she became pregnant by the great king. In due course the Ark was stolen by their son Menelik, the first emperor of Ethiopia. For the Christian Amhara the story of the Ark was their foundation myth, like it was the foundation myth of no other society on earth.

But was there any historical basis to these tales? In Arab folklore the Queen of Sheba is called Bilqis and is associated with the pre-Islamic south Arabian kingdom of Saba. In fact there is no evidence at all that the Queen of Sheba ever existed. However, her alleged union with Solomon generated countless legends throughout the world. In the Ethiopian retelling of these legends, the story and the substance of the Ark had become deformed. At the most it had become a pretty, Christian altar box with crosses on it. It was used to celebrate the Christian sacrament. It had been metamorphosed into something tame, domesticated, safe, and obviously far from the Ark of Moses. It had been transformed into something it was not.

There was not the slightest indication that the object in the chapel of the St. Mary of Zion Church in Aksum had any great antiquity or was connected with the original Ark or with original Arks in any way. Quite the contrary: it has been proved without a shadow of doubt that it did not.

But even conceptually, this fake, Christian Ark described by Abu Salih, and something even more ornate described by later visitors to Aksum, was not the Ark I was seeking. It was not the Ark.

THE TOMB OF HUD
THE PROPHET OF GOD

"That's not what the Mossad thinks!" said Reuven. After my Ethiopian trip I had telephoned Reuven from London. He was reluctant to accept my findings on Ethiopia and claimed that even Israeli intelligence agencies thought the Ark was there. But in my own mind I was quite sure: the Ethiopian connection had drawn a blank.

Over a drink at his London club a few weeks later I set out what to me were the sound reasons for believing that the Ark was probably not, nor ever had been, at least for any great time, in Ethiopia.

Reuven shook his great head and sighed. "I believe in Ethiopia but I guess you'll just have to keep following your nose."

This I did, and my nose led me to the deserts of south Arabia.

* * *

In October 1995, a few months after my trip to Ethiopia with Daud, I was doing some research on the Yemenite Jews in the Hadhramaut—a remarkable valley system that cuts through the *Rub al-Khali*—the Empty Quarter—the great Arabian desert in the southern part of the Yemen. Here I stumbled on a solution to a problem, a major problem that had occupied me for a long time.

Initially this did not seem to be very closely linked to my quest to find the Ark, but in due course it would provide a decisive clue that helped me to proceed with my detective work.

The problem had to do with the Lemba tribe of southern Africa that I had been studying on and off for many years. When I lived in Sevias's hut in his village in Zimbabwe, he and his friends frequently spoke of a tradition that connected them with a place outside Africa, "in the north," called Senna. The Lemba believed that they were of Israelite extraction. They believed that they left Israel and settled in a place called Senna. From Senna, they had "crossed Pusela" and about fourteen of them had arrived in Africa, where eventually they prospered and reconstructed Senna in two or more places.

"We have come from a very remote place called Senna," goes one version of their tradition, "on the other side of the sea. We crossed Pusela. We were on a big boat. A terrible storm nearly destroyed us all. The boat was broken into two pieces. Seven men went north or were lost, seven men settled in Africa."

First, I had discovered that there was once a city on the east coast of Africa mentioned by the early medieval Arab geographers. It was called Sayuna, which was similar to Senna. Sayuna was situated not far from the medieval town of Sofala, somewhere near the modern town of Beira on the Mozambique coast, far down the east coast of Africa. There is no trace of either Sofala or Sayuna today save some great clumps of blackened stone on the beach pounded by the waves. Intriguingly, the name Sayuna is identical to the Judeo-Arabic word for Zion. The tribe had asked me to locate their original Senna across the sea "in the north." Finding out about Sayuna was a starting point.

There was also a town called Senna on the Zambesi River, which entered the Indian Ocean not far from where I thought Sayuna had once been. This Senna had been a busy entrepot town for several centuries and had been mentioned by the Portuguese from the sixteenth century on. I was sure that Sayuna on the coast and Senna on the Zambesi had been the towns referred to in the Lemba's narrative. The Lemba claimed to have made their way from the coast or from the Zambesi, inland, where they constructed a further city before being dispersed over a large area of southern Africa, frequently living in small groups among other tribes. However, until I got to the Hadhramaut, I had no idea at all where the original lost city of the Lemba was to be found.

"I've spent the last eight years looking for a lost city," I explained.

It was the autumn of 1995 and I was in the town of Tarim in the Hadhramaut, in the home of the mufti, or religious head, of the town. I was speaking to one of the mufti's guests, a white-bearded old Hadhrami called Sheikh Abdul Rahman Karim al-Mallahi, who was a poet and playwright with a passionate interest in the history of Arab navigation.

It was oppressively hot in the *mafraj*, or sitting room, of the mufti. Carved shutters filtered out the blinding white light of Tarim but little of the heat. We were sitting on the floor, propped against the cushions that lined the room while the mufti's sons brought us flag-shaped raffia fans, cold water, and tea. We had just eaten a lunch of rice, goat curry, chillis, and a fragrant salad of bananas, tomatoes, and onions. I was now telling the mufti and Sheikh Abdul the story of the Lemba. I explained that they had Semitic customs and Semitic clan names, and that they had originally come from somewhere called Senna. This was their lost city that I had failed to find. What followed was one of those rare and infinitely exhilarating moments of scholarly discovery.

Sheikh Abdul said: "You have been looking for this place for many years—and now, *insha-allah*, you have *found* it." I looked at him open-mouthed. He stood up and bore down on me, smiling broadly, his white gown billowing around him, and put his arms gently around me. "You have *found* it. It's only a few hours from here."

He asked the mufti if he had a map. The old mufti rose slowly from his cushion and hobbled to the corner of the *mafraj* where there was a leather Arab chest bound with brass strips. He took from it an old hand-drawn chart, which he spread out in front of me.

"This must be your Senna," he explained, indicating a point right at the eastern end of the *wadi* (valley or dry riverbed).

"I've looked for this place on hundreds of maps," I said, "and I never found anything."

"It's just a small place now," explained Sheikh Abdul, "but once around a thousand years ago, before the great Senna dam burst, it was an important town."

He explained that the people from the eastern end of the *wadi* always used to seek refuge from poverty, war, and starvation in Africa.

"Those west of Tarim always traveled to the East—to Singapore or to Indonesia and embarked from the ports of Aden or Makullah. Those *east* of Tarim went to Africa. For reasons to do with tides and winds, Sayhut, which is close to Senna, was good for Africa; the other ports were good for the east. Senna was once important, there is no doubt of that. But you'll see for yourself—we'll take you there tomorrow."

The next day we drove together in a rickety Toyota Landcruiser down the *wadi* to Senna. Sheikh Abdul Rahman Karim al-Mallahi wanted me to see the place for myself.

It was one of the most exciting and fulfilling days of my life. I had discovered my lost city.

Probably.

Senna has a wild and stark beauty I have never seen anywhere else. It thrilled me. I rejoiced in it. I could not forget that for the Lemba this was the Senna to which they expected to return after their death. This was the place Mathivha and my Lemba friends had asked me to find on their behalf. This place was the key to their history. This was the culminating moment in a quest that had taken me many years. I knew that there was no real, absolute proof of the identification, but the pieces of the puzzle seemed to fit together incredibly well. My evidence was circumstantial but I thought it was pretty damned convincing nonetheless.

The town is joined to the sea and to the ruins of the medieval town of Sayhut, on the shark-infested southern coast of the Yemen, by a riverbed called the Masila, which I thought could be a corruption of the Lemba's Pusela (*we left Senna, we crossed Pusela*), which is otherwise meaningless.

The clans in the area of the Senna in the Yemen, as I discovered, have a great number of the identical clan names of the Lemba. The Lemba clan names were intriguing because they were not African names, but Semitic names. Clan names such as Hamisi, Sadiki, Seremane, Mhani, which were found among the Lemba in southern Africa, were all found here in the Hadhramaut. In addition, the proximity of Senna to Sayhut meant that it would not have been difficult to get from Senna to Africa. According to Sheikh Abdul, a big Arab sailing dhow, with the monsoon winds in the right direction, could go from Sayhut to the Mozambique coast in a couple of weeks or so.

Three days after my initial trip to Senna with Sheikh Abdul and the mufti, I went back down the valley by myself. I wanted to speak to the head man of Senna to see if I could find anything more about the constant emigration from the area. The mukhtar, or head man, was dressed in a spotless *futa* and a shawl was wrapped around his shoulders. His beard and hair were dyed a dull red with henna. With great shouts of welcome—*ahlan ahlan*—he showed me up to the second floor *mafraj* of his substantial clay-built house. To accommodate me he used *al-lughah al-fushah,* or classical Arabic, rather than the Yemeni dialect which I did not understand very well as he explained something of the history of the house and his family.

The *mafraj* was decorated with ostrich shell, swords, *djam-biyyehs,* and photographs of his castle, ruined grievously in one of the perpetual intertribal conflicts that had bedevilled

Hadhrami life for centuries. He clapped his hands and shouted in English, "Bring drink for English!"

A gloomy-looking youth arrived bearing an earthenware pitcher of water and some glasses. The mukhtar courteously introduced him as his slave and also wished me to make the acquaintance of a young, discouraged-looking girl who was sitting in a corner, fiddling with the beads on her shawl. She was, he told me, the whore of Senna. Over ginger tea, dates, and grapes from his orchards he listened to my story about the Lemba.

"With names like Sadiki, Mhani, Seremane, and all the rest," he boomed, "those Lemba folk have to be our people. People from here always went to the east coast of Africa. Some of them may have gone inland like your people. If they'd stayed here they would have starved to death. They just walked down the Masila and took a boat from the port of Sayhut. We used to have great stone-built dams hundreds of years ago. When the dams burst, and we could no longer store the water that comes down from the mountains of the Yemen, Senna started to die. Before, it was a large city. Now it is as you see it. Just tell those Lemba people from me that they are welcome to return whenever it pleases them, *in sha-allah*, if Allah wills. They are welcome! *Ahlan wasahlan.*"

Over the next few days I discovered a number of local customs that appeared to be at the root of analogous Lemba traditions. However, local customs, identical clan names, and the ruins of the stone dams of Senna, of great antiquity, were not the only features of the area to contribute to my understanding of the Lemba story.

In the pre-Islamic era there was actually a Jewish kingdom in Himyar—what is today the Yemen—that extended right into the area around Senna. It was at the time the only Jewish state in the world. Himyar was an Eldorado of the ancient world— rich beyond belief on the profits of the trade in frankincense and myrrh, indispensable items in the religious systems of the ancient world.

According to mainly Arabic sources, a certain Dhu Nuwas had seized the throne of Himyar at some point between AD 518 and 523. At this time the Ethiopians held a good deal of territory in southern Arabia. Dhu Nuwas attacked and destroyed the Christian Ethiopian garrisons in a number of their strongholds, notably Najran, on what is today the Saudi frontier, and having stamped out Christianity throughout his realm he and his nobles embraced Judaism.

In addition, there were significant links between Himyar and the Jewish community in the land of Israel and Jews from elsewhere settled in south Arabia at the time. We know that at the time of the death of the prophet Muhammad in about AD 632 there were Jewish tribes in the *Wadi* Hadhramaut and there were Jews there at least until the end of the fifteenth century, when they were expelled. The Jews in the area preserved links with the land of Israel and no doubt with the Jewish oasis towns of the desert. The historical presence of Jews in and around the town of Senna seemed to provide some strong supporting evidence for the Lemba's claims to be of Israelite stock.

* * *

On the research trip, during which I discovered what I was almost sure was the Lemba's Senna, I also came across the famous Ahqaf Islamic library—which is reputed to have more than 300 ancient Klamic manuscripts which do not exist anywhere else in the world, as well as hundreds more that do. It seemed the ideal place to seek unknown works on the connections over time between Jews and Muslims. It occurred to me that this library could be of great importance for Reuven's mission to find Muslim texts that might reconcile Muslims to Zionism.

Some weeks after my return from the Yemen, I telephoned him from London and told him about the library. He was immediately interested. He insisted that Daud pack his bags and spend some time working in the manuscript collections of the Yemen. Daud was only too happy to oblige. Once I heard that Daud was going to be in the Yemen, I arranged to make another short research trip myself and when I told Reuven this, despite his promise to Clara never to go anywhere dangerous without her, he decided to join us.

While Daud initially undertook his researches in various libraries in Sana'a, the capital of the Yemen, Reuven and I drove in a rented car from the highland city toward the Hadhramaut. I wanted to tell him about my recent findings and share with him the beginnings of a hazy idea I had about the Ark.

As we made our way down the *wadi* we could see palms swaying in the heat haze at the edge of the valley floor, and black-robed women with high straw hats tending the alfalfa fields. The river that irrigates the fields, orchards, and palm groves of the *wadi* flows underground from the mountains of upland Yemen until it reaches the ancient town of Tarim. Thereafter the *wadi* changes its name to the *wadi* Masilah and the river flows mainly above ground through Senna and down to the sea.

Reuven was enchanted by the beauty of the place, but kept reminding me that this was where Usama bin Laden was from and that this was one of the great world centers of extremist Islam.

I had never had quite this impression. In all the months I spent in the Yemen I found it the most hospitable place I had known, a place where strangers were utterly unlikely to be robbed or abused in any way. However, I knew that things were beginning to change. In the previous months a number of foreigners had been seized and there were now small groups of radical Islamists living as semioutlaws in the least accessible parts of the country, such as the hinterland of the Hadhramaut.

Tarim, with its 360 mosques and enormous mud-built palaces constructed out of the fortunes made by Hadhramis in places like Singapore, is hidden behind a mud wall with impressive turrets and gatehouses. It is one of the most intensely Islamic places on the face of the earth. We drove through the dusty tracks of the town to Qasr al-Qubbah—a decrepit but lovely hotel on the edge of town, surrounded by lush gardens and palm groves, which had once been the palace of a Hadhrami warlord.

A couple of edgy, dead-eyed men arrived at the hotel from the capital Sana'a at the same time as us and immediately threw themselves on the ground in the shade of some bushes to chew the narcotic privet-like plant called *qat*. While the drug was active they were happy and animated, but by the end of the day their supply was finished and in the Hadhramaut the drug was unobtainable. It grows only in the mountainous regions of the country. Over the next few days the men's waxy white Yemeni faces turned ashen. They stayed slumped on rugs in the garden. When new guests arrived they would bleat *"qaaat qaaat"* and hold out their hands imploringly. It was never clear what the men were doing there and Reuven regarded them anxiously whenever we passed them.

Despite the presence of the life-giving little river, the valley floor around Tarim is dry where it is not irrigated and the desert plateau above the valley system is one of the driest places on earth. The area is as arid as the Egyptian desert, if not more so. Rainfall is little more than 60 millimeters a year.

"You told me to follow my nose," I said to Reuven as we took a cooling drink on the hotel terrace. "My famous nose has brought me here to Tarim. And now it is beginning to twitch. If you think about it, in ancient times the Ark could either have been taken to Egypt or Ethiopia or it could have been taken south into the deserts of Arabia. It could have been brought here."

Looking at my twitching nose, Reuven laughed. But what I was saying made a lot of sense. If there was good reason to suppose that in the sixth century BC the Ark had gone to Elephantine in Egypt—as it was the closest thing on earth to the Jerusalem Temple—so by the fifth century AD was it not reasonable to suppose that the Ark might have been brought here to the only Jewish polity on the face of the earth?

Reuven was mildly skeptical that southern Arabia would produce anything of value in the quest for the Ark. But initially he was in a genial mood, and enjoyed the danger of being an

Israeli (albeit an Israeli with a Dutch passport) on the loose in such a conservative, Islamic country. In the evening we would sit under the palm trees in the garden of the great house and discuss the mass of conflicting traditions about the peregrinations of the Ark that we had managed to piece together.

There were countless Arab legends claiming that the Ark had arrived in Arabia. As Rabin had told me, the second book of Maccabees explained that the Old Testament prophet Jeremiah had taken the Ark from Jerusalem, before the Babylonians captured the city in 587 BC. He took it across the river Jordan and into Arabia. Broadly the same story is picked up by the medieval *Tractate of the Temple Vessels,* which initially had excited Naki and me so much. The Arab historians claim specifically that the Ark was discovered by the Jurhum tribe, which controlled parts of northwestern Arabia, in the sealed cave where Jeremiah had hidden it and that they took the Ark to Mecca.

One morning, as Reuven and I were having breakfast in the garden, we saw Daud limping energetically toward the main entrance of the Qasr al-Qubbah. With a triumphant gleam in his eye, he shouted "Eureka!" He had left his big gold cross and black shirt in Sana'a, and was dressed in the jacket of his black suit and a rather unwholesome looking *futa,* which revealed a pale and scrawny pair of shins. As he approached our table I noticed something odd about him. His hair was plastered with some thick, opaque unguent and there were rivulets of grease flowing down his face.

"Daud—in the name of Allah the Merciful—you will forgive me if I point out that you appear to have half a pound of melting lard on your head."

He explained that it was ghee, or clarified butter, that had been given him by a friendly Bedouin he had met in the bus from Sana'a.

"That Bedouin chap was wearing very nice makeup, especially around his eyes, and kept his hand on my knee all the way from Sana'a to Habban," Daud giggled. "He seemed to have taken a liking to me and was worried that the slight dandruff I sometimes get would spoil my suit. So he gave me a pot of this wonderful ghee."

Daud then pointed at the brief and unsavory cotton skirt he was wearing and stagily whispered "camouflage"—for Daud, like Reuven, I soon discovered, was convinced that Tarim was a hotbed of Islamic terrorism and he fondly imagined that the wearing of the *futa* would enable him to pass for a local Muslim.

In Sana'a he had been looking at documents from a corpus of literature called *Israiliyyat*, the statements and observations of Jews who had converted to Islam in the seventh to eighth century AD. *Israiliyyat* writers of particular note were Abu Kaab al-Ahbar, who is said to have accompanied Umar ibn al-Khattab, the second caliph of Islam, on his first visit to the Temple area in Jerusalem, and Abu Rihana, who is said to have been related to the prophet Muhammad by marriage. Another of these ancient sources was the eighth-century Arab historian Wahb ibn Munabbih, who was almost certainly of Jewish origin and hailed from south Yemen, not far from the Hadhramaut.

Daud had unearthed masses of Arabic references to the Ark. According to some, the Ark was buried in Kalwadha, once a large town near Baghdad. However the main argument for this was the similarity between the name of the town and one of the Arabic names for the Ark—*kilwadh*. Folk etymologies such as this are common throughout the world and I did not believe that this constituted proof that the Ark was ever really in Baghdad. Other Arabic texts spoke of a "wooden chair"-like object being carried into battle (as a guarantor of victory) and venerated by Shiites in the early years of Islam, apparently in conscious imitation of the Ark. But there is nothing to say that this "wooden chair" was not actually the Ark itself, for the Ark was also a chair, as it was the throne of God.

I was very excited by this. But what had excited Daud most, and in turn excited me, was a passage from Wahb ibn Munabbih that claimed that the children of Israel were still marching with the Ark at the head of their armies long after the death of King Solomon. According to him, the Ark had returned to the old peripatetic life it had had before it was incarcerated in the Temple. If the stories about the "wooden chair" being carried into battle in the early days of Islam had any substance, the tradition of an active Ark had been brought up to relatively recent times.

Ibn Munabbih's version of events was a radical departure from the usual Jewish tradition. But what he recorded could well have been based on alternative Jewish traditions, since lost, that had been kept alive by the Jewish communities of the Arabian oases close to Medina about which almost nothing is known except what we find in sparse Muslim sources.

"What he says," said Daud, scraping his scalp with the very long nail of his little finger, "is that the Ark was not shut up, uselessly doing nothing, after the construction of the Temple but went before Israelite troops when they marched against Arab armies. After one battle, despite their possession of the mighty Ark, the Israelites were crushed. I know, *ya-achi*, that this seems pretty unlikely on the showing of recent Arab–Israel military encounters. But thus it was. And the Arabs carried the Ark off in triumph."

Daud had absorbed some of the passion that Reuven and I shared for the history of the Ark and also had a particular fondness for it. What had happened to the Ark in Mecca appalled him. For despite warnings given by a member of the Jurhum tribe, al-Harith ibn Mudad al-Jurhumi, the captured Ark was thrown onto a stinking pile of dung.

"Which is what you would expect in a primitive Islamist hellhole like this," he added, looking contemptuously at the crumpled figures of the dead-eyed *qat* eaters.

That evening, over an ice-cold and illicit gin and tonic taken on my terrace, Daud told us the rest of the story. The people of Mecca were punished for this *lèse majesté* and a plague was sent killing most of the population. The survivors had the good sense to remove the Ark from its insalubrious resting place. It then stayed on in the family of Hamaysa ibn Nabd ibn Qaydar ibn Ismail "until the time of Jesus."

Daud had found other old Arabic texts that described how the Ark was sealed in a cave somewhere not far from Mecca, where it still was in the seventh century AD, at the time of Muhammad. These stories seemed altogether remarkable to me because they came from early, knowledgeable sources: Jews of the Arabian oases whose knowledge of the world was enriched by the travelers and merchants who used the trade routes that passed through their oases. *These sources were giving us an alternative history of the Ark right up to the eighth century.*

Other astonishing Muslim sources maintained that the Ark had been in existence since the time of Adam and that it had once contained pictures of all the prophets including the

Prophet Muhammad. Alexander the Great took these images out of the Ark and eventually they came into the possession of the Byzantine emperor of Muhammad's time. Other Islamic traditions such as Ibn Hisham—which Daud was particularly enthusiastic about—contain precise lists of the people into whose hands the Ark fell after its arrival in Arabia: very many of these were Yemenis.

Reuven was not overly impressed by these Muslim traditions and was particularly contemptuous of the *Israiliyyat* stories. He saw them as being misunderstood versions, or self-serving reworkings of Jewish legendary material from the Midrash.

"Even Muslims don't take the historical stuff in these narratives seriously. I guess that's because the writers were Jews. Converts perhaps. But still Jews. But why the hell should *we* take seriously the word of Jewish *renegades?*"

In his heart Reuven was still convinced that the Ark was in Ethiopia and he kept hinting that I return there to undertake a systematic search of old churches and monasteries. He was also convinced that the men who had accompanied the Ark from Jerusalem to Ethiopia at some point in the past were likely to have been Falashas and thought therefore that the hiding place of the Ark could well be revealed by penetrating the inner secrets of the Falasha community. He wanted me to mount a proper expedition, to take along Ronit, to hire appropriate people, vehicles and *matériel*, and get the Falasha leadership in Israel involved in the hunt.

One sweltering night Reuven and I sat on a kelim in the garden drinking ginger tea next to a limpid pool of water, pumped up from the water table. I tried to explain to him in rather more detail why it was that I thought the Ark might have passed this way at some point in its life.

Maybe I had suspected all along that my Lemba tribe of southern Africa were somehow involved in the Ark story. Given the extraordinary similarity of the Lemba's sacred drum—the *ngoma*—and the Ark, and given the Lemba's association with the lost city of Senna, I was beginning to wonder if some important clue that might lead us to the object of our long quest was not waiting to be found here in Arabia.

When I spoke of the wealth and novelty of the *Israíliyyat* literature, Reuven yawned. When I spoke of the lost Lemba cities—of Senna, multiple Sennas, and Sayuna, perhaps Zion— he closed his eyes and pressed his clenched fists against his temples. When I told him about my discovery of the Lemba's lost city, he showed little interest. When I talked of Lemba history and all the other things that I had being trying to piece together in an attempt to link them with Arabia, he became impatient and said I was wasting my time and his.

Reuven was not at ease. He was convinced that the *qat*-chewers were Islamists who were planning to kidnap him. They rarely moved from their rug in the garden and seemed to be watching us. One of them had a satellite phone. There had been a welter of kidnappings of foreigners over the previous months and Reuven feared that if he were caught, the truth of his identity would emerge, and he would finish up with his throat slit.

After a few more days, suffering terribly from the heat and primitive conditions, and feeling guilty for having lied to Clara, he hired three heavily armed guards, took a taxi back to Sana'a and returned to London.

* * *

Daud and I stayed on in the hotel. Daud spent several more days working in the Ahqaf library and I spent my time reviewing my notes. I was devoted to the task of trying to find out what had happened to the Ark but I was also anxious to try to establish *what* it actually was. I still did not know. It was a complete enigma.

I had by now realized that in ancient times, before all the cultic affairs of the Israelites were concentrated exclusively in the capital, Jerusalem, there had been Arks, probably of different sorts, wherever Jehovah, the God of Israel, was worshiped. These early Arks appear to have had the form of a simple wooden container and were used for magic purposes including divination.

With the centralization of the cult of Jehovah, all deliberate mention of other Arks, of multiple Arks, had been suppressed. What happened to the other Arks we do not know. Perhaps they were destroyed, perhaps they were hidden or lost. But after the centralization there was to be only *one* God, *one* Temple, and *one* Ark. Anything that suggested the contrary was purged from the text. This I thought was the point where the original, simple wooden Ark of Moses, which itself was but one of other sacred Arks, was reinvented for public consumption as a golden object with fancy cherubim on top. But who knows what was actually hidden in the Holy of Holies?

In the shady, sweet-smelling gardens of Tarim, I gave more thought to the frequent overlaps between the curious biblical artifact, called the *ephod,* and the Ark. The *ephod* is supposed to have been created in the desert at the same time as the Ark. *Ephod* is usually translated as "apron" of the high priest, or as a priestly shoulder cape or a mantle. There are very detailed descriptions of how it was constructed but the descriptions give little clue as to its overall purpose and do not correspond to the conventional view of it.

It had a clear magic function of some sort and was used for purposes of sorcery and divination. We know that when it was being used for consulting God it could be held in the hand.

In some biblical passages, the *ephod* was something that apparently was worn or carried by a strap. However, in other places, it was something not worn but carried around by the priests, sometimes made of gold, sometimes of silver. Gideon, one of the judges in premonarchy Israel, made an *ephod* out of 1,700 shekels of gold, which represents about 53 pounds. Micah, one of the minor prophets of the Old Testament, made a solid silver *ephod* in his sanctuary. In the temple of Nob, probably somewhere near Jerusalem, the sword of Goliath, the mighty Philistine warrior slain by a stone from the sling of a youthful David, was wrapped in a cloth and placed behind an *ephod*. Presumably then it was a substantial free-standing object behind which something as substantial as the sword of Goliath could be placed.

The Ark had the same holiness and divination function as the *ephod*—and indeed if Ark is substituted for *ephod*, in the majority of cases it makes total and perfect sense. A number of important scholars have argued that *ephod* and Ark were one and the same thing.

This line of reasoning suggested to me that there were probably multiple Arks, that their function was essentially religious but hazy, and that they could perhaps be constructed of different materials. They seem to have all disappeared after the centralization of the cult in Jerusalem. Reviewing the hundreds of pages I had written about the *ephod* and the Ark made me realize I still did not really understand what either one of them really was. Even if they *were* one and the same thing, I still did not know what that thing was.

One day Daud said he had done as much library work as he could. We could now concentrate in the remaining time on local traditions that might cast light on the movement of the Ark. Traveling round the *wadi* Hadhramaut and interviewing elderly men and women, we soon discovered that some of the *Israiliyyat* stories disparaged by Reuven live on in the oral traditions of the Hadhramaut. In the villages and hamlets that shelter along the arid sides of the *wadi*, a memory had been preserved of the arrival of the Ark in Arabia at some remote time in the past. It was widely believed that the Ark had been hidden somewhere in Arabia in a sealed cave, perhaps in the *wadi* Hadhramaut itself.

Ibrahim was a honey-gatherer who was only too happy to talk. "My grandfather used to tell us stories about the Ark," he explained. "According to my granddfather it was in one of the caves in the cliffs of the *wadi*. But the cave mouth had been sealed so cleverly that it was indistinguishable from the surrounding rock face. Even a bee would not get in it. Lions and snakes protect the secret of the place."

A number of the people we interviewed suggested to us that one of the more plausible hiding places was at the eastern end of the *wadi* in the vicinity of one of the most remarkable ghost towns in the world. This small, eery desert town of stone-built houses, situated an hour's drive to the east of Tarim, is clustered around the tomb (*qabr*) of the prophet of God Hud. *Qabr* Hud is visited once every twelve months by the Muslim faithful, who keep houses here, built into the cliff face of the *wadi's* side. They are used for only four days out of the year, yet some of the houses are palatial.

Hud was a presumably Hebrew prophet who brought the message of monotheism to the ancient pre-Islamic people of Ad. The annual pilgrimage to his tomb is very ancient, and in the past, for the people of south Arabia, this *hajj,* or pilgrimage, rivaled the *hajj* to Mecca.

The people of Ad were the citizens of an ancient city and area known in Arabic as Iram, which was at the center of trade routes crossing the Empty Quarter. The lost city of Iram—which Lawrence of Arabia called the Atlantis of the Sands—came to light in 1984 when archaeologists examined photographs taken of the Persian Gulf Coast from the space shuttle *Challenger*. Vanished cities were visible from space and one of them proved to be Iram, the capital of the people of Ad, in the heart of the Empty Quarter.

According to Islamic tradition, the people of Ad were the great-grandchildren of Noah and were chastised by Hud for their decadence, polytheism, and wealth. The Hud of the Quran can almost certainly be identified with the biblical Eber, the great-grandson of Noah's son Shem. Eber is the origin of the word "Hebrew" (*ibri*) and Hud is a word that is derived from the Arabic word for Jew (*Yahud*). *Qabr* Hud was probably the center of some pre-Islamic Judaic cult.

According to the people of the eastern end of the *wadi* there was some connection between the area of the tomb of the prophet of God Hud and the legend of the Ark.

Ten days after Reuven's departure to London, Daud and I decided to visit Hud's tomb and the ghost city that surrounds it, to find out about links that might exist between the Ark and this desolate place.

In the shadow of an acacia tree, a Bedouin was resting near the fast-flowing stream that passes though the *wadi* at the foot of the tomb. High above him, a desert eagle was making lazy circles in the noon sky.

He had languorous green eyes smeared with black *kohl* and long hair greased with ghee. He was nursing a Kalashnikov wrapped in a piece of shiny, purple cloth and had a silver *jambiyyeh* with an elaborate scabbard stuck into his belt.

"*Salamu aleykum,*" I said.

"*Aleykum salam,*" he replied.

After a particularly long exchange of pleasantries with Daud, whose well-greased hair seemed to meet with his approval, he asked what we were doing in this uninhabited place that was known to be a refuge for silver desert foxes but not for man.

"This and that," I answered evasively and went on to ask him about the prophet Hud.

He eyed me narrowly and explained. "The prophet Hud, peace upon him, was a Jew. There are better and greater prophets than Hud. Moses, peace upon him, and Aaron, peace upon him, for instance. They were great prophets, peace upon them. Hud ..." he made a dismissive rocking gesture with his slender hand.

"But Moses, peace upon him, and Aaron, peace upon him, were Jews too."

He spat on the sand.

"And the Ark of the Covenant. Have you heard of this?

"They say here it was once in Mecca but then it came into the possession of certain righteous Muslims from the Yemen who hid it in a cave. The Ark, peace upon it, is guarded by lions. This is what I learned."

He pointed limply in the general direction of Mecca and then up at the cliff walls of the *wadi* behind Qabr Hud.

I heard similar accounts from a number of Hadhramis. Was it possible that the Ark had indeed been hidden somewhere in the Arabian desert as some of the rabbinic texts suggest? Had it been kept in Medina, the ancient Jewish oasis town of the Hijaz in northwest Arabia among the Jewish tribes who lived there, such as the Banu-lnadir, the Banu Kainuka, or the Banu Kuraiza? Or had it been kept in one of the Jewish oases of Khaibar, Fadak, Wadi 'I-Qura, or Taima slightly farther to the north? Had it been brought to the Hadhramaut in some remote time in the past? Perhaps at the time of the Judaizing Himyarite state?

For fugitive priests hoping to find a safe hiding place for the Ark, the great Arabian desert with its powerful Jewish communities ready to give a helping hand along the route might have been an ideal solution. In addition, in the desert, acacia wood would last indefinitely. It was one of the driest places on the face of the earth.

There were elements in the puzzle that seemed unlikely to be sheer coincidence. Very ancient traditions surrounding Hud connect the Hadhramaut with the ancient Hebrews. More recent traditions maintain that Jews had lived in the *wadi* from before the time of Muhammad until the fifteenth century. And there were traditions connecting the Ark with the Hadhramaut.

I also believed that the town of Senna—just a few miles away from *Qabr* Hud—was associated with the Lemba and therefore with their traditions of the *ngoma*. And the similar-ities between the *ngoma* and the Ark were significant. There were sufficient connections between the area and the Ark to make it worthwhile making further enquiries.

Daud and I camped out at *Qabr* Hud for several days, spend-ing most of the time climbing in the nearby cliffs searching for caves and crevices, examining the cliff wall minutely for signs of some long-sealed cavern. We found a few likely hiding places and we dug around a bit with a shovel and a pick I had bought in Tarim. One particular cave, all but sealed with a great boul-der and with signs of plaster sealing the cracks on one side of the mighty stone, looked promising, but all we found inside were signs of the passage of goats and shepherds.

We had brought a good supply of water, whisky, canned sardines, cans of Egyptian *ful*, onions, and Arab bread, and in the afternoon to escape the heat we would return to *Qabr* Hud to eat and rest. At night we would spread our sleeping bags close to the great rock that marks the resting place of the prophet, and under the desert sky surreptitiously sip from plas-tic cups the Laphroaig that Daud had smuggled in from Cairo.

Late one night while we were camping out near the tomb, some armed men crept stealthily up to where we were sleeping. We heard nothing. Gently, they shook us awake. I recognized the gloomy face of the slave of the red-bearded mukhtar of Senna. He explained that he and his friends had been sent by his master, the mukhtar. It was dangerous for us to stay even another hour. Word of our interest in the Ark had spread throughout the sparsely inhabited valley and had come to the attention of some well-armed Muslims from another country. They had discovered we were camping out here and were themselves heading toward the tomb of Hud, the prophet of God. The mukhtar's men did not know what they planned, but they could guess. They advised us to return immediately to Tarim.

We bundled everything into the car and took their advice. Daud was an extraordinary off-road driver. He did not know the meaning of fear or prudence. With squealing tires, he drove off incredibly fast and slowed down only when, in the pink light of dawn, he saw the minarets of Tarim on the horizon. We were conscious that we had had a narrow escape.

A few days later we drove back down the *wadi* to thank the mukhtar of Senna for his timely warning. By way of thanks I took him a present of a vat of local honey from the *wadi* Da'un in the Hadhramaut, which is much prized in the Yemen. He told us that the men who were looking for us were Islamists from Saudi Arabia, Iraq, and other parts of the Muslim world.

"They would have killed you," he said grimly. "There is a rumor in the *wadi* that you have second sight, and that you are looking for the sealed, dark cave where the holy Ark of the prophet Musa is hidden. If this is so we should honor you, not kill you. In the holy Quran is it not written, 'Shall the blind and the seeing be held equal? Shall the darkness and the light be held equal?' These men who tried to capture you think they are riding the winged steed of Islam, but they are riding the donkey of the devil. As the holy Quran teaches us, 'The only guidance is the guidance of Allah.'"

Thanking me for the honey, he unbuckled his belt and took the *djambiyyeh* out of its silver sheath. Pointing at the blade he showed me the Arabic inscription: "Allah save you from that which you fear the most." He thrust it into my hands and insisted that it was a present. It would keep me safe, he said, until I found what it was I was looking for, or until what I was looking for found me.

While I was in the Hadhramaut with Daud, I had an almost permanent sense of frustration. I felt that I was in the middle of a puzzle from which I would never extricate myself. The clues were vague and formless and took me in opposing directions. I tried to be systematic and to check off paths that had been eliminated. But this was not always easy.

One of the more perplexing areas concerned the close similarities between the Falashas and the Lemba. I still had not eliminated the Falashas from my hit list. They could still potentially have useful information to impart. They certainly had a lot in common with the Lemba. They were both African metalworking groups, strongly associated with the magic arts. They both claimed to have come from ancient Israel. They both had legends that associated them with the lost Ark.

The Falashas claimed to have come from a place called Sennar. The Lemba, at the other end of the continent, also claimed to have come from Senna, phonetically almost identical. Was there a connection?

Had the Lemba really left Israel millennia ago? Had they traveled by way of the Nile to Elephantine and then on to the Sudan and Sennar on the Blue Nile? Was their original town Sennar on the Blue Nile, and not the Senna in the Hadhramaut and had they had some connection in ancient times with some of the Judaizing populations of the area? Or had they come from Sennar in the Sudan to Senna in the Yemen bringing with them the Jewish traditions that they maintained with such tenacity? And did the Falashas have some connection with the south Arabian Senna—similarly rich in Judaic associations? Or was the Senna of the Lemba a corruption over time of the Sayuna on the coast—a name that had a remarkable similarity to the Arabic word for Zion?

We do not know much about Sayuna, this possible African Zion. According to Abu Abd Allah Muhammad al-Idrisi, the twelfth-century Moroccan cartographer, Sayuna was a "town connected to the land of Sofala and peopled by groups of Indians and negroes and others." In the thirteenth century, Hassan ibn Said, an Arab philosopher and historian, described Sayuna as the capital of the kingdom of Sofala, where the people worshiped "idols and stones that they anoint with the fat of large fish. Their principal resources are gold and iron. They wear the skins of panthers." On a number of early European maps there is a Senna on the coast somewhere near where Sofala was: it is altogether likely that this Senna represents the lost Sayuna of the Arab geographers.

The little we know tells us that the town was settled by a cosmopolitan mix of people with some bizarre and outlandish religious customs. What more likely destination could there be for fugitive south Arabian Jews fleeing persecution by Muslims than this Sayuna/Zion just beyond the outer limit of Islamic influence? It seemed more than reasonable to suppose that the Lemba had settled the area, called the town either after their home town of Senna or after their original Zion, before moving inland to build more Sennas (or Sayunas).

It was tempting to try to draw bold and dramatic conclusions, but there was not enough evidence to draw them. Not yet. No dead bones, no scrap of parchment, no tiny inscription. Nothing.

During the days we camped at *Qabr* Hud I wondered if there had been any connection between the Lemba and *this* place, at some time in the past. Was there any connection between their stories of the *ngoma lungundu* that they claimed to have brought, carried on poles, on the shoulders of priests, from Senna, and the local Arab traditions that claim that the Ark had been brought here and was still hidden away in a cave at the time of the prophet Muhammad? It seemed as if there might be some connection.

But during all the years I had spent in libraries in Europe and the Middle East I had come across only a single reference that seemed to create a possible linkage between Arabia and the Lemba's *ngoma lungundu*.

In the twelfth century, Abu Abd Allah Muhammad al-Idrisi, the Arab geographer, wrote a few words about al-Banyes, a town not far from the town of Senna on the Zambesi and close to the town of Sayuna on the Islamized and Arabized coast. "The inhabitants of al-Banyes," wrote al-Idrisi, "worship a drum called *Arrahim*, as big as *Albaba,* covered with skin on one side only and attached to a length of cord with which one beats the drum—it makes a terrible noise that can be heard about three miles away."

The word *Arrahim* is odd. It is not a Bantu word. Its origins come from outside Africa. It sounds exactly the same as the Arabic word ar-Rahim, which means the Merciful One—a common designation in Arabic for God. The idea that a drum could be worshiped and called by one of the sacred names of Allah would have been deeply offensive to a Muslim. Yet al-Idrisi passed over it without the slightest comment. The word *Albaba* is unknown.

Al-Idrisi relied upon travelers and other oral sources for much of his information. As L and R are interchangeable in many languages—and particularly in African Bantu languages—is it possible that what he actually heard was *Errohim*—a Bantuized form of *Elohim*, the Hebrew word for God? And al-Baba, "as big as al-Baba," could this be another drum or another object and perhaps an echo of some sort of association with the priestly Lemba ancestor Buba? What was the terrible noise it emitted that carried for three miles? Was it possible that someone had seen the Buba priests carrying the *ngoma lungundu* from the coast of Africa toward the interior? Was the reference to incredible noise a reflection of its frequent association with fire, death, and explosion? This was the slimmest of leads, and there was little else in the Arabic sources that could help.

All I had were dried bones with hardly a vestige of historical meat clinging to them. First of all it is unclear what reliability can be placed upon the old Arab and *Israiliyyat* legends. In addition, my idea that the Senna of the Hadhramaut was the revered Senna of the Lemba was perhaps a little circumstantial. And there was no proof of any connection between this Senna and the Sennar mentioned by the Falashas and the Qemant.

One night at *Qabr* Hud under a perfect sky, a thin crescent of moon hanging over the desert like a question mark, I tried out on Daud a tentative theory that was beginning to form in my mind.

The Lemba, I conjectured, came from Senna in the Hadhramaut. Prior to that their roots were in Palestine. They may have spent some time in Ethiopia and before that in Sennar. Perhaps they crossed from Africa to Arabia by way of the narrow straits of Bab al-Mandeb, in dhows or rafts. Once in Arabia, the Lemba continued guarding the Ark, which they kept safe in their Arabian oasis strongholds and which they used in their battles against the pagan tribes of Arabia.

After the rise of Islam in the seventh century, they lived a precarious existence in the Hadhramaut, suffering persecution under their Muslim rulers. They settled right on the edge of the *wadi,* close to the desert of Mehra. Perhaps some of them converted to a version of Islam and took the Ark with them in their wars with neighboring tribes. When the mighty Senna dam cracked in around the tenth or eleventh century, they went down the *wadi* Masila/Pusela to the south coast of Arabia. The great port for Africa, Sayhut, was at the bottom of the *wadi* and there they embarked in ocean-going dhows for southeast Africa. On the African coast, somewhere in the vicinity of present-day Mozambique near the Zambesi estuary, they created a town that they called Sayuna/Zion where there was already a mixed population of people from the interior, from the Arab world, and perhaps from India.

They took the Ark of the Covenant with them.

They went inland and settled in the Zimbabwe/Venda areas and contributed to the great medieval civilizations that flourished there in Mapungubwe and Great Zimbabwe from about the twelfth century on. I explained that all the dates—Muslim persecution (which started in the seventh to eighth century), the rise of Sayuna/Zion, perhaps in the early twelfth century, the collapse of the Senna dams in about the eleventh or twelfth century, the rise of the medieval African kingdoms in the eleventh or twelfth centuries, fit together rather well.

Having made my pitch, I rose and performed a gracious, hopeful little bow.

"Bollocks, *effendi!*" roared Daud, whose gift both for English demotic and for rigorous analysis were sometimes a little trying.

"First of all, there is no proof that the Lemba ever came from Palestine. Second, there is only circumstantial proof—strong circumstantial proof admittedly—that they came from Senna in the Hadhramaut.

"There is no proof that they are connected with the Falashas or the wretched Qemant or that they ever spent time in Sennar.

"As far as all the local legends about the Ark we have heard— well, it is tempting stuff. Seductive stuff. These Arab stories have the veneer of respectability because they are very, very old. Al-Idrisi, Hassan ibn Said, the *Israiliyyat*—they're all great stuff. They really are seductive; they are much older than anything in Ethiopia. They are as seductive as a certain widow I know in Cairo," he added, raising one eyebrow.

"But until such time as you find some hard evidence, over and above their oral traditions and circumstantial connections, linking the Lemba to Israel and to Arabia, that's all it is, *ya achi.* Bollocks. But I believe that there may be another theory. I don't have even a shred of evidence but a little voice keeps whispering in my ear, *effendi.*"

After a lengthy silence Daud, hesitantly at first, came up with his new theory. It was the Egyptian Copts who had rescued the Ark, he suggested, pious Egyptian Copts who had kept it safe for centuries, and it was a diminutive, dandruff-ridden Egyptian Copt who was destined to find it.

I offered my friend my views on this hypothesis.

It had not been easy to reconstruct the early history of the Lemba and, as Daud had been swift to point out, my reconstruction was based upon some sketchy evidence. There was little if anything to go on. In sub-Saharan Africa, at least in the interior, there are no written records. We are dependent upon oral tradition.

On the coast, the Arabs left some accounts—such as the one of al-Idrisi—of what they saw and heard. It looked as if at some point the Lemba must have had a connection with the sophisticated coastal, semi-Muslim civilization and then had moved into the interior where they almost certainly played a role in the advanced stone-building Zimbabwe civilization. However, the first written mention of the Lemba—by this name—does not occur until 1728 when an official of the Dutch East India Company posted in what is today Mozambique noted that the nation of the Lemba "were said to be rich in gold and were trading with the Portuguese in the direction of Senna." It is fair to conclude that by the eighteenth century the Lemba were already long settled inland.

At the time of my nocturnal walk to the sacred cave at the base of Dumghe, in 1987, the claims of the Lemba to be of Israelite origin seemed, at best, to be pretty farfetched. The idea of their being, in addition, the guardians of the Ark of the Covenant always seemed utterly unlikely. Totally farfetched. As Daud said, probably rubbish.

By 1996 I had discovered quite a lot more about them. I had perhaps identified their place of origin—the Senna in the Hadhramaut. I thought the Sayuna/Zion on the coast had a lot to do with them. I also thought that it was possible that the Sennar of the Falasha and Qemant traditions and the Senna of the Lemba were somehow connected.

I was drawn to the hesitant belief that the Lemba indeed were what they claimed—a tribe descended from some ancient Jewish or Israelite community. After so many years of work I had a theory, a series of theories. And they were appealing because they seemed to answer a lot of questions. But the evidence was thin on the ground.

There simply were not enough clues.

However, this was soon to change. The vital proof I had been seeking was to emerge from a completely unforeseen quarter.

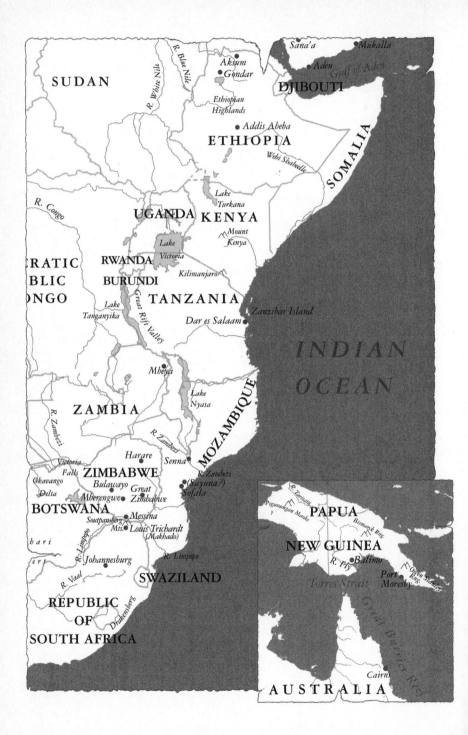

10

THE
MOSES GENE

As I was tramping round the hot, dusty tracks of the Hadhramaut trying to find some clue to help me unravel the history of the Ark and the mystery of the Lemba, another Welshman was also showing an interest in this remote African tribe.

His name was Trefor Jenkins. He was born and brought up in Wales. He studied medicine at King's College, London, and at Westminster Hospital. In 1960 he became medical officer at the Wankie Colliery Hospital in Zimbabwe (then Southern Rhodesia) and moved to South Africa where, after a short spell as a senior house officer at the University of Natal, he moved to the Department of Anatomy at Witwatersrand University, where Phillip Tobias stimulated his interest in the history of African peoples. In 1965 he joined the prestigious South African Institute for Medical Research (SAIMR), finally becoming professor and head of the Department of Human Genetics in the School of Pathology at Witwatersrand and the SAIMR.

I did not know Jenkins at this time although we were to meet later. Jenkins already had a keen interest in ways in which genetics might help our understanding of African history. Through Margaret Nabarro, an ethno-musicologist, who had made the study and support of the Lemba tribe her life's work, Jenkins got to know about the secretive and enigmatic Lemba people. Who were they? How had their strange Judaic rites penetrated unto the heart of Africa? How had the mysterious legend of the *ngoma,* with all its biblical resonance, reached this remote part of the world?

One day Jenkins had the inspired idea of putting the Lemba's claims to the test in a completely new way. With the forward march of modern genetic science, it had just become possible to test sizeable groups of people for markers that might be able to connect a group to some spot on the globe. Jenkins had the idea of trying to determine the origin of the Lemba by collecting genetic material from them and analyzing it.

One tribal tradition that I had first heard from the old chief Mposi in Zimbabawe insisted that the original Lemba immigrants from the north, from Senna, were males who subsequently took local African wives. Nabarro also knew of this tradition and passed it on to Jenkins who decided therefore to concentrate on male DNA, and specifically the DNA of the Y chromosome which is found only in men.

The DNA molecule may be seen as an extraordinary handbook of instructions designed essentially to reproduce and sustain life. The DNA molecule contains four different chemical bases, each represented by a letter: A (adenine), T (thymine), C (cytosine), and G (guanine). The data of the code generated by sequences of these letters are stored in the chromosome portion of the DNA double helix.

Jenkins argued that if the Y chromosome of the Lemba, which passes down only the male line, could be shown to originate in some specific part of the world, it would be possible to determine where the Lemba were from. It would be possible to say whether they were originally from Africa, or, as they claimed, from somewhere else. Were they "the white men who came from Senna" as they liked to say, or simply Africans with some strange customs and beliefs?

Jenkins's article analyzing his data was published in *The American Journal of Human Genetics* in November 1996. He was able to show that "fifty percent of the Lemba Y chromosomes are Semitic in origin, forty per cent are Negroid, and the ancestry of the rest cannot be resolved. These Y-specific genetic findings are consistent with Lemba oral tradition." He was also able to show subsequently that another of the Lembas' traditions was correct: the founder group was indeed seven or eight men.

Jenkins's pioneering efforts reached a wide audience with the transmission of the BBC Television series *Origins* and the book of the series, *In the Blood: God, Genes and Destiny* (1996) by Professor Steve Jones, an outstanding geneticist at University College, London. The practically unknown Lemba were thus brought to the attention of millions of people worldwide.

In his book Steve Jones noted:

> *In the pedigree of the Lemba there is a surprise. Most of their genes— blood groups, enzymes and the like—unite them with the African peoples around them. However, those on the Lemba Y chromosome ... have a different origin. On a family tree of the world's male lineages the*

Lemba are linked, not with Africans, but with the Middle East. The Lemba legend of their origin contains a hidden truth.

The first I heard of this was in mid-November 1996 when Professor Mathivha, the spiritual head of the South African Lemba, telephoned me in London to share the news that Jenkins had shown that what Mathivha called "the secret of blood" had proved what Mathivha had been saying for years, that the Lemba had come from outside Africa at some point in the remote past.

"You must be pleased," I said.

"Not *pleased*, Parfitt. We always knew it to be *true*. We had no *doubts*. We knew we came from outside Africa. We knew we were white people from the north. The only thing is we had black skins. It was the others who had the doubts. They thought we were just black people like all the others. They are the ones who should be astonished. They are the ones who should be pleased."

But he telephoned me back later that evening and said that the discovery that his tribe were actually from the north was the most important thing that had happened in his lifetime and the most useful weapon in his battle to prove to the world that the Lemba were originally non-Africans who had come from Senna.

I immediately walked over to the new British Library next to St. Pancras Station in London, to take a look at Jenkins's article for myself. It was extraordinary that the Welshman had been able to find what looked like real, hard evidence that could really begin to resolve the mystery of the Lemba.

What Jenkins had shown was that the Lemba definitely came from some area of the Middle East. This was amazing for them and it was amazing for me. This was the first *real* proof of my theory and I was initially overwhelmed. Sitting in a greasy little café near St. Pancras Station, I felt a wonderful sense of closure. Finally the proof I had been looking for had come to hand. I now knew more or less where the Lemba were from. My theory was largely substantiated.

But as I thought more about it, I realized that Jenkins had not suggested anything about the Lemba's specific ethnic or religious origins. He had proved that the tribe's claim to have come "from the north" and from outside Africa was true, and that was a massive step forward, but he had not proved precisely where they were from and he had not proved that they were indeed descended from Jews.

It seemed possible that a larger Lemba sample and more detailed anthropological information about each DNA donor might reveal something that could cast more light on their ethnic and religious origins. Jenkins had shown they were from the Middle East. The part of the Middle East from which they were most likely to have come was south Arabia. It seemed therefore a good idea to compare south Arabian and Lemba DNA.

In December 1996 I set off for Africa to see if I could do anything further to solve the intriguing puzzle that had dominated my thinking for so much of the previous years. My aim was not to elicit oral traditions and memories but to gather DNA. Instead of my usual pen, notebook, and tape recorder, this time I went armed with a DNA collection kit.

I flew into Harare, the capital of Zimbabwe, and picked up a battered rental car, which I drove down to the Mposi area near Mberengwe, in the central part of the country. At the beginning of the trip I spent a few nights with my old friend Sevias. I had been back once or twice over the previous years and had kept in touch with the old man and his family and friends by letter. He was always eager to know how my research was progressing. Now he was flummoxed. What could a cotton bud do to unveil the secrets of his ancestors?

I explained that every one of his tribe carried around a coded history of his ancestors' passage across the earth, over time and over place. Each man and woman contained in their genes the history book of their ancestors.

"Will this help you get those secrets that we did not want to tell you?" asked Sevias, smiling as he opened his mouth for me to take a sample.

"I'm hoping it will," I replied.

Once Sevias had agreed to give his DNA, everyone else in the kraals nearby followed suit.

In Africa the transmission of history was often the responsibility of guilds, or specific elders, or chiefs. Ordinary people had nothing at all to do with it. The idea that everyone's genes were equally useful, that everyone's individual history book was equally valid, was an idea that the Zimbabwe Lemba received with joy. Everyone wanted to help.

After a few days I drove the car down to the frontier crossing at Beit Bridge, left it with the rental car agency with little regret, and took a bus down to Louis Trichardt. I immediately went across to see Professor Mathivha, who soon got a number of neighbors in to give their DNA. One of them was a very old toothless Lemba man.

"Will this tell us where we came from?" he asked. "Will it tell us which route we took across Africa and will it tell us where Senna is and how to get back there?"

I nodded. I hoped very much that the clue that had thus far evaded me might be found in the tribe's DNA.

I had enlisted the help of Magdel le Roux, a lecturer in Pretoria who had been researching the Lemba for many years. Together we collected DNA from 136 Lemba men scattered over a pretty wide area between Zimbabawe and the South African capital, Pretoria. The next stage was to collect DNA in south Arabia so a comparison could be made.

The following year, in 1997, the geneticist Neil Bradman and I went to the eastern end of the Hadhramaut where I had been before with Daud and Reuven. During our visit, Neil and I collected 120 male DNA samples, some from Seiyun, a few miles down the *Wadi* from Tarim, some from Senna itself. Once it was explained that the research might cast light on the history of the Hadhramaut, most people were happy enough to participate, although one or two men refused to participate on the grounds that it was un-Islamic.

The first results clearly showed a significant similarity of markers between many of the Hadhramaut Y chromosomes and those of the Lemba. This seemed to confirm beyond any doubt that the Lemba actually had some past contact with this part of south Arabia. This was the most remarkable confirmation of my own theories about the origins of the Lemba and a confirmation of the place from which their mysterious *ngoma* had almost certainly come. But these results still left the question of the *religious* origins of the Lemba as open as they had been before. Were they really Jews?

A parallel study with which I was also involved and that was concerned with the genetic origin of Old Testament priests was beginning to produce startling and exciting data. Somewhere between the thirteenth and fifteenth centuries BC the Israelites left Egypt and were led by Moses for many years through the desert areas of the Sinai, Negev, and Trans-Jordan. The Bible tells us that during this period the tribe of Levi was selected for certain religious duties that included carrying the Ark of the Covenant. Both Moses and his brother Aaron were members of this tribe, and descendants of Aaron in the male line were designated priests.

According to Jewish tradition, *only* males from this direct line going back to Aaron could be permitted to serve as temple priests and as servants of the Ark. This strict rule was allegedly implemented from the first tabernacle in the wilderness until the destruction of Herod's Temple by Titus in 70 AD. It was essential for the priestly line to be kept intact, as the Bible states that the priesthood should last forever—it would be "a covenant of everlasting Priesthood."

With the destruction of the Second Temple by Titus two thousand years ago, the Temple priests (*cohanim*—plural of *cohen*) lost much of their function. The things they were chiefly involved with—notably caring for the Temple and organizing and carrying out sacrifice—stopped being relevant when (a) the Temple was destroyed and (b) the sacrifice of animals was terminated.

Priestly status is transmitted exactly in the same way as the Y chromosome. The Y chromosome is inherited by men from their fathers, whose sperm cells contain either an X or a Y chromosome. When these male sperm cells fuse with the female egg cell, which *always* contains an X chromosome, the sex of an ensuing baby is established: XX combinations producing girls, and XY combinations producing boys. The Y chromosome passes from father to son and that is the only way it can be transmitted. Priestly status passes from father to son—and that is the only way the status of priest can be transmitted. You cannot be appointed or promoted to the priesthood—you are one if your father was one.

A number of geneticists had the same inspiration in about 1997. By testing the Y chromosome of priests, they argued, it should be possible to see whether today's priests are genuinely descendants of some distant ancestor. The two key players in the unravelling of priestly descent were two remarkable and energetic men: Neil Bradman in London and Karl Skorecki in Israel.

Skorecki and his team produced the first paper (Hammer, Skorecki, Selig, Blazer, Rappaport, Bradman, Bradman, Waburton, Ismajlowicz, "Y Chromosomes of Jewish Priests." *Nature*, 1997); and Bradman's team, some of whom had collaborated with Skorecki, published in the same highly prestigious journal the following year (Thomas, Skorecki, Ben-Ami, Parfitt, Bradman, Goldstein, "Origins of Old Testament Priests," *Nature*, 1998).

Among Jewish priests (*cohanim*) it was found, amazingly, that over 50 percent of the sample had one specific constellation of markers that became known as the Cohen modal haplotype (CMH). The CMH may clearly be seen as a marker for the descendants of the priests of the Jerusalem Temple.

In addition, the research demonstrated something utterly extraordinary—more than extraordinary. It showed that the priests who carried the CMH were descended from a single, common male ancestor who lived around 3,000 years ago. It was reasonable then to suppose that this distant common ancestor could have been Aaron, the brother of Moses, who lived at about this time and was the founder of the priesthood. As brothers have the same Y chromosome, it was as if we had discovered the Moses gene.

It was a world-shattering discovery with all kinds of implications. Who would have thought that Mr. Cohen down the block was really descended from the Jerusalem Temple priests? Who would even have thought that the original Temple priests were really, as they claimed, descended from a common ancestor?

Even though he was no longer actively involved, Reuven telephoned me regularly and was always keen to know how things were going. When I told him of the discovery, he was finally convinced of the usefulness of this new tool of historical research.

"I realize now," he said, his voice faltering, "that you finally have a way of following Rabin's advice. *You can follow the priests!*"

Reuven told me that the discovery was received with joy by the organizations in Israel dedicated to rebuilding the Temple, as now they had a way, as they saw it, of selecting authentic priests for future temple service. For others of his friends, the discovery appeared to be a confirmation of holy writ: after all, the Bible had prophesied that the Israelite *cohanim* would be "a covenant of everlasting Priesthood." And thus they appeared to be.

But for me there was an even more astounding implication and one that Reuven had spotted immediately. We had a way of trying to track the passage of Temple priests across the pages of history.

* * *

Mathivha had told me years before that the *ngoma lungundu* had been carried on poles inserted into its rings from Senna and down through Africa by the priestly caste of the Lemba—the Buba clan. No one else could touch it—otherwise they would be put to death.

Mathivha had told me that Buba, the founder of the Lemba priestly clan, was the individual who originally led the Lemba ancestors out of Israel.

When my colleagues tested the Lemba DNA samples for the presence of the CMH—as a way of testing for potential Jewish antecedents—they had a mighty surprise. Almost exactly the same proportion of Lemba males carried the CMH as did the overall Jewish population. But even more extraordinary was the fact that the CMH was found in more than 50 percent of the Buba clan, the Lemba priests, the guardians of the *ngoma lungundu*.

The CMH is virtually nonexistent in non-Jewish populations. It occurs among the Lemba priests at almost precisely the same frequency as it does among Jewish *cohanim*. More than half the Lemba Buba priests have the same common ancestor as 50 percent of the *cohanim*. This same common ancestor who lived more or less 3,000 years ago may reasonably be taken to be Aaron or someone close to his generation.

Which meant that the Buba clan were in direct line of descent from the priests who once served in the Jerusalem Temple.

The research demonstrating the presence of the CMH in the Buba clan was published to international acclaim in 2000. "Y Chromosomes Traveling South: The Cohen Modal Hapolotype and the Origins of the Lemba—the 'Black Jews of Southern Africa'" (Thomas, Parfitt, Weiss, Skorecki, Wilson, le Roux,

Bradman, and Goldstein) appeared in *The American Journal of Human Genetics*. Even before the official publication of the article, the story caught the attention of the media. In the United States the *Nova* series on PBS made a documentary. CBS's *60 Minutes* carried the story, and in the UK, Channel 4 aired a documentary that I wrote and presented—*In Search of the Sons of Abraham*. Newspapers the world over carried the story. The Lemba became internationally known. To their delight they were invited to visit

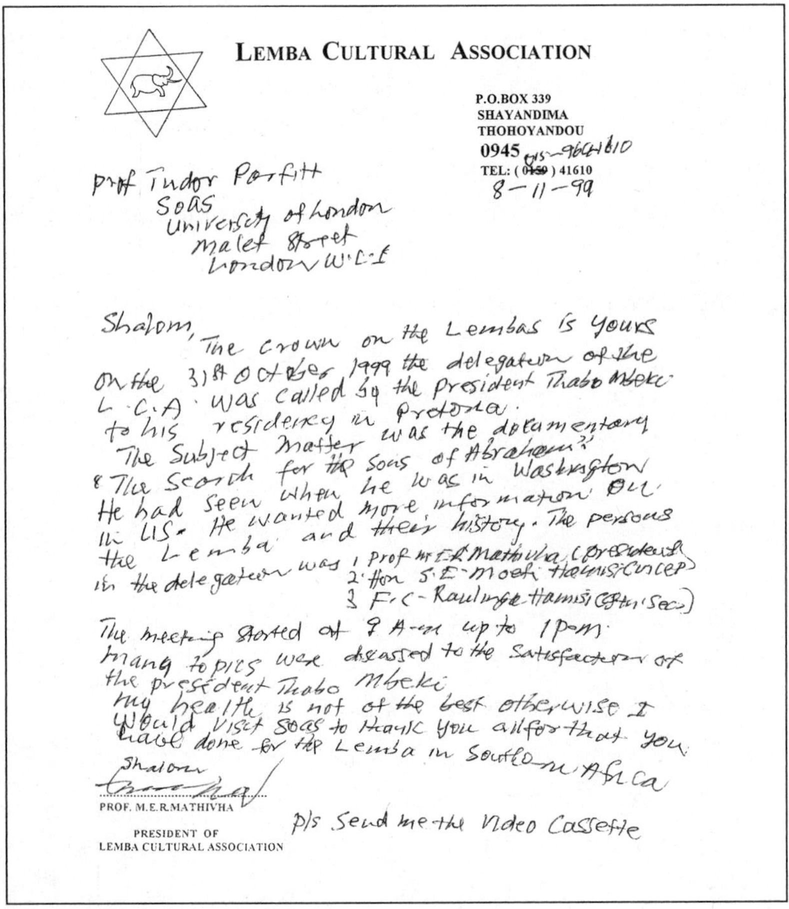

LEMBA CULTURAL ASSOCIATION

P.O.BOX 339
SHAYANDIMA
THOHOYANDOU
0945
TEL: (0159) 41610

[Handwritten letter:]

Prof Tudor Parfitt
SOAS
University of London
Malet Street
London W.C.1

015-9641610
8-11-99

Shalom,

The crown on the Lembas is yours

On the 31st October 1999 the delegation of the L.C.A. was called by the president Thabo Mbeki to his residency in Pretoria.

The Subject matter was the documentary "The Search for the Sons of Abraham". He had seen when he was in Washington in US. He wanted more information on the Lemba and their history. The persons in the delegation was 1 Prof M.E.R Mathivha (President) 2. Hon S.E. moeti (Vice/Cincep) 3 F.C. Raulinga Hamisi (after/Sec)

The meeting started at 9 A-m up to 1pm. Many topics were discussed to the satisfaction of the president Thabo Mbeki.

My health is not of the best otherwise I would visit SOAS to thank you all for that you have done for the Lemba in Southern Africa.

Shalom

PROF. M.E.R.MATHIVHA

PRESIDENT OF
LEMBA CULTURAL ASSOCIATION

P/s Send me the Video Cassette

President Thabo Mbeki in Pretoria. The South African president had seen the *Nova* documentary while visiting the United States and wanted to hear more of the Lemba's strange history.

What was taken up at the time was the amazing way in which genetics was able to confirm the pretty unlikely oral tradition of the tribe: a tradition that normal historical and anthropological methods had failed to fully confirm. In addition, the genetic trail had led to the Lemba priestly guardians of the *ngoma lungundu*. One priestly line ran straight from ancient Israel to the Buba clan of the Lemba of southern Africa.

With this new evidence it was no longer too farfetched to imagine that a secret priestly guild had preserved one of the Arks of ancient times, perhaps one of the purged Arks, or the original Ark of Moses, and transported it across the Arabian desert perhaps by way of Ethiopia, perhaps aided by the Falashas, and concealed it in some hiding place, perhaps in the Hadhramaut, in the vicinity of Senna. With the rise of Islam and the persecution of Jews, the Ark was again taken by the priests. This time to southern Africa.

I began to feel that my quest could be nearing its end. The codes of blood had revealed something, but there were other puzzles to crack before I could finally claim that my quest was over.

THE FIRE
OF GOD

Years passed during which I carried on publishing in my fields of study. I made a couple of short trips to southern Africa, hoping to push closer to my goal. But in vain. The great clue I had been handed on a plate had fleshed out my theory, but it had not helped me find the Ark. But nonetheless I was making some slow progress and had at least managed to eliminate some suspects.

One of the issues that had interested me was to what extent, if at all, the Lemba were connected with the Falashas, and to what extent, if at all, there had been a connection between their Senna in the Hadhramaut and the Sudanese Sennar of the Ethiopians' traditions. As further genetic data emerged from DNA studies from the late 1990s on it became clear that there is a distinct genetic connection between Jews throughout the world. However, there was no connection between other Jewish populations and the Falashas, and it appeared therefore that the position taken by Steve Kaplan and a good deal of modern scholarship was correct: the Falashas were simply an

Agau tribe with their roots in Ethiopia. There was no genetic link between them and the population of ancient Israel. And there was also no genetic connection between the Falashas and the Lemba. This suggested that the Lemba had come directly to southern Africa from Arabia and that their connection, if there was one, with stories of the Ark had little, if anything, to do with the multitude of legends about the Ark in Ethiopia.

The Senna/Sennar, Lemba/Falasha question could be safely eliminated. I was delighted to be able to mentally put a cross next to this whole confusing area that had cost me so much sleep over the years.

In January 2002 I was once again working on different aspects of the history of the Lemba tribe, hoping to solve one or two of the outstanding issues in the hopes that a clearer understanding of their past might lead me to my ultimate objective. This involved returning to South Africa. The first thing I did when I arrived was to telephone Professor Mathivha—the elegant, erudite, and charismatic leader of the South African Lemba. In his characteristically enthusiastic way he boomed:

"Parfitt. We have to see you. We have to push forward. We have not got all the time in the world."

He gave me the address of a farm owned by a wealthy Lemba on the slopes of the Soutpansberg Mountains and told me to be there at four o'clock the following day. There were some people he wanted me to meet.

There were three men there. Plus me. Mathivha, the spiritual head of the tribe, my old friend Samuel Moeti, a Lemba politician who had had a distinguished career as member of Parliament and mayor of the Venda capital of Thohoyandou, and William Masala, a saintly man who sat throughout the meeting with the Bible open in front of him.

We were sitting round a cherry-wood table laid with fruit, mineral water, and crystal glasses. Mathivha had called the meeting to discuss a matter of great importance for the tribe. They, like me, wanted to know the whereabouts of the *ngoma lungundu*. They believed now that the *ngoma* was the Ark of the Covenant and that the Buba priests had brought it from the land of Israel via Senna. They believed that it was the *ngoma* that had guided them from Senna and that it was the *ngoma* that would take them back.

The genetic work done on the tribe had corroborated their oral traditions beyond any reasonable doubt. It was now doubly important for them to find the *ngoma*.

However, the Lemba tribe were not the only people interested in its whereabouts. A local mayor had made a speech a few days earlier setting out his plans to search the entire area for traces of the *ngoma*. The king of the powerful Venda tribe had set his heart on acquiring it. Some of these people would stop at nothing, said Moeti. They would kill to get it.

As the papers that day were full of reports of a man who had been murdered for a pair of steel-rimmed glasses, I was prepared to believe it.

As we sat on the terrace watching the sun go down over the veldt and sipping at our drinks, I was formally commissioned, once again, to continue with my quest for the *ngoma* with the full support of the tribe. I had received an unofficial commission from Reuven to find the Ark, and a more formal commission from the Lemba elders to find the *ngoma.*

I now had two quests.

Or was it one?

The following day I had arranged a meeting with some Lemba elders in a shabby township near Louis Trichardt. I arrived too early and had half an hour to kill, so I stopped at a bar on the outskirts of town and ordered a beer. At a table in the corner I noticed a couple of young Lemba I had met once or twice before. I sat down and started chatting. They were reserved and suspicious but, anyway, they listened to what I had to say. I told them that I had seen Mathivha. Moeti and Masala and that they had asked me to look for the *ngoma.*

Their faces registered shock and resentment and the two of them immediately tried to dissuade me. It was a task for *them,* the young men, not for a middle-aged white man from another country. It was a sacred thing. I had no right to be involved with it in any way. No doubt my motive was financial. I was trying to rip them off. One of the men, referring, I suppose, to the DNA tests, accused me of having sold their blood for money. Our eyes met. He had been drinking beer for hours and his eyes were yellow and angry. The other man took my hand in an iron grip and forced me into an arm wrestling contest. He was younger and stronger than me and the violence was seeping out of him. He stank of beer. His eyes bulging, he slammed my hand on the table with such force that the skin over my knuckles broke.

"Just leave it alone, man. This is a new South Africa now. We don't want whites mixed up with our affairs."

"I guess you're right," I said, wrapping a handkerchief around my bleeding hand. To change the topic, I asked them the quickest way to get to the little village of Elim, where I had a meeting with some other Lemba people later in the day. They grudgingly drew me a map and I left to carry on with the interviews that I had arranged in the township.

The interviews over, I drove off in my hired car and sped down the dusty track that led from the township to the main road. My hand still hurt and I felt a sense of grievance. There was a bend ahead, and thorn bushes on both sides of the track obscured what lay ahead. I slowed a little into the bend, my mind still turning over the events of the morning.

As I turned the bend I could see a felled tree barring the road. Behind it, just a few yards away from me, three hooded armed men were flagging me down. *If I stop*, I thought to myself, *I'm dead.*

I crouched low over the wheel and crashed around the barrier.

Bullets shattered the rear window. I kept my head down and accelerated through clouds of thick red dust into the veldt.

The only people who knew I was taking this particular track were the young Lemba. Was this significant? Had they planned this? Or was this just a random criminal attack such as happened every day in South Africa? If these were Lemba, were they really out to kill me? Some of the tribe wanted me to investigate their past and their association with the *ngoma*; others perhaps did not.

A few days later I went to see Mathivha in his bungalow. I told him what had happened and he shrugged. He was convinced it had nothing at all to do with his people.

Once again he urged me to carry on with my search. He was sure, he said, that the *ngoma lungundu* still existed. It was not just a myth or a figment of their imagination. It was a real thing that had been discovered and actually seen and held by a white man in the 1930s or 1940s. The name of the white man, he said, was Harald von Sicard, who was a missionary and scholar who had worked with the Lemba for many years. He knew that von Sicard had found the genuine article because the Lemba historian Phophi had confirmed it.

This he knew for sure. Subsequently the *ngoma* had been recovered by the tribe and hidden. No one knew exactly where but a number of weighty tribal authorities thought it had been on Dumghe at some point. According to him it was now probably to be found in the mountains of Venda, south of the Limpopo. Some of the more venerable elders of the tribe knew where.

"So ask them where it is. Ask the elders!"

"The elders won't tell me. They won't tell me a thing like that."

"Will they tell me?"

"You'll have to see. If not, you'll just have to look for it."

A few days later I was sheltering from a tropical storm in a cave high in the mountains close to the border with Zimbabwe. I took out my sleeping bag from my small rucksack and spread it on the ground. I poured myself a coffee from my thermos flask and gave myself a tot of Laphroaig. As the storm outside raged, I wrote down a list of the reasons I had for believing that the *ngoma* was none other than the Ark of the Covenant.

- All the Lemba legends represent the *ngoma* as something the tribe had experienced with fear and awe, as the very voice and essence of God. The same thing can be said of the Ark.
- The *ngoma* was the dwelling place of God. So was the Ark.
- The *ngoma* was never allowed to touch the ground. Nor was the Ark.
- The *ngoma* was connected with death, fire, smoke, and noise. So was the Ark.
- The *ngoma* was looked after by priests. So was the Ark.
- The two sets of priests derive from a single common ancestor who lived at about the time of Moses and Aaron. Only the high priest was allowed to touch the *ngoma*. Only the high priest was allowed to touch the Ark. Anyone else touching the *ngoma* would be struck down. Thus it was with the Ark.
- According to Lemba traditions the *ngoma* was the same size and shape as the original simple wooden Ark of Moses.
- The *ngoma* was carried on poles. So was the Ark.
- The poles of the *ngoma* were fitted into carrying rings, as were those of the Ark.
- According to the Lemba the *ngoma* was made of very hard wood. So was the Ark.
- There were magic things secreted inside the *ngoma*. There were magic things originally hidden inside the Ark, including the magic staff of Aaron.
- The *ngoma* could be traced back to south Arabia. There were ancient traditions that traced the passage of the Ark to south Arabia.
- The *ngoma* had been brought to Africa at some time in the distant past and had been seen and authenticated in fairly

recent times. It had been seen by the German anthropologist von Sicard and even photographed in the Bulawayo Museum in about 1947.
- The Ark, on the other hand, had disappeared from history.

The storm did not let up. The rain was pouring down and it was getting dark. I decided to sleep in the cave. I finished off the whisky and lay looking out at the night. I felt a comfortable glow of achievement. It seemed to me that the evidence was beginning to mount. But over the next few days further points of comparison began to present themselves as I reflected more deeply on the *ngoma* narratives I heard from the elders in the remote Lemba *kraals* in the mountains.

One dramatic occasion that occurred over a hundred years ago was recounted by many of the old men. It had been a time of war and hunger.

Enemies in their multitudes were at the door. Suddenly there was a terrible noise, black smoke, and fire shot out from the *ngoma,* which was kept behind its plaited fences in an enclosure next to the house of the king. Many people died as a result of the *ngoma*'s eruption but none of the people killed was Lemba. All the Lemba survived, as *they* were in a state of ritual purity and had remained true to the one God.

What killed the others was the fire of God.

Another widely recalled tradition had it that many, many hundreds of years before—one of my informants put the date at 1600—an alarm had gone out from the royal *kraal*. No one knew what was wrong. The people rushed toward the king's house. Again flames, smoke, and terrible noise were seen coming from the part of the royal enclosure where the *ngoma* and the other sacred items were kept behind their plaited fences. The sacred objects that had been kept inside the *ngoma* were consumed in the fire. The *ngoma* alone survived. But barely. It was terribly, mortally damaged by the fire. The fire had come out of the *ngoma*. A new *ngoma* was somehow fashioned from the old with all the terrible power of its father.

Before I left for South Africa I had spoken to Reuven. By chance he had some diamond-related business in Johannesburg and elsewhere. We had arranged to meet toward the end of January in Messina, a small mining town just near the Limpopo River on South Africa's northern border with Zimbabwe.

Messina is a dusty little town whose copper seams had been worked in the distant past by Lemba miners and produced the raw material for the famous Lemba coppersmiths.

I drove up to Messina the day before my meeting with Reuven with the intention of visiting the ancient ruins of Mapungubwe that may have been the Lemba's first point of settlement in this part of Africa well over a thousand years earlier. I was driving back at a leisurely pace thinking of the passage of the tribe through this area. I was daydreaming, enjoying the spectacular views on all sides and the gaunt beauty of gigantic baobab trees when I saw an open Jeep racing over the high veldt along a track, which was converging with the one I was on.

As the Jeep flashed past, sending up clouds of dust, I saw that three khaki-clad white men were inside it. One of them was Reuven. I sounded my horn and the Jeep skidded to a halt.

"I thought you were coming tomorrow," I said, but Reuven cut me off with a hoot of joy and a great bear hug.

He had put on a good deal of weight since I had last seen him the year before. His beard had become long and straggly and he had gone back to something like the orthodox clothing he wore when I first met him, although his long coat was in unorthodox cotton twill, of course beautifully cut, and he was wearing a black Panama hat. Dusting himself off with a pristine white handkerchief, he explained that he had changed his plans slightly. He had needed to come up to Messina a day early to meet someone at the Venetia diamond mine, the world's most productive, which was a mile or two down the road.

He bade farewell to his companions, took his briefcase and a small holdall from the Jeep, and climbed into my car.

We drove to a point where we could gaze down at the crocodile-infested trickle, which was the Limpopo. The long drought had taken its toll of the Limpopo as well. Under this same glittering sky the Lemba priests had carried the *ngoma* from the north. According to Mathivha, the *ngoma* had once been concealed somewhere near here in a cave—perhaps for many centuries.

"This was the way the Lemba came," I said pointing down at the river. "This is where they crossed into southern Africa. They were led by the *ngoma lungundu.*"

I had had a further insight over the previous few days. The traditions that connected the Ark/*ngoma* with fire, smoke, and noise, with death and destruction, with smoke and battles, were beginning to suggest to me that there was something very specific about the way it was used.

I spelled it out over a drink later that afternoon at the Cloud's Inn Hotel, an hour's drive south in the direction of Johannesburg.

"You see, Reuven, I think we have misunderstood the true nature of the Ark. It was, after all, the ancient equivalent of a weapon of mass destruction. Many people have suggested the Ark was a primitive but powerful device of electrocution, something like a giant Van der Graaf generator, that was capable of emitting a lethal electrical charge. Others have said that the stone tablets inside the Ark were meteorites that retained some radioactive or other destructive force and yet others have suggested it was some kind of Leyden jar that could preserve electrical charges and emit them. In the centuries when it had been incarcerated in the Temple it became little more than a good-luck talisman, a palladium. Its powers were probably forgotten.

"But the Ark was *not* a palladium," I said, my voice rising. "When it was installed passively behind the walls of the Temple it lost much of its true purpose. But once it was taken from the Temple, once it was freed from the Temple, it had a chance to work once again as the early Ark had worked. And that's what the Arab accounts suggest. The Ark went back to doing what it was originally meant to do.

"And that's what the *ngoma* is. The *ngoma* is the freed Ark! The *ngoma* is the functional Ark. Dangerous, menacing, loud, and ambiguous. Yes ambiguous! You know, Reuven, even the smoke that came out of the Ark was ambiguously poised between the smoke of battle and the incense offered on the altar."

Hearing the conviction and passion in my voice, Reuven gave me a dry, amused look as if all of a sudden our roles were reversed. Smiling to himself, he stroked his beard and for a few minutes said nothing. He stood up and walked over to the edge of the forest where the monkeys were chattering and leaping from branch to branch. He returned and sat down.

"You are getting a bit carried away," he said. "But the notion of the Ark as a weapon of mass destruction is certainly true to the texts."

"Just think of it. The Ark and the *ngoma* are completely identical in this respect," I replied. "Their guardians usually won battles when they had their weapon and usually lost them when they didn't. The Ark and the *ngoma* may have been fairly uncomplicated, conventional weapons. I understand that in pre-colonial times local people in southern Africa, including the Lemba, had perhaps independently invented primitive guns. They probably made more noise than anything else. But the principle was there."

"And what in God's name do you think they used as gunpowder?" asked Reuven impatiently.

"I'm not absolutely sure, but I do know that saltpeter is found throughout southern Africa. And with saltpeter and charcoal you have something that makes a very loud bang. The Lemba in Messina and elsewhere were miners and metalworkers. They knew about fire and they knew about digging up useful things. It is more than likely that they discovered low-grade explosives. The same argument might be applied to the Ark. It is almost inconceivable that the ancient Egyptians, whose knowledge of mineral compounds for medicinal purposes was so sophisticated, similarly did not have some knowledge of the power of saltpeter mixed with charcoal, as both things were readily available throughout Egypt."

"Yes, I suppose that's true," said Reuven softly. "Saltpeter is potassium nitrate and potassium nitrate occurs as a crust on the earth's surface, particularly under rocks and in caves and it forms naturally in certain soils throughout the world including, as I recall from my time studying chemistry, in southern Africa and Egypt.

"Or another possibility is that there was something incredibly inflammable like petrol or *naptha* in the Ark. You recall that Aaron took fire to burn his sacrifices, but the Ark burned them instead and that his sons Avihu and Nadav brought the wrong kind of fire close to the Ark and were incinerated."

"Whatever technology was used in the Ark," I said, "is lost to us now. You can speculate until you are blue in the face but it does not really get you anywhere. But it is perhaps the same technology that we find in the *ngoma*. But this won't help us because the people who knew exactly how the *ngoma* worked are all dead.

"Probably we'll never know exactly *what* the technology was, anymore than we know exactly how the technology of the secret weapon of Byzantium worked. It was called Greek Fire and caused devastating damage to enemy fleets, but when Constantinople was destroyed in 1453 the secret of Greek Fire went up in smoke. Anyway, I'm convinced the Ark/*ngoma* was a weapon."

Reuven nodded. "There is one little thing. If it was used as a weapon and kept bursting into flames, is it really likely that the same object survived over millennia?"

"You have a point, of course. The Lemba say that perhaps the original Ark, which brought them from south Arabia, destroyed itself almost completely and that many hundreds of years ago a son of the *ngoma* was fashioned out of it by the priests. The power remained. The essence remained."

"If you ever found it you could tell when it was made."

"How's that?" I asked.

"Through radiocarbon dating."

But Reuven's mind was on other things.

"A weapon," he muttered. "Yes. I agree. You remember that ancient prayer that Moses uttered when the Ark was placed before the armies of Israel. *'Scatter your enemies, and let those who hate you flee from in front of you.'* That is self-evidently a prayer you'd say over a dangerous weapon. And from what you say, the *ngoma* too worked as a kind of weapon." Reuven placed his glass on the table before him and, raising both hands, looked directly at me.

"Let's just slow down a bit here," he said. "The Ark and the *ngoma* no doubt have many, many things in common but they were not the same thing. The *ngoma*, my friend, is a *drum* and the Ark is a *box*. That's an essential difference. There's never been any suggestion that the Ark was a *drum*. The two things are opposites."

Thoughtfully, I went to the bar, got us a couple more drinks, made myself comfortable, and observed with a smile, "Sometimes, Reuven, as our friend Daud is perhaps too fond of remarking, opposites are one."

I explained that the Biblical text was immensely old and described a world that is almost completely closed to us. For political and religious reasons the text had been altered over time and deliberate attempts had been made to suppress a good deal of the function and true history of the Ark of the early strata. The Biblical account is a purged version of a much more ancient narrative that existed in the oral tradition and that included elements many of which have been forgotten. The descriptions of the Ark and its functions were mainly written at a time when the Temple was the predominant feature of Israelite life.

The Ark and the history of the Ark and its tabernacle had to fit in with the concept of temple and in many ways the story of the Ark and the tabernacle is a precursor to the story of the Temple. There was no way a simple acacia weapon/drum from Africa or from the desert could fit into that scheme of things.

There were hints in the text that could cast light on the true function of the ancient Ark. One hint I thought was to be found in the passage where God spoke to the prophet Nathan, explaining that the Ark had not lived in a proper house *"from the time I brought up the people of Israel from Egypt to this day."* This verse suggests that the Ark was there at the beginning of the Israelites' trek across the wilderness, not fabricated en route. It was something that came with them from Egypt. It looks as if this is a slip that the scribes' efforts to rewrite the text had missed. I thought there was some hint of this in the account of the crossing of the River Jordan. The Ark was credited with opening up a dry path for them to cross into Canaan, their Promised Land. When they crossed the Red Sea, a dry path also opened up. But it was the rod of Moses that was credited with the miracle. But perhaps it was really the Ark.

"You remember," I said, "the first thing the Israelites did when they got to the other side of the Red Sea? Moses's sister Miriam danced and played the drum. She was carrying it. She did not even have to unpack it. This was the drum she carried from Egypt. This was the very first thing that happened to the

Israelites as they crossed from Africa to Asia. We hear the beat of an elemental African drum, which in the Egyptian religious system was closely connected with the struggle between good and evil.

"And don't forget that a possible etymology of the word *aron* (Ark) in Hebrew supports a connection with music and drumming. You remember years ago when I told you about that conversation I had with Naki about the etymology of the word *aron*. Among other things it could be connected with the Hebrew root RNN and mean something like 'I make a ringing noise.'"

Reuven took a sip of his whisky and sat stroking his beard for several minutes. He seemed to be lost in thought. Stretching himself and smiling slightly he said, "Yes, OK, I agree that there is some support for the idea of the Ark as a musical instrument. It's often in musical processions, it's often accompanied by trumpets. It appears to make a musical noise. You remember when the Ark goes up to Jerusalem it does so 'with noise, and with the sound of the trumpet.' Going round the walls of Jericho it looks like it is forming part of a military band."

"'*And it came to pass,*'" he quoted sonorously, "'*when Joshua had spoken unto the people, that the seven priests bearing the seven trumpets of rams' horns passed on before the Lord, and blew with the trumpets: and the ark of the covenant of the Lord followed them.*'

"'*And the armed men went before the priests that blew with the trumpets, and the rearguard came after the ark, the priests going on, and blowing with the trumpets.*'"

All of a sudden Reuven leaned toward me, looking as if he had seen a ghost. His face had gone pale and the hand he reached out to touch my arm with was trembling. Looking me straight in the face he said slowly, "Often enough we have spoken about the similarity of the Ark and the biblical *ephod* that was made by Moses in the desert at the same time as the Ark. If we are going to agree that the *ephod* and the Ark are or could be the same thing, as I have often thought was the case and as many competent scholars have suggested, and if that same thing has got something to do with a *drum* as you are suggesting, just think, just *think*," he was shouting now and waving his arms wildly, "of that passage in the book of Exodus in the Bible describing how the covering for the *ephod* should be made."

I didn't know what he was talking about.

Reuven reached hurriedly into his briefcase and pulling out the Hebrew Bible with which he always traveled, and pointed out the passage. I read it slowly, then I read it again. A shiver went down my spine as I absorbed the inescapable implication of the lines. It was immediately clear to me that the cover of the *ephod* was a decorative casing for a drum. It could be nothing else.

What the Bible explains is that the *ephod* was connected to the breastplate of the high priest by two golden chains, and on each side of the *ephod* there are gold rings attached to this golden chain. The harness is exactly what you would expect of a drum harness, designed to leave the hands free for playing the instrument. At the bottom of the cover of the *ephod* there were bells and round red and blue baubles filled with beads, like rattles—the "pomegranates" of the text.

Reuven took back his old battered Bible, put on his reading glasses, and read aloud in Hebrew:

And you shall make the covering of the ephod all of blue, and there will be an opening in the top of it, in the middle, and around it there will be an interlaced pattern, around the hole, like the hole of a tahrah, so it will not tear ... and round the bottom you will put blue and scarlet pomegranates ... with gold bells in between them. The gold bells and the pomegranates are to alternate around the bottom (of the ephod). Aaron must carry it when he ministers. The sound of the bells will be heard when he enters the Holy Place before the Lord ...

"What's a *tahrah*?" I asked.

Reuven did not know.

"I'll go and look it up," I said and walked slowly over to my room to get my classical Hebrew dictionary, wondering how it was that I had never appreciated the significance of the description of the *ephod* cover. When I got back I placed the dictionary on the table between us and looked up *tahrah*. Brown, Driver, and Briggs tentatively suggests "linen corselet," which makes little immediate sense and is not derived from any etymologically similar root.

"Listen, Reuven," I said hesitantly, "if one were to connect the word *tahrah* with the most obvious root HRH (to burn, be kindled) it could most simply mean 'stove,' 'a place where fire is kindled' or something like it. 'There will be an *interlaced* pattern around the hole (which is) like the hole of a stove.' Don't you see? The top of the *ephod* could be either a drum, if it had its lid on, or the mouth of some primitive weapon or noise-and-smoke-emitting object if it did not, and around it was an *interlaced pattern* to fortify the covering—'so it would not tear' in the event of its exploding, or maybe the interlaced pattern was actually on the *ephod* itself to fortify *it*, 'so it would not break,' perhaps something like chain mail. There is a hole in the cover, at the top, to enable the drum to be played or for the drum to do its other tricks associated with sound and fire."

I remembered that in the Midrash the thorns that were burned by the Ark gave off the sweet smell of frankincense. Perhaps the Ark/*ephod* was also a kind of censer in which incense and other things could be burned according to the ritual needs of the moment. And I was also reminded of the famous altar that, like the Ark, was created in the wilderness of Sinai in that strange frenzy of ritual, object construction when Moses came down from Mount Sinai. Like the Ark, the altar was in the form of an acacia box. It had almost the same dimensions (two cubits high, one cubit wide, and one cubit deep). Like the Ark, it had carrying rings at each corner. The incense was burned each morning and evening in a golden censer placed on top of the box. Perhaps the altar, ephod, and Ark were originally one and the same thing. When the bowl was placed on the box, no doubt it was placed inside the hole of the *tahrah*.

All of a sudden my mind was flooded with images that had been projected onto the back wall of my mind by the powerful illumination emerging from the idea of *ephod*/Ark as drum. When David, for instance, danced before the Ark, with all his might, he was dancing with an *ephod*. He was naked at the time, causing offense to Michal, his wife, who never again slept with him after this.

The suggestion is that he was exposing himself, and that the *ephod* did not cover his private parts. If it was a drum/Ark he was playing, it is not difficult to imagine what he was doing with his penis. Was he standing naked, dancing and playing the drum/*ephod,* which was supported around his neck by a chain? Did it have a covering with its bells and pomegranates ringing? Was he lewdly thrusting into the open bottom part of the cover of the drum/*ephod*? Was the drum/*ephod* in fact the Ark? Was the king dancing before the Ark but with the *Ark* strapped to him, with its skirt and its bells?

Reuven seemed breathless with excitement as the implications of this conversation sank in. "I don't know much about etymology but the idea of the Ark as an instrument of music is compelling. Once you have seen as we just *have* seen that the *ephod* is a kind of drum, you cannot read the description of it and its cover in any other way. It can be carried around, it can be used for divination as the *ngoma* and other African drums are, it makes a noise, it is accompanied with trumpets. It gives new meaning to phrases like 'Make a joyful noise unto the Lord.' The top of the cover is left open so it can be played and the fringe of the cover has bells on it to accompany the drum. And you know," he said, sipping again at his whisky, "I've just realized that there is another little clue."

He explained that the Ark, like the *ephod,* had a blue cover. But rather strangely it was also covered with the skins of an animal called, in Hebrew, *tahash,* which used to be translated as "badger." Recent translations of the Bible have suggested that *tahash* should be translated as seal or dugong. These aquatic herbivores, which are sometimes around fifteen feet long, live along the coasts of the Red Sea. In Arabic this animal is still called *tukhas.*

The dugong are easily caught and their skins are large enough to use as covers and tent flaps. Reuven suggested that the original association of a leather cover and a hollow acacia box immediately suggested some kind of leathered drum. It was covered with a blue cloth, like the *ephod,* and sealskin leather. Sealskins are used by many peoples, including the Inuit, as drum skins.

"And the size of it," I replied. "Have you ever paused to reflect on the size of the Ark? It is two cubits long. One cubit is the distance from your elbow to the tip of your middle finger. If you were playing a drum two cubits across, resting your elbow on the rim, you would strike it bang in the middle—at the point of maximum resonance!"

Reuven grinned at me. "You know," he said, "in the kabbalistic work the *Zohar* we are instructed by the sages of blessed memory that the tales and stories in the Bible are just the outer garment of the Torah. We are strictly enjoined to look *beyond* that. In fact those who do not look beyond will be deprived of a portion in the world to come. We have discovered the outer garment of the Ark. We too have looked beyond that. We are following the rabbis' sacred injunction!"

"That's actually a very modern perspective," I said. "There are people like Carlo Ginzburg, a historian at UCLA, who instruct us to push way beyond the simple clues of historical evidence to suck out a lost reality that conventional history misses."

"And there are so many hints in the Bible," Reuven continued, ignoring me, "that there was actually more than one Ark. Most obviously there was that awful moment when King David seduced the wife of one of his officers—Uriah the Hittite.

David hears that the lovely Bathsheba is pregnant by him but in a shabby attempt to cover up his activities suggests to Uriah that he should spend the night with his wife. The pregnancy could then be attributed to her husband. Uriah, who was no fool, gave the best possible reply to his flawed king: that while the Ark and the soldiers of Israel were on the field of battle he would not dream of going to his comfortable home and making love to Bathsheba.

"The problem is that at the moment of the conversation the Ark was in *Jerusalem*. The troops were far away in Rabbat Ammon. So what was the Ark that they had with them on the field of battle?"

"I'm sure about the multiple Arks," I agreed. "An old Oxford friend of mine, Professor Philip Davies, who's had an outstanding career as a biblical scholar at the University of Sheffield, argued very convincingly that the *ephod* and the Ark were completely interchangeable terms." I remembered the articles in which he argued this very well. One was published in the *Journal of Theological Studies* in 1975; the other in the *Journal of Northwest Semitic Languages* in 1977. "Thinking about it now, I can see that he is right. This implies that until the centralization of the cult in Jerusalem, there *were* multiple Arks because *ephods* are popping up all over the place."

Reuven stopped short as if he had just had an inspiration and, taking a pencil out of his pocket, wrote a couple of words in the square characters of the classical Hebrew script on the back of a beer mat on the table.

Pushing the beer mat over to me he said, "I've just realized that "Ark" in Hebrew, אָרוֹן, looks quite similar to *ephod,* אֵפוֹד, which might begin to account for some of the confusion."

As the sun set over the hills, I told Reuven more about the complex African traditions regarding the *ngoma* and the connection between these and the Ark. I explained its role in the southern movement of peoples, the many local stories that attached to it, and the possible ways in which these could be interpreted or explained.

Reuven's earlier euphoria soon dissipated. He stifled a yawn, shot a pair of immaculate white cuffs complete with gold cufflinks, and nodded encouragingly. With a flourish he put his reading glasses back in his pocket. Checking his gold Cartier watch, he set his face in an attentive mold. But it was not very convincing. He could never get very passionate about African history.

"It's extraordinary to think that the Ark of the Temple or one of the early Arks might have got this far," he said, cutting me off and looking out with little interest beyond the terrace at the heartrendingly beautiful forests of the Soutpansberg. Monkeys were trooping across the lawns to the trees behind the hotel where they slept and the setting sun was covering everything with a shimmering golden veil.

"It is extraordinary but people traveled in ancient times much more than we imagine," I said. "The area around the Limpopo was connected by trade routes to the Middle East, India, and even China. It was not nearly as cut off from the outside world as one imagines. All kinds of things came here. One of them was the Ark. The clues that suggest that it is hidden somewhere in these hills are adding up," I added, nodding in the direction of the Soutpansberg.

"Over all these years," he said slowly, "the search has con-tinued worldwide but no one has come up with anything. It's funny. I don't much like the idea of the Ark being hidden in sub-Saharan Africa. For some strange reason I'd have preferred it to be in Ethiopia. But I now see you are right. You followed Rabin's advice and you set out to try to follow the trail of the priests, and the new technology has helped you. Your DNA argument that traces the passage of the priests down here is very persuasive."

He said this judiciously, stroking his beard.

"In addition, I must say that I don't know of anyone who disagrees with your reconstruction of Lemba history. The idea that the Buba priests brought the *ngoma* from Arabia is entirely plausible. The passage from al-Idrisi might very well refer to the arrival of the *ngoma*/Ark on African soil—the Ark *was* God and the word he uses is the Hebrew word for God. And it is clear from what you told me that the Lemba *ngoma* traditions are very ancient and certainly predated any Christian mission-ary influence."

Reuven had a particular loathing for missionaries who tried to convert Jews and he puckered his nose in distaste. And he was entirely right about the antiquity of the *ngoma* traditions.

"This has been a critical conversation for us. I know that. The pieces are beginning to fit together."

He smiled. His teeth were still a brilliant white and, despite the dark hollows under his eyes draining his lined cheeks of color, he was still a handsome man. He held his hands out toward me in supplication, palms uppermost.

"Just tell me one little thing. Just one bloody, little thing. Where *is* it? I'm not long for this life, you know. I want to see it before I die. Find it. Do radiocarbon dating and we'll be getting close to an answer."

He was smiling as he said it but there was an underlying seriousness in the way he spoke.

"I thought I was close a few years ago," I said. "I told you of my nocturnal adventure in the cave in the Mposi tribal area. Of course I didn't know what the *ngoma* really was all about then but in any case I was scared off. I was a coward. I know it. I feel ashamed of that. But you know I returned to the cave on Dumghe in 2001. And I was *still* scared. Most of the people I knew in the villages had died including the old chief. There was a terrible drought and there was no one out in the fields, because there *were* no fields. Everything had dried up. So I walked over there and forced myself down the path, behind the boulder and into the cave. I felt an overpowering fear, but I forced myself. I was so scared I wanted to throw up."

"You have to learn to control fear. I learned that when I was a kid in my garret. Anyway, what did you find?"

"I forced myself to go into the first aperture and then through a small hole at the back, into a second. There was nothing there. No wild animals. No two-headed snakes. No lions. Piles of bat dung, a few bleached bones, and that's it."

"I'm sure *we* are on the right track," he said leading the way into the dining room. "I *know* we are on the right track. But being on the right track is not the same thing as *finding* it. You know," he continued enthusiastically, "the rand is pretty weak at the moment and locals up here in the Limpopo Province work for peanuts. That's what they told me at Venetia. They're *happy* to work for peanuts. I could literally hire an army of assistants. We could afford hundreds of them. Even thousands of them for a short-term project."

He called out to a passing waiter, pressed a ten-rand note into his hand, and asked him how much he earned a week.

"You heard what he said? You heard? They work for *less* than peanuts. We could comb this entire area. We could get into every last damned cave between here and the Zimbabwe border. We could comb the Limpopo Valley. Even go back to your precious Dumghe and Mberengwe. Why don't you give it one last try?" he pleaded. "There's so much depending on this. Put everything into it. Organize yourself for once. Make a last big effort. While there's still time. Listen. I'll change my plans. I'll call the office and let them know I'll be here for a couple of weeks. I'll tell Clara it's got to do with business." Reuven reached for his cell phone.

"Hang on, Reuven. You know, I don't think it would, er, really help," I said gently. "There are too many vested interests here. It would need authorization from the top. Maybe the president himself."

"For God's sake, I *know* Thabo Mbeki," said Reuven querulously. "I saw him just a few days ago. I know Mandela. I know half the ministers. If we need to cross the border into Zimbabwe, I know Mugabe. I do business with Mugabe."

"Amazing," I murmured. "The problem is that I am quite sure it wouldn't *work*. It would require the cooperation of both the Venda *and* the Lemba tribes. They never agree on anything. They both want it. Without official sanction and local cooperation, a large-scale operation like the one you suggest would simply be impossible. In any case, whoever is hiding it would soon move it somewhere else. Then we'd never find it. The whole thing has to be done much more quietly."

"You haven't changed," he said in a completely different tone of voice. He looked at me for a long time with something like contempt in his eyes and shrugged. "You've never really put your back into this thing. I gave you every chance, I was prepared to give you all the financial help you needed and what did you do? You as good as spat on my money. You've never understood that without money you get nowhere in this life. Without money you're nothing. You could have mounted a proper expedition in Ethiopia to finally close down that chapter. Even Israeli intelligence people thought that that's where it was most likely to be.

"I remember years ago asking you if you really understood what a man of vision was all about. I'm beginning to realize that you never *did*. You still don't understand that the redemption of Israel—the state of Israel—is tied up with the Ark, that with its discovery the Muslim world will finally accept that Jews belong in the Middle East, in their own divinely appointed state. And the combination of the discovered Ark and the confirmation of the priestly code going back to the time of Moses may be a sign that the time is now ripe for the rebuilding of the Temple and messianic days ..."

As he uttered these words, his eyes shining, he looked like an unusually well-dressed but peevish Old Testament prophet.

"*That* is the vision," he said, his voice rising. "An Israel secure within the frontiers promised by God. An Israel that is no longer hemmed in on all sides by murderous neighbors. A divinely appointed state accepted by the whole world, with its own Temple rebuilt in Jerusalem, the capital of the world, awaiting its own Messiah. That vision is worth effort and massive investment.

"*You* have given it neither. The returns on that investment of time, money, and effort would have been fabulous. *Fabulous*. In financial terms too. You would not be sitting here today wondering how you will manage in old age on a lousy London University pension! The calculation of the return on the investment you might have made but didn't is obviously a calculation you never entered into. To be truthful, you were not cut out for it. You drink too much, you've been too hung up on the wrong sort of woman, and you're a bit of a dreamer. One thing I can now see for sure: you'd never have made a businessman."

"I guess not," I replied, biting my lip. I knew what he meant.

But I also knew that Reuven's reasons for wanting to find the Ark were not entirely mine.

We had an early night. Over breakfast Reuven hardly said a word. We went for a short walk in the forest and he asked me one or two terse questions about the *ngoma* and half an hour later his driver came to drive him down to Johannesburg. Later that day Reuven would fly back to Tel Aviv. He waved unenthusiastically from the window of the Mercedes.

That was the last time I ever saw him.

* * *

For a couple of weeks I wandered miserably around the Soutpansberg mountains. Reuven's low opinion of me hung like a
millstone around my neck. I crisscrossed the land from east to
west, from south to north. With his caustic words ringing in my
ears I climbed higher and higher in the mountains along
narrow tracks that skirted the ravines, I walked through forests
protected by dense creepers. I slept rough in the hills, rigging
up a mosquito net from the branches of trees. I forced myself
to take crazy risks.

Wherever there were Lemba enclaves in the remote villages
I was made welcome. They looked after me, always showing the
greatest consternation that I was traveling around on foot.
Discreetly, I let it be understood that whereas I believed that I
had uncovered the central mysteries in the history of the
Lemba and principally the original Senna and Pusela of their
traditions, there was still one last thing I wanted to find before
I died: the Ark—the *ngoma lungundu.*

But of course I always heard the same thing. The individual
who held this secret was always someone much older and wiser
than my interlocutor. The man who had information about the
resting place of the *ngoma* I would have to find myself.

I went to see Mathivha a couple more times in his retire-
ment bungalow in Sibasa. He now liked to spend his days on
the terrace looking out at his fruit trees and getting his papers
in order. He repeated what he had said so many times before.
The Ark was hidden somewhere in the mountains. Perhaps
somewhere near Tshiendeulu, high in the Soutpansberg range.
Certain members of the elders knew. But he himself could
neither tell me *where* it was nor precisely *who* knew where it was.

One day, sitting with a cup of tea on his terrace in Sibasa, I asked him if there was only one *ngoma*.

"They always made copies of the Ark. Some of its power was passed onto the copies. But the real *ngoma*—the real Ark, the one that all the elders thought *was* the real thing—was the one found by the old white man I told you about, near the Limpopo, when I was a young man about sixty years ago. That is what the elders told me. All the others hidden away in caves and caverns are copies of that original *ngoma* and they still have some of its magic, some of its power. All of these copies of the original Ark are worth finding, wherever they are in the world. They are worth finding because they will lead you to the true Ark itself."

I thought to myself that the tradition of multiple Arks, of Arks spawning Arks, and inheriting the power of their forebears, was entirely consistent with what we know of the Ark/*ephod* in the Bible.

Toward the end of February I had to return to London. My sense of the passage of the Ark was clearer now, and I had a much more robust idea of what the Ark actually was. But I had found nothing very concrete. I had poked around more caves than the most seasoned speleologist. I had interviewed scores of senile, toothless old men. They never had the information I was seeking. They never failed to send me elsewhere. There was always someone else, somewhere else, who was older and wiser still and who would be sure to be the repository of the precious secrets. I was never able to track down these elusive and venerable elders.

It slowly dawned on me that the tribal sages to whom I was regularly referred as the final sources of information and authority simply did not exist. I began to feel that my time in southern Africa, promising though the leads undoubtedly were, was coming to an end. I thought I had seen the light. I thought I had glimpsed the truth and it was difficult therefore to turn away my gaze.

The passage from the Quran quoted by my friend the mukhtar of Senna came to mind. "Shall the darkness and the light be held equal?"

But perhaps, in spite of myself, I would have to look elsewhere.

12

THE SACRED
FIRE POT

I had made a good deal of progress over the years. But I had thus far failed in my attempt to actually locate the Ark, to locate any Ark. And this was critical for Reuven. It was possible, I thought, that now I should go somewhere else, do something else, look somewhere else. I also wanted to make a great effort to redeem myself in Reuven's eyes. When we spoke on the telephone he predictably urged me to go further afield, go to more exotic and more remote places. Or to go back to Ethiopia to put to rest the sneaking suspicion he still had that the Ark was still there. Organize a proper expedition. Spend his money.

He was encouraging and charming. It was not at all that he doubted my identification of the *ngoma* and the Ark, he simply thought it might have moved on. All the irritability he had shown in South Africa had disappeared. He just urged me to keep on looking. To widen the search. Perhaps the *ngoma* had been taken far away. It could be on the other side of the world by now.

* * *

In March 2003 I was invited by the distinguished Semitics scholar Professor Alan Crown to give a series of lectures at the University of Sydney in Australia. Soon after my arrival the telephone in my hotel room rang.

"Are you the man who proved to the world that the Lemba tribe are Jews?"

"I suppose. In a way you could say that," I started.

"That's it then. I discovered on the Internet that you were lecturing in Sydney. I've got another job for you. A big job. For generations my people, my tribe, have known that we were Israelites. Our holy traditions tell us that we came from the land of Israel many, many thousands of years ago. We are one of the lost tribes of Israel. This is what the elders passed down from generation to generation. You proved the Lemba were Jews by genetics. You took cells from their mouths. I saw the *Nova* documentary. I read all about it on the Internet."

He told me that he had collected 500 strands of hair from the men of his tribe and that he was flying down from Papua New Guinea to Sydney the following day to deliver them to me.

"You will do for us what you did for them. You will find this lost tribe. God bless you," and he hung up.

Tony Waisa and I got on from the start. Earnestness and honesty shone from his dark, wedge-shaped face. He was a passionate believer in his tribal traditions and knew more about the oral history of his tribe than any man alive. The tribe in question was the hunter-gatherer, formerly cannibalistic, headhunting Gogodala tribe, which lives around the steamy, estuary wetlands of the Fly River in the western province of the great island of Papua New Guinea.

He had brought with him half a dozen fat folders of computer-generated notes, charts, and analysis, all beautifully presented and bound, showing how this unlikely story could be true, tracing the dispersion of the lost tribes in general and the Gogodala in particular. He begged me to return with him to Papua New Guinea and take cheek samples from the Gogodala and to observe their Judaic customs firsthand.

"That might be difficult," I replied. "I have teaching responsibilities. No, I don't think I could do that. Not just at the moment."

As we sat in the sun-filled lobby of my hotel, Tony looked at me sternly. Rubbing his high bridged and prominent Papu nose, he seized my arm and said, "But you've got to come. I've come all this way to make you come. And you will never regret it. Our lagoon is beautiful. The people are beautiful and pious, even though we were cannibals until a few years ago. We live a wonderful life, fishing in the lagoon, hunting in the jungle. We are still hunter-gatherers—we don't cultivate anything except flowers, Jewish flowers. We are a unique Jewish tribe and we still are keeping up our Jewish customs. Perhaps not all of them, exactly, but many of them. Most of them. You *will* see. I am sure you will come."

He held his arms wide like a showman at a fair, extolling his wares. "We are, as you will see, the veritable and genuine Jews of Fly Swamp."

He told me that according to their tribal traditions a white man would come from a distant land to take them back to where they came from—to the land of Israel. This individual was a messianic figure called Bogale. I was perhaps Bogale. In fact I was almost certainly the Gogodala messiah. His doubtful, hesitant smile suggested that he realized that this suggestion was not quite enough to entice me. He paused again and started slowly and diffidently.

"It may sound strange to you but we do in fact have the proof, even without genetic testing. The genetic testing, though, would be the scientific testimony that would persuade the authorities in Israel to take us in. We have many, many stories that connect us to the Jews' homeland. But it is not just stories. As I said, there is hard proof. When you have heard what the proof is, you will surely come. You see, we still have the ancestral canoes that brought us from the land of Israel. They are buried in the lagoon."

I asked him how on earth a canoe could get all the way from the Red Sea to bloody Papua New Guinea.

"These are very big canoes of war. They can take fifty men rowing. In those days the sea was much lower than it is today. You could hop from island to island, take your time. That's what we did. That's what the elders told us. We went to Yemen and then to Africa. We stayed there for a long time. Then we got in our canoes and came here."

"Where in Africa did you go?"

"It was so long ago. We have lost the details. But when we came here we were already black. If we had been white the cannibals who live all around us would have gobbled us all up to the last man, woman, and child. Yes, we came down here slowly, visiting other continents. We took our time but finally Fly Swamp is where we ended up. We brought with us holy relics from Israel. And that is the main proof we have." He smiled piously at me.

"What holy relics might they be?" I asked cautiously.

"Oh, the Ark of the Covenant and the rod of Aaron. That's it. That's all we have."

I called Reuven later that night. I imagined that he would pour ridicule on the idea of the Ark being in the wilder reaches of the Pacific. But he did not. He listened carefully without interrupting and said, "You've come to a standstill in Africa. It could be that your reconstruction of the journey of the Ark is close to what happened but that at some time in history the priests took it farther afield. According to you, there is nothing in Ethiopia and you have found nothing in the rest of Africa except stories—very enticing stories, I grant you. But stories are not the Ark. I want to find the Ark itself. You've done a good job so far—it is fair to say that you have got further than anyone else." His tone had become irritatingly judicious.

"But what do we do now? I've always said that the priests would have taken it far away. As far as was humanly possible. With stocks of food and water, a good vessel could get from Eilat to Papua New Guinea with no problem, particularly with the monsoon winds in the right direction. Or, if your theory about south Arabia is true, they could have followed the monsoon winds from one of the Arabian ports. They would have had no difficulty getting to India or Indonesia, as the Arabs did later with similar vessels, and to follow the Indonesian islands down to Papua New Guinea would not be impossible by any means. Or it might have been taken from the port of Sofala and gone via Madagascar to the islands farther east. You yourself are always saying that in ancient times people traveled around the world much more than we imagine. It's worth a try. Go have a look! What can be lost by taking a fresh view, by thinking outside the box?"

I promised to give some thought to organizing an expedition to Papua New Guinea.

"Really?" asked Reuven. "You are finally going to organize a proper expedition? *Yedidi*, my friend, I see you in a new light."

"I would not rely too much on that light," I answered grumpily. "Anyway, I'll think about it."

I bade farewell to Waisa and told him I would respond to his invitation when I was back in London.

In England the weather in spring 2003 was awful. There was a week of persistent drizzle. It was cold. London appeared drabber than ever. Tony Waisa telephoned from the Papuan capital, Port Moresby. He now told me that he had seen the sacred artifacts with his own eyes and so had other members of the tribe. The reeds surrounding the part of the lagoon where the Ark was had died back and it was clearly visible in the sparkling, blue water of the lagoon. He spoke less now about the genetics project he had first wished me to get involved with. He mainly spoke about the Ark. He was trying to get me hooked.

How he knew I was searching for the Ark, I do not know. I had not advertized the fact that the quest to find the Ark was a consistent feature of my life. Indeed very few people knew. I suspected Reuven had somehow managed to tell him. He had contacts among diplomats and politicians throughout the world and undoubtedly knew someone from Papua New Guinea, but he admitted to nothing.

Over the last few days, Tony told me, the level of the lagoon had dropped even more and there was a fear the reeds would return to obscure the canoes. In any case, if I wanted to see the Ark I would have to bring in a professional diver to extract the treasures. The water was too deep for even the experienced swimmers who were to be found among his people. If I waited too long it might be too late. Hearing this, I started making tentative plans to leave.

I spoke to my dean at SOAS who gave me some research leave.

The first thing that occurred to me was that this adventure I was preparing for would provide the most striking example, if one was needed, of the worldwide importance and resonance of the Ark. As I prepared myself for this trip, not least in my mind was the question of illness. I had had dengue, or break-bone, fever a couple of times and various other exotic ailments. I was anxious to avoid repetitions. I felt some mild apprehension about going to Papua New Guinea. I knew Africa, India, and the Middle East pretty well and had spent time in some pretty wild places. But for me Papua New Guinea was *terra incognita*, it was the end of the world, and its dangers were unknown. Whatever they were I was anxious to avoid them.

Maria and I had patched things up but predictably she was not very enthusiastic about this trip. As she was excessively fond of remarking, I was not as young as I once was and, according to her, I should be taking things easier. Anyway, I was anxious to avoid trouble.

I was similarly anxious to avoid Papuan wild-pig ticks, which attack your crotch (I had heard you can remove them with Sellotape), crocodiles (you are recommended to poke them in the eye with something very sharp), but particularly, a horrifying and simply unimaginable variety of nasty snakes.

When I was told by a botanist friend in London of the luxuriant wealth of snakes to be found on the great island, I phoned

Reuven and told him the trip was off. I hung up the phone on him for the first and only time in our relationship and felt a surge of agreeable power. He called me straight back, laughing his head off. Scoffing at my fear, he shamed me into reconsidering. The next day he called me at the university and, for the very last time, my old friend Reuven talked me into doing something about which I had the most profound reservations.

Reuven urged me to make proper preparations for this journey. He wanted every detail to be planned beforehand and called incessantly with suggestions and advice. Through the good offices of some evangelists I had met on my trip to Australia who were conducting a mission among the Gogodala, I had secured the services of an experienced Australian diver for the task of bringing the canoes, along with the Ark, to the surface.

The evangelists had a particular interest in the Gogodala because they believed the Gogodala story and believed in addition that the Gogodala were a genuine lost tribe of Israel. As they explained to me, Jesus would never return until *all* the lost tribes had gone back to Jerusalem, to the Holy Land, and had accepted the Word of God. They wanted to encourage the Gogadala to return to the Promised Land. Their mission to the Gogodala therefore had cosmic implications. At least for them.

I had reservations and concerns about the evangelists' activities and the effect they would have on the Gogodala but I had even graver concerns about the likely effect of the trip on *me*.

I was not exaggerating. There really were a lot of snakes in Papua New Guinea. One, the Papuan taipan (*Oxyuranus scutellatus canni*) was a three-meter-long, fast-moving snake with the third most toxic venom of any snake in the world. I had read that as the result of its egregious nastiness it was apparently in the process of becoming the dominant species, above man, *above man,* in the grasslands near the Gogodala villages. When I thought of *Oxyuranus scutellatus canni,* unknown parts of me became deliquescent.

I'm not good on snakes and it was of little comfort to recall that *if* the Papuan taipan failed, which I did not expect it would, as the mortality rate after a bite is 100 percent, there were always death adders, the Papuan blacksnake, the Papuan brown snake, the New Guinean small-eyed snake, and the Papuan *mulga* snake: the bite of each and all of them is equally lethal. There were many, many more. I spent the long flight from London to Port Moresby in preparation for the hazards of the grasslands, gravely reading the pile of scholarly material on the Papuan snake population published by that admirable body, the Chicago Herpetological Society. It was not a fun read.

Viewed from above, Port Moresby appears as a dense concentration of the vibrant greens of tropical foliage and the reds of slashed earth, overlooking a stupendously beautiful bay circled with reefs.

In reality, as I was to discover, it is a filthy, smelly, sprawling, dull, crime-infested, gratuitously violent shantytown of horrible, gray metallic corrugated roofs clustered around a small, repellent center with drably modest high-rise buildings. I did not like it.

Waisa met me at Port Moresby airport along with a few hundred Gogodala men and women who were living and working in the capital. They were wearing grass skirts, carrying traditional weapons and banners, and their skins were painted with traditional designs. Both men and women were bare-breasted.

Stars of David, I was amazed to discover, were painted on just about every part of their body: faces, chests, arms, and breasts. There were more Israeli flags to be seen than in Tel Aviv on Independence Day. They were astonishingly delighted to see me and some of them dashed toward me, eying me closely, banging their spears on the ground and shouting "Bogale, Bogale."

From Port Moresby, I took a Twin Otter that would fly me in stages from the capital to the western province over the swamps, grasslands, and rain forest of western PNG. I put my herpetological reading matter away in my rucksack and forced myself to enjoy the flight. T. S. Eliot said somewhere that a first condition of understanding a foreign country is actually to smell it and here in the tiny, decrepit plane, every opportunity was afforded the traveler to fulfill this injunction: people, chickens in cages, bundles of sago, dried fish, they all had their distinctive and pungent odor. I breathed deeply, closed my eyes, and felt a moment of pure happiness. Perhaps, after all, my long search would finally be rewarded in this most unlikely place.

We flew west down the coast following the line of waves crashing against the barrier reef like folds of lace fringing a blue infinity of sea and sky daubed with patches of turquoise and aquamarine.

I was accompanied on the flight by Waisa, one of the best mannered men I have ever met.

"You have a wife?" he asked.

I showed him a photograph of Maria I had as a screensaver on my laptop.

"I have never seen such a beautiful woman," he said awestruck.

"Neither have I," I replied, feeling the hard knot in my stomach that usually accompanied thoughts of Maria.

Thereafter he became even more attentive to my needs. I was without my woman and would need his help. In former times he would have provided me with a woman during my stay but the missionaries had changed all that. He spent the flight worrying about the sleeping arrangements in the Gogodala village in which we would be staying. It would be only a hut, he explained. A reed hut built on—he searched for the word—stilts.

"So wild creatures cannot get in," I suggested helpfully.

"Only snakes can get in," he replied. "No animals, only snakes."

My fears returned. I had impregnated my sleeping bag with an Australian product called Shoosnake, suggested, after some research, by Reuven. While I was wondering to myself how efficacious Shoosnake was likely to be, Tony filled me in on the Jewish characteristics of his tribe.

He told me that they were getting more Jewish all the time. They now lit candles on Friday evening, the beginning of the Jewish Sabbath, and refrained from all work on Saturdays. They no longer ate pork. They were starting to circumcise their young boys. While most of them were still Christians, some were now refusing to go to church and wanted to worship in a specifically Jewish way. They were not only Israelite in origin; they were becoming Israelite in practice. They were anxious to prove to the outside world that they were Israelites. This was my role—to let people know. They were anxious to recover the Ark and to return it in triumph and glory to Jerusalem. Along with themselves.

According to Tony, the priests who attended the Ark and who brought it from ancient Israel were called Guwali; and the high priest who was principally in charge of it was called Tilaki. I tried without success to find some echo of ancient Hebrew in these names.

Waisa called the Ark the Covenant Box. "In the Gogodala language there are three names for the Covenant Box. *Melesa, Ila Sokate,* and *Awana.* The one we use most is *Ila Sokate.* It means the fire pot."

"Why is that?" I asked.

"Because it shoots fire at people. It shoots other things too. Some while back we had a contractor come to the place in the lagoon where the Ark is and they put chains around the canoes and tried to pull them up. Then the water rose suddenly, the contractors and the people helping them got terribly ill, and they had to stop. It was the Ark that shot something at them that made them very sick. It has always been trouble.

"When we first got here to the swamp hundreds of years ago twelve of the priests tried to steal the fire pot just for themselves. These were priests who wanted to hide the Ark in a secret place without letting the others know. There were two boats altogether. The twelve thieving priests took one boat and left the other priests and all the people in the other boat. They took the fire pot and the *pasia batala*—the priest's rod of Aaron—and the others had to chase them for fifteen kilometres in the other boat. That is how we got to Fly Swamp. This was when the fire pot acted. It shot fire and sank the thieving priests' boat off the shore of Balimo and it has been there ever since. It went down nose first. That was the end of them. The other boat was just behind it and the fire pot shot fire on that one too and it sank in the same place, but the other priests and people all scrambled off."

Pointing out of the window he indicated islands and inlets that the canoes had passed by on their epic voyage. He went on to tell me what the tribe recalled of its arrival in the lagoon.

"We were not wild savages when we arrived. And we did not eat people—we learned to do this after we arrived here. The women were very modest and wore veils. They did not show their faces. Later the missionaries put a stop to that. In those days the men had clothes, proper clothes, weapons, eating utensils. Each one had his own bowl," he added proudly.

"Since we have been here the other tribes have always been at war with us. Twice a week they would come and capture Gogodala people and eat them. They were many and we were few. And with all the eating we got fewer.

"The reason that we survived at all was because of the fire pot, because of Malesa, which looked after us. We are the people of the covenant and this is the land of the covenant. This protected land we call 'the place where Melesa rests its head.' When the cannibals came in great numbers, Malesa, the fire pot, the Ark of the Covenant, would shoot flames at them. From time to time still it shoots fire out of the lagoon, usually at times of grave danger."

Tony Waisa's description was eerily reminiscent of the biblical and later rabbinical accounts of the Ark. The tribe might have picked up some of this from the missionaries, but where would they have got the rabbinic stories? In the Bible the fire that came out of the Ark was called *the fire of God.*

"Recently some Muslim terrorists came to attack us. They had automatic weapons but they were no match for the Ark. It shot fire in the air and they fled. They are a great danger to the people of the lagoon."

Islamic terrorists were not what I was worried about.

I asked Tony about snakes in the lagoon.

"There are dangerous water snakes all over the place. And crocodiles. They often take the children. But you never see them near the fire pot. They keep their distance."

I drew some small comfort from the fact that the Ark, according to the Midrash, was also a powerful weapon against snakes and scorpions. If it was in the lagoon, perhaps it would keep *Oxyuranus scutellatus canni* and other horrors at bay.

Pointing out of the plane window, he said that it was along this deserted coastline that his ancestors, the Temple priests, had traveled by canoe from Israel hundreds of years ago. I felt a mild frisson. *"Follow the priests,"* Rabin had said. Was it really possible? Was it possible? It was known that the water level *had* dropped since biblical times and that it might well have been possible to navigate from island to island without having to traverse great expanses of empty ocean. The monsoon winds made the journey more or less feasible.

"You know in the Bible," said Tony, "there is a lot about the fleet of Tarshish sent by the great King Solomon and how it would return with a cargo of gold and silver, ivory, parrots, apes, and monkeys. Some people believe that this was India. But I think it was Papua New Guinea. The round trip took three years. That's about the length of time it would take in a great canoe of war. We have many apes and monkeys here. And parrots." Tony had a good memory and an intimate knowledge of the denizens of the tropical rain forest he grew up in. He started enumerating the parrots to be found in his native lagoon: pygmy-parrots, buff faced pygmy-parrots, orange-breasted fig-parrots, double-eyed fig-parrots, tiger parrots, modest tiger parrots, red-faced parrots, pink-faced parrots. He did not know which ones they took to King Solomon.

Waisa said that when we got close to our destination, the large Gogodala village of Balimo, the plane would fly right over the very place where the great ancestral oceangoing canoes had been found and, no doubt, I would be able to see them from the air.

If the weather was right, I might even glimpse the Ark gleaming through the crystalline water.

The plane swept in from the coast skimming over the rain forest before coming in to land on a large patch of cleared ground. As the pilot banked to make his final approach, I craned my neck to get a good look at the lagoon but it was not possible to see the canoes from the air, although it was a bright day and the lagoon was blue and translucent.

As the plane came in to land, I saw a crowd of hundreds of people standing with banners in the middle of the field.

Stepping down from the Twin Otter, I saw that a broad pathway lined with people had been strewn with reeds and branches. Waisa explained that all this was in my honor. This was in honor of Bogale.

There would be a vehicle to take me to my accommodation; all the other people out there would accompany me by foot to the village.

Most of the people were wearing Western-style uniforms, including those of the Boys Brigade, and carrying Israeli flags. One or two elderly men were shouldering muskets and when I got close to them they saluted and shouted, "Bogale!"

They had formed two long, tightly packed lines, a kind of guard of honor, through which I was expected to walk.

I had never before been received like this. People looked at me with awe and veneration. I felt like a visiting deity. Except I was wearing baggy cotton trousers and no socks.

"Shalom!" someone shouted out. "Bogale! Bogale!"

"They are greeting you as our Messiah," whispered Waisa.

"Oh," I said.

I was more than ready for a drink, although Waisa had told me that in his devoutly religious Gogodala mileu, drink was frowned upon. I was glad I had packed a couple of bottles.

Eyes fixed firmly on the ground, my attention especially attuned to anything that looked like it was about to slither, I minced hesitantly down the avenue of flags and banners. In places the grass and branches were quite high and would have provided a safe hiding place for small to medium-size reptiles.

Some of the men had drums and guitars and they sang songs of welcome in which the words Jerusalem, Israel, and Bogale were occasionally discernible. "Halleluiah Bogale," they shouted, throwing more reptile cover in the form of palm fronds at my feet. I waved vaguely at them, bent down and sprayed my Timberlands with Shoosnake, keeping my eyes on the ground and doing my best to avoid the deeper patches of strewn reeds and branches. The cries of "Halleluiah" and "Bogale" got louder and louder, and more and more devotional.

With a sigh of relief, I reached the truck. Except for a communal tractor, it was the one and only vehicle in Balimo. Indeed there was little need for more than one vehicle in Balimo, as Balimo had no road connection with the outside world. The only way in or out was by air or by canoe.

The driver was a muscular, dwarflike man who was accompanied by a very pretty, younger wife. She sat in the middle of the bench seat with the two of us on either side. She rested her very small, pretty hand on my shoulder and smiled at me. I attempted a smile but it was difficult—my mind was elsewhere.

The driver was worried about the weather. It was gray and sultry; there were puddles everywhere. "If it rains again," he said, "the next plane will not be able to land; you'll have to stay here!" Wiggling her shapely bottom, the young woman giggled and said that sometimes the plane could not land for weeks on end. Blimey.

The truck left the airfield and nosed its way through longer grass and clumps of *pandana* palms, the shoots of which are eaten, the dwarf told me, and that used to be used to make the characteristic woven veils the Gogodala women used to wear. I kept the side window closed and tried to concentrate on what he was saying. While his wife caressed my cheek I made every attempt to follow what was happening around me. Singing songs of praise and cheering, the crowd followed the truck, which advanced at a stately pace in the direction of Balimo.

A man was walking alongside us, not part of the procession. He was carrying an animal over one shoulder wrapped in a large leaf and held a wooden spear in his hand. "It's a wallaby," said the driver. "And the man is the village school headmaster. The wild pigs and the wallabies make the best meat. Now there are many in the village who do not want to eat pig. They are the Gogodala who believe they are Jews. Not all of them think that but many of them do. They say that they have found the Ark of the Covenant. That's what they say. I've heard it many times." He shouted out of his open window at the teacher. The teacher suggested we get out and inspect his wallaby.

"Professor from England want your wallaby. OK? He's come to get the Ark of the Covenant! OK? He wants that fire pot! OK?"

The teacher explained that if I really wanted the wallaby it would be brought to the hut on stilts where I would be staying. It would not be very expensive. If, on the other hand, I wanted to see the Ark, the people were all ready to accompany me to the lagoon. They'd got all their equipment together: ropes, shovels, and long sticks to beat back the reeds and to protect against the snakes. Moreover the Australian deep-sea diver had already arrived on a previous flight. But before we went to the place the Ark was hidden, there would be a big meeting, just to talk over plans.

We were following a rough track overgrown with the long grass of the savannah, pitted with potholes filled with water. Suddenly the driver swung back to the right and we found ourselves cruising right down the center of the grass airstrip.

"Much flatter," said the driver.

"Wouldn't do at Heathrow," I said.

He looked at me questioningly.

"Heathrow—the London airport," I explained.

"They have restrictions there, do they?" he asked disdainfully.

We arrived at a kind of sports field with a wooden pavilion at one end. Again there was a double guard of honor: this time people were carrying not only flags but palm fronds, and the branches of nameless trees from the rain forest. Some carried placards: one read "*Holy God bless Israel the Lost Jews refugees living in exile (PNG).*"

Farther along there was a sort of *tableau vivant* of utter destitution consisting mainly of skinny little boys carrying worn-out cooking pans, oil lamps, and an old plastic bowl. On their grimy little chests, I could discern smudged Stars of David. A couple of men behind them carried a roughly written legend: "*Blood brothers we are tired of living in poverty. Please take us home quickly as possible!*" At the end of this phalanx of frond waving, placard-carrying people there was a group of elders carrying aloft the Jewish seven-branched candelabrum.

"Take us back, Bogale!" they pleaded. "Take us back!"

That evening there was a tribal assembly in the great thatched meetinghouse, open on the sides, the bamboo floor raised on stilts. In the center of the room a bamboo fire smouldered sullenly.

About a hundred men were sitting around ready to debate the purpose of my visit. They wanted me to prove that they were Jews. They were quite sure I would succeed, as the tribal prophecies had predicted I would do just that. But if I did manage to prove their Jewishness to the satisfaction of the Israeli authorities, as I surely would, what would happen next? Here in Balimo, after all, the Gogodala were allowed to wander around freely. But would the Israeli authorities be so lenient? Where would they live in Israel? Were there rain forests in Israel? Who would pay for the accommodation and for the flights? Would they be able to take their bows and their spears? What would they hunt? What would they eat? Were there wallabies in Israel?

The discussion became heated. There were occasional pauses, particularly as it got later and the men became tired. In the silences I could hear a strange *tut tut* sound. I had read in the literature of the Chicago Herpetological Society that one of the nastier Papuan snakes made a sound something like that. I looked up at the thatch and peered between the bamboo poles of the floor but saw nothing. It left me feeling a little uneasy.

We walked back to the hut-on-stilts where I would be staying. It was surrounded by palm trees and there were clumps of snake-friendly bamboo growing adjacent to the wooden stilts. This building had been put up years before by the Australian missionaries who had brought Christianity to Balimo. My room had a window covered with rusting metal mesh; there was a mosquito net over the incredibly short single bed at the bottom of which, at the point where my feet would extend over the mattress, there was a significant aperture. I sprayed the room with Shoosnake and placed a pile of books over the hole. The hut was a few yards from the water's edge. They advised me not to approach the water after dark. Various creatures, of different sorts, lived there. They were better avoided.

On the front porch of the house there was a prosperous-looking cat. "Best snake catcher in Balimo," said Waisa pointing proudly at the admirable animal. "Nothing will get into your room. Except possibly ..." his voice trailed off.

The dinner that first night was not at all bad. Fish grilled between sticks of bamboo, sago palm, and roast wallaby. I had brought with me a couple of bottles of Elliot Rocke Estate Semillon from the Mudgee region in New South Wales. To restore my flagging spirits I decided to open one. I offered Waisa and his Gogodala friends a glass but everyone shook their head with disapproval.

"We only drink kosher wine," said Waisa primly, "and you can't get kosher wine in Papua New Guinea, although I think it could be ordered from Israel, couldn't it?"

I nodded slowly. The wine was a dream. A snake-banishing dream.

"Is it kosher?" Waisa whispered after dinner, pointing at what was left of the wallaby. "Er ... not absolutely sure," I muttered, taking a furtive swig from my hip flask.

My task, it was agreed at the meeting, was threefold. To locate the war canoe, extract the sacred fire pot, and collect Gogodala DNA. The last of these was straightforward. I had brought my kit with me from the genetics lab in London and for the next few days I sat on the raised bamboo floor of the meeting house as I inserted swabs into willing cheeks and put them into specially prepared tubes along with a preserving agent.

Finding the canoes proved more problematic. Three days after my arrival, we tried to locate the sunken boats but reeds had taken over the riverbed where it had last been seen and it was utterly impossible to get even close to it.

I was sitting in the meeting hut the evening after the abortive attempt to find the canoes when Waisa ran across the village square and vaulted onto the bamboo floor. Panting, he pulled me to my feet and insisted I come with him immediately to see a miraculous event.

"The Lord Yahweh is among us," he said. "The Lord Yahweh will show us the way to the Ark. Bogale is here among us. Bogale has come! This is why the place is being shown to us now."

Over the previous few days strange events, signs, and portents had already been evident in the village. Some women had been granted the gift of speaking in tongues. They had had visions. They had dreamed of the Ark. Others had seen it with their own eyes, shining below the surface of the water, clearly visible through the ubiquitous reeds. It gave off a strange light. It was made of shiny gold and there were golden angels at each end. There were golden poles attached to the carrying rings, and they could be seen through the water when the light was right.

A young girl who had taken her small dugout canoe out to the place had actually touched one of the golden carrying poles. Sometimes flames would shoot from the Ark, high into the sky above the lagoon. One man had heard a loud bang exactly there where the fire pot was. Others had seen Israeli planes circling over the rain forest. It was only the wet weather that had prevented them from landing and that had forced them to return to Jerusalem.

Now Tony held my sleeve and guided me to a house set a few yards inside the rain forest. We would be shown now exactly where the Ark was hidden. Some women from the tribe were engaged in a kind of prayer meeting centered on the mysterious fire pot.

They had entreated God to guide their every action and their every word. The dwarf's pretty wife had been so guided to write a prayer on the blackboard.

Peace, peace, peace.
Yahweh, Yahweh, Yahweh.
Malesa, God, fire pot.

Another woman hobbled up to the board and asked the ancestral spirits to direct her hand as she drew one of the canoes of war. The question was: where in the boat was the Ark to be found? Her hand hovered for a while over the blackboard. Then with a rapid movement she drew the fire pot, square in the hold of the boat: the tablets of the Law were next to it, crudely depicted. The Ten Commandments included the injunction not to smoke hashish.

As the women expressed themselves in various ways on the blackboard, others joined in with ecstatic snatches of song and prayer.

> Yahweh God is the God of War!
> This is the cry of the people!
> Malesa is the fire pot
> Steaming beneath the water.
> We call out to the God of Fire
> Ouwah! Ouwah!
> Oh God of Fire!

And looking at me they joined together and cried out:

> Bogale is here!
> Lead us Bogale, lead us!

The women carried on praying at the top of their voices. Some were dancing, beating their breasts, entreating Yahweh God to show the way to the Ark.

Then silence fell. Total, eery silence.

"The spirit of God has fallen," whispered Tony.

A shriveled, bent old crone called Bibiato stepped forward to the blackboard.

"Write, sister Bibiato," the women whispered.

Bibiato was illiterate. She had never written a word in her life. When the missionaries had come from Australia with their books, their schools, and their clinics she was already a grown woman—too old to learn these new things. She was brought up a cannibal. She closed her eyes and held up a scrawny claw. Someone put a piece of chalk into it. She started to make forms—her eyes still closed—and then more weird shapes and squiggles, which everyone agreed was a kind of writing. There were gasps of astonishment from all round the room. Then she drew a kind of pot. The atmosphere in the room was now electric. More than electric.

"*Malesa*, fire pot, *Malesa*," the women cried out. "Sister Bibiato will take us there. She will take us to *Malesa*. She is the one chosen to find the Covenant Box."

They installed Sister Bibiato on a chair set on top of a low table. They brought flowers and garlands and placed them on and around her throne. She was the heroine of the moment. Yahweh God was acting through her.

The next day it was raining heavily. The warm, fragrant mists rolled into the village from the lagoon. It seemed unlikely that the rain would ever stop. "Sometimes it rains for weeks on end," said Tony.

It poured all day. But the warm, torrential rain did not stop us.

The tribe's tractor came to the place where the women were still praying. They had been praying all night and the room smelled of sweat, anxiety, and holy desire. Bibiato, the spirit of the Lord Yahweh still upon her, was led out and placed on the tractor, still covered in garlands made of water lilies from the lagoon.

"Sister Bibiato. The bride of Yahweh! The bride of the Covenant Box!"

Hundreds of Gogodala followed the tractor on foot. When we arrived at the lagoon shore Bibiato was handed down from the tractor by the women with great ceremony. They shot triumphant glances at the men. It was the *women* of the Gogodala who were going to find the Ark. Not the men.

Bibiato looked around her fearfully but marched without hesitation to a length of shoreline covered with tall reeds. She pushed her way into the shallow water trampling the reeds under her bare feet.

"Go, Bogale," the women urged. "Be there with her. Stay close. Stay with Sister Bibiato."

There were women's hands pushing me into the water behind her, to be there when she found the Ark.

The old woman waded on through the reeds. I was soon covered in leeches. I pulled them off one after the other and flung them back into the water. Traces of my own blood floated on the surface of the lagoon all around us. The water got deeper. I wondered if the blood would attract crocodiles, which was more or less acceptable, or water snakes, which was not. I took a pull at my hip flask and kept my eyes on the reeds.

Tony was following close behind. The water now was up to my stomach and all I could see of Sister Bibiato was her head, which was bobbing on the surface of the water like a small coconut. I asked Tony if she could swim.

"The Lord Yahweh will teach her to swim, if necessary. The important thing is that she is pure in heart.

"He who cleans his body from evil will be used," added Tony, who knew his New Testament.

Bibiato stopped bobbing, and steadied herself with outstretched arms. She looked out at the endless expanse of reeds. She did not know which way to turn. She clambered up onto a dense clump of reeds and pressed her knuckles into her eyes.

She looked all around her and then plunged into even deeper water. Tony whispered in my ear: "She is fighting the battle between the forces of light and the serpent of darkness."

So was I, in a different way.

I thought I felt something brushing against my legs in the churned-up water. I gritted my teeth, took another swig of Laphroaig, and kept going.

Then Bibiato stopped again. She climbed onto another clump of reeds and looked around her. Then she looked around her again.

In the simple way of a little girl she said very quietly that she did not know where to go.

The men started muttering. The heroine of the evening before, the illiterate woman who had miraculously written, was now forgotten.

All we had before us was an old woman with no teeth who did not know what to do. She was diminished. The women seemed diminished too.

The men now took over. Shoving the women to one side they headed into the water. The trick was to balance yourself with a stick and to step quickly from one clump of reeds to the next. There was great activity all around me, beating down the reeds, trampling in the muddy shallows. A man pointed out a water snake that was thrashing about in the reeds, its back broken by one of the men's sticks.

The Australian, a big tough abalone diver from Tasmania, pushed his way into the deeper water of the crocodile-infested lagoon and splashed around a bit but failed to see anything. The lagoon was choked with reeds. He found absolutely nothing. There was not the slightest sign of sunken canoes, hidden treasure, golden objects. Nothing.

What Tony had described as a crystal-clear lagoon in which the great canoes could be seen clearly was in reality a dank bog in which something might one day be discovered, but not now and not by us.

Reuven was fond of a Hebrew expression that translates: "There were no bears—not even a forest." He would have used it now.

When we had made our way back through the reeds to the stony shoreline, Waisa was perhaps slightly, just slightly, crestfallen. He had no explanation. But his belief in the stories of his ancestors was in no way dented. From a bag he had slung over his shoulder he extracted folders with more text, charts, maps, and diagrams of the Ark that he had hoped would help us track down its last hiding place.

He showed me a photograph of a colorful Gogodala drawing. A pot painted with a Star of David was surrounded by a serpent with the head of a bird. This was the traditional representation of the Ark, he told me.

As we walked back to Balimo from the lagoon, he announced, his eyes shining with excitement, that the evening before he had chanced upon an old woman whom he had not seen for many years.

"A very, very old woman," he started, "a very, very, very old woman who has very, very old memories. Ancient memories from ancient days. She told me last night that the box is there. The fire pot is down there. She says it is called Awana Taba." He paused and looked at me triumphantly and said, "Taba is Hebrew, isn't it?"

"Yes, Tony. More or less. It is almost Hebrew."

"Well, there's your proof," he said, giving me the thumbs-up sign.

Some days later he told me that the location of the canoe was now known to him. Sister Bibiato had been mistaken. But there was a sure sign. He said that at the time of our fruitless search there had been a terrible bang, like an explosion. Subsequently the place from which the noise had come was identified by some Gogodala fishermen as the place where the Ark languished.

The Ark had wished to identify its hiding place. The time was ripe for Bogale to make the long-awaited discovery. It was not Bibiato but Bogale who was destined to find the Ark.

"Possibly," I said. "Or possibly not."

He shook his head, made his thumbs-up sign and laughed lugubriously. Everything was going to work out. I would see. The signs were clear. But as we waited for the correct portents to manifest themselves, he would take me the following day to visit the smaller Gogodala villages dotted over and around the lagoon.

That morning I got up early and wandered around the village, sticking to the well-trodden paths. In the past, on Wednesdays and Saturdays, the Gogodala men would take out their great canoes of war to hunt down their traditional enemies. They would eat them over the following days. All that has now stopped. Cannibalism and headhunting have been replaced by obsessive religiosity and, more bizarrely, rugby league. Every Wednesday and Saturday the Gogodala men now play rugby matches against the five surrounding tribes who used to eat them. That morning I saw two teams playing with the utmost ferocity. Only three or four in each side had boots— the rest were barefoot.

When the game was over they came together for a feast, which consisted not of people but of sweet, hot milky tea, buttered scones, and pikelets.

While the young men were trying to kill each other on the rugby field the rest of the population were wandering around the rain forest picking fruit, fishing in the lagoon, or attending lengthy prayer meetings in one of the twenty or thirty small churches located in and around Balimo.

Waisa came in search of me, bearing a basket full of fruits I had never before encountered. He sat me on a chair in the middle of a long wooden canoe of war and set the basket at my feet in case I felt hungry during our journey. We traveled across the mist-shrouded lagoon for many hours. There was nothing much to see: when the mist lifted you could see an endless expanse of water lilies, pink and white, great flocks of water-birds, and occasionally isolated pairs of egrets, pied herons, and kingfishers. There was the occasional heavy, oily splash of a crocodile, to which the Gogodala paid not the slightest atten-tion. Nonetheless, I happened to know that the estuarian croc-odiles here were the largest crocodile species in the world and in fact the world's largest living reptile. They are also man-eating.

Wherever we went among these small isolated communities, we heard the same sort of thing. Everybody had heard that the ancestral boats had disappeared along with their precious cargo. The Ark had disappeared too. The golden Ark had gone. But they put a brave front on it. In the meantime there were more pressing things to discuss.

Everyone told me about new and disturbing revelations. A Russian submarine had been spotted at the mouth of the lagoon; white men in military uniforms had been observed in the rain forest not far from Balimo. They were looking for the Ark. That's what they said.

The son of the village chief had had a Soviet "detection device" implanted into his shoulder, and he still had the scar to show for it. Al-Qaeda operatives were passing freely from the border with the western part of the island, Irian Jaya, part of Muslim Indonesia, to Balimo. Uniformed Hamas people had been seen in the jungle. Nobody knew what they were looking for. It was rumored they were after the Ark.

All this was because the word had got out that the Gogodala were Israelites, that they possessed the holy Ark. They were the guardians of the fire pot, the custodians of Malesa. People were getting ready to leave, to return to where they had come from millennia before. Israeli planes would be landing to take them and the precious Ark back to Israel. It would be returned to the Temple from which it had been snatched before the destruction of Jerusalem.

Once, in the Yemen during my quest to discover the lost city of Senna, I had been given a Jewish-made silver *djambiyyeh* with the words in Arabic written on the blade: "God preserve you from that which you fear the most." I wish I'd had it in my bag on the way back from the island to Balimo. I knew what I feared the most.

In the boat, the men were anxious to learn a little Hebrew. "Teach us Hebrew, Bogale. When we go to Israel we will be able to speak to the people. Bogale, teach us Hebrew!" I taught them a few words and expressions and we talked in general about Jews and Arabs, about conditions in Israel, and the threat to the Gogodala from the barbarian Muslims of Irian Jaya, the Indonesian and partly Muslim section of the great island, the border with which was not far to the west of the Fly estuary.

We talked about Malesa, the holy Ark, the fire pot, how mysterious it was that all of a sudden there was no trace of the ancestral canoes that had been clearly seen so recently and whose illustrious cargo had been visible to the naked eye. We spoke of the chances of finding the Ark in the lagoon and the need to mount a great expedition to locate its hiding place. My scepticism had long since given way to tired disbelief. They spoke of tribal secrets, of elders' anecdotes, of ancient traditions passed down from generation to generation. I seemed to have heard all this before. They spoke of their deep conviction that I, Bogale, was the one who would bring the Ark to the surface and lead the people back to the Holy Land. Bogale, Bogale, they sang. You came to take us back, to find the Ark. Bogale, Bogale.

We were drifting down a kind of overgrown backwater. They had cut the outboard motor and were paddling gently, pushing the reeds away. There were high rushes and trees with over-hanging branches on both sides and the canoe was edging slowly under the dense foliage. I tried to avert my gaze from the infested reeds and wished we could get back to open water where there was nothing worse than crocodiles to worry about. I was taking a spine-bracing gulp of Laphroaig from my metal hip flask when my heart stopped.

I glimpsed first a two-headed snake. My mind entered a madness zone as I recalled the Lemba tradition that maintained that a snake with two heads guarded the Ark. I looked around in panic. Was the Ark hidden somewhere in these reeds? Looking down again I realized that what I had seen was two sickeningly smooth olive-green ends of the same snake. There was a flash of metal from a heavy Malay kris and two halves of a python, thrashing around, fell into the boat, at, over and around, my feet.

"What's the matter, Bogale? This is a gift from God Yahweh!" The simple joy manifest on everyone's face did something to calm me.

"We'll have a good dinner tonight," said Waisa, rubbing his hands together. "This creature is a great delicacy for us, as I am sure you know. This is what we usually eat at weddings."

"It won't be on the menu at my wedding," I muttered, thinking tenderly of Maria. Waisa looked at me with some concern etched on his dark, angular face.

"It is OK, isn't it?" he asked. "It is kosher?"

I replied very firmly and with as much authority as I could muster: "Sorry, python is not Jewish food, Tony. It's not kosher, Tony. Not kosher at all."

Thinking outside the box, as Reuven called it, had led me to having to confront my greatest fear. It had also led to my being mistaken for a messiah. But it had also led me to a new understanding of the worldwide resonance of the Ark and the radically different ways in which its meaning was interpreted by different peoples. But as for the physical Ark of flesh and blood, it was not here. It obviously, clearly, and most evidently was not here. Not with the best will in the world. Even if it had been here, I had no desire to spend any more time looking for it. Not here. Not here in this snake pit. If it was here, which it wasn't, it could stay where it was, in its reed-choked, snake-infested lagoon. I thought briefly of my father, who would have stayed the course, snakes or no snakes. But not me.

Suddenly I longed for Maria, for salsa dancing, for London beer, for decent wine, for drizzle, for world-class Chinese food, for Maria in bed, for real newspapers, for theater, I longed for the classrooms and libraries of Bloomsbury. Libraries. I had always thought in my heart of hearts that the hiding place of the Ark would be revealed in some dusty tome in one of the great libraries of the world; the Vatican, the Bodleian, the British Library. This would be my next adventure.

Back in Port Moresby I telephoned Reuven and told him the bad news. The Ark was not in the Pacific. I told him I was coming back to London. I told him that he could, if he wished, pay for me to follow a course of aversion therapy. I told him that for the foreseeable future I planned a sedentary, scholarly existence.

13

WATCHDOGS
OF THE KING

It did not help. For five years the trail went from cold to colder. In 2004 I had a serious operation that laid me up for a good while. During my long convalescence I received an awful piece of news. Reuven had died suddenly of a heart attack. This was in the autumn of 2005. It left a huge hole in my life and without his encouragement and energy I was tempted to give up my quest for the Ark. I spoke about it with my father, who encouraged me to keep going if I could.

"You're dead for a long time," he said. "Do what you have to while you can." During the time, I was too weak to do anything else. I spent a lot of time in libraries, both carrying on with my usual academic work and Ark-related matters.

I was by now even more sure that the analysis that had led me to believe that the Ark's last manifestation was the *ngoma lungundu* was correct. It was almost certainly somewhere in Africa. But where?

It was February 2007. I was irritable and tense. I was fed up with books and libraries and academic papers and theses. I was fed up with SOAS, fed up with my colleagues. I felt I needed to breathe, to move, to travel again.

After my illness my doctor had ordered me to give up difficult journeys. I had been ready to hang up the old Timberlands I always used when traveling. But now that I was feeling better I wanted to take them out and oil them. I wanted to cram a few possessions into a canvas bag and take off. In the back of my mind the poem of Kipling hammered away as it periodically did.

"Something hidden. Go and find it. Go and look behind the ranges—something lost behind the ranges. Lost and waiting for you. Go!"

Those who had been a part of my quest for so many years were no longer there to participate in it or to encourage or discourage me. It wasn't only Reuven who'd dropped out of my life. The blindingly beautiful Maria had left me without a word in 2006 and returned to her native land. My teacher, David Patterson, had died of cancer the year before, in 2005. Shula Eisner, my oldest Jerusalem friend, had died the same year, also of cancer. Doniach and Rabin were long dead. Mathivha had died in 2003 and Samuel Moeti in 2005. Daud too was dead. He had died of an AIDS-related condition in February 2006. He still had not completed his thesis.

I was now on my own.

I was trying to keep warm in my old stone chateau in the Languedoc. The central heating system had failed again. The beagle had pissed on the dining room floor. Again. Without Maria, the once beautiful house had fallen into disorder. There were empty bottles everywhere. Empty memories. The log fire in the kitchen was spluttering and smoking, and a damp, inimical chill was rising from the flagstones.

The phone call came like a bolt from the blue.

Magdel le Roux was the South African scholar from Pretoria who had played an important role in the genetic study that had catapulted the Lemba tribe to international attention. She had also written a good deal on the Lemba, including an important book that was published in 2003. She was aware of my interest in the legends of the *ngoma lungundu* and had called me with the enticing, if unlikely, news that the *ngoma* had been found.

Perhaps not exactly *found* but rather that someone she knew had a very good idea where it was.

"Are we talking about *the ngoma*, Magdel, or just *any* old *ngoma*?" I asked.

"Oh *ja*. *The ngoma*. There is someone who knows where the original *ngoma* is, isn't it. Anyhow, that's what he says."

That someone was a South African *aventurier* called Richard Wade who, for an as yet undisclosed sum, was prepared to guide me to a remote cave in an undisclosed and almost inaccessible part of the Soutpansberg mountains, which lie between South Africa and Zimbabwe, where, he claimed, it was located. He was not yet prepared to tell me exactly where it was or how he had come by the information. I felt a rush of adrenaline. My first thought was to call Reuven. Then I remembered.

Reuven was dead.

I booked a ticket with British Airways from Toulouse via London and two days later found myself in Magdel's house in Pretoria.

Richard Wade was difficult to read. He was a big, blond-haired, blue-eyed, good-looking man, rather overweight, who looked soft but sounded tough. He was dressed in khaki bush clothes and serviceable high-sided desert boots. When he observed me glancing at his boots, he explained that there were the deadliest snakes in the hills at this time of the year.

My heart went cold. Calling up my last precious ounce of bravado, I replied jauntily: "According to the tradition the *ngoma* is guarded by snakes with a head at both ends."

"Whatever," he replied shortly. "Anyway you should take precautions."

"Do you think *I* need boots?" I asked.

"Won't help," he replied, "they go for your face." My stomach lurched. The aversion therapy I had followed had not been as successful as I might have hoped.

Wade rattled on with tales of his family. He told me he came from distinguished stock. In the 1830s a Wade ancestor of his had been the military secretary to the governor of the Cape of Good Hope Colony.

"He was a bit of a disaster, like most of the Wades. He was directly responsible for the Sixth Kaffir War and the flight of the Boers in the Great Trek!"

Another nineteenth-century ancestor of his, Thomas Wade, was the famous inventor of a standard of transliteration from Chinese called the Wade-Giles system. On his mother's side, there were generations of Dutch aristocrats. Richard's family had been rich and he had had a privileged upbringing in South Africa. He loved the country and knew it in a way few white South Africans did. He told me that he had spent many years living in a hut in a Zulu village.

Richard had been interested in the Lemba for many years, was writing an MA dissertation on the tribe, and was involved in new and exciting archaeological work.

"That book you wrote about the Lemba was the book *I* was always planning to write," he said. "The DNA research you were involved with was the research *I* was always planning to do!"

I smiled and shrugged. We discussed his fee and the equipment that would be necessary for the expedition. He insisted that I rent two big four-wheel-drive vehicles. This was a seriously expensive undertaking and I regretted no longer having Reuven's bottomless bank balance at my theoretical disposal if I needed it. Clara was still alive but was deeply opposed to anything to do with the Ark. She had cut herself off from all of Reuven's interests. In any case, I would never have asked her. Thinking of my bank balance, I told him that one vehicle would have to do. Richard took this with ill grace.

"With one vehicle we're taking big risks. What happens if we have a breakdown? We'd be murdered within the hour." He looked very upset. "Listen, I don't advise it. I really don't. If we're taking only one vehicle we need to go in fast and get *out* fast." Richard explained through clenched teeth, the muscles in his cheeks working overtime: "They might just let you get near it, but they'd never let you get away alive. Have to be in and out before they realize you're there."

He told me of the scores of whites who had been killed in the Soutpansberg mountains over the previous few years.

"It's not like it was before in your day. Now, this country is the murder and rape capital of the world. You might like to know," he said pointing at my chest, "that these days they use white men's skins to make their drums. I understand and fully appreciate that you want to find the *ngoma* but I imagine you don't want to finish up on it—or in it." He gave me a sardonic smile.

317

"But it's not just that. The discovery of the *ngoma* could cause a war. It really could cause an actual *war*. Between Zimbabwe and South Africa or between tribal groupings. The Venda tribe want to get their hands on it just as much as the Lemba. A hell of a lot hangs on it. There are incredible commercial implications as well."

He told me that at the Mapungubwe site some ancient bones had been discovered that had been declared Lemba ancestral property. The Venetia diamond mine, which Reuven had visited a few years before, is adjacent to the Mapungubwe site. Increasingly in South Africa, so Richard explained, ancestral rights over territory had overwhelming significance. Many white-owned farms had been taken over by local blacks because ancestral burial sites were located on the farming land. The fear was that such rights could compromise the extraction of diamonds at Venetia and that was the reason the area had been declared Lemba territory, because it was known that the Lemba were from elsewhere and were unlikely to make a fuss. Nonetheless the bones that had been declared the bones of their ancestors were in a lab in the University of Pretoria and Lemba demands that they be reburied on Lemba land had fallen on deaf ears.

"All this means that Lemba sensibilities are heightened at the moment," said Richard. "For the first time, thanks in part to your putting them on the map, they have achieved a lot of political power. Now anything to do with their ancestral lands or ancestral artifacts is red hot. Anybody poking around in caves up there at the moment is likely to finish up dead."

Richard had brought all that was needed for the expedition. There was vodka from Finland, cognac from France, and

Bodington's beer from England. There was a mixed case of wine. There were soft drinks and water in an icebox. There were Russian sausages. There was biltong. Tons of it. There was good wholemeal bread. There were biscuits. There was a well-oiled ox-hide whip (for the snakes), and the biggest knife I have ever seen. There were piles of maps. There were compasses, cameras, and tape recorders. There were leather hats to keep the sun off. Blankets to keep off the cold. It was as if we were setting off on the Great Trek. But it was a well-organized ex-pedition—just the sort of thing Reuven would have approved of.

Just before arriving at Magdel's, Richard had been to the university library at UNISA—the University of South Africa—to photocopy some Ordnance Survey maps of the Soutpansberg, which had been prepared by the British during the Second World War. He checked through his maps and provisions and finally said that we were ready to roll.

On the long drive up north from Pretoria, Richard spoke about his passionate interest in the astronomical data found in archaeological sites throughout Africa. He was persuaded that the Lemba had once been master astronomers and that the key to the understanding of the intriguing stone-built sites in Zimbabwe and the border regions in the north was to be found in the stars. I listened attentively and took the occasional note. This was fascinating stuff. My spirits began to rise. I thought of the rugged hills of the Soutpansberg, their cliffs and their caverns. "Something lost behind the ranges. Lost and waiting for you. Go!"

We stayed at a small private hotel on the road between Louis Trichardt, now renamed Machado, and Messina. Over dinner, as the good South African wine started to loosen tongues, I tried to elicit some more precise information about his plans but Richard was reluctant to say anything about where the cave was or how exactly we would get there. He told me simply that he had got his information from an old Boer civil servant, Pieter van Heerden, who thirty years before had been the inspector of Bantu education for the Soutpansberg-Sibasa circuit.

Van Heerden had once been accompanied by a Venda priest to a cave high in the mountains and there had been shown the *ngoma*. Shortly before his death, van Heerden had told Richard about the cave sheltering the *ngoma* and how to get there. On his deathbed he had sworn that what he told him was the truth, the whole truth, and nothing but the truth.

Just before we turned in, he dropped a little bombshell. He said that we would need to get official permission before we could enter the area where the cave was.

"I've had tribal permission for years," I groaned. "From Mathivha and Moeti as well as the other elders. They formally asked me to look for the bloody thing. If we ask for tribal permission now, everyone will know what we're doing. I thought we had to get in fast and get out fast. Your words, Richard."

"That's not enough these days. You need official government permission to be doing research. You also need the permission of the king of Vendaland. Listen," said Richard petulantly, "I'm not going in without permission. I don't want to get killed. I've said I'll take you there and I will. We have a deal and I shall honor my part of it. But is has to be done properly and go through the correct channels."

My heart sank as I thought of the weeks of protracted haggling that could so easily occur if we went through official channels. This, after all, was Africa. But I could see Richard's point. He was working here, he was apparently a serious man, and he had to do things by the book.

"It may be possible to get permission within a day or so. Certainly within a week. The new Lemba men who are running the Lemba Cultural Association until replacements are found for Mathivha and Moeti are coming out to meet us at Dzata," he said. "They'll help us. I'm taking someone else along too, someone called Norbert Hahn."

When we got down to the hotel dining room the following morning, Hahn was waiting. He was kitted out in khaki shirt and shorts, wore a battered leather hat and stout boots. He had a serviceable knife stuck in his leather belt. He was unshaven, lean, and very tough looking. Hahn was a botanist and had worked in and around the Soutpansberg most of his life. From Richard's body language it was clear that he now expected Hahn to take control. Hahn asked Richard to go and check the vehicle. After finishing off a good Boer breakfast, we went out to the waiting 4x4, where Richard was checking his equipment and scrutinizing his Ordnance Survey maps.

We headed down the long hotel drive and swung north on the Great North Road until we reached the turn-off for Witvlag, which took us onto a dirt road flanked by acacias. There was still a handful of white farmers operating to the east of the highway, but most of them, Hahn said, had gone. Too many had been killed. They had to sell their farms for next to nothing. Nobody wanted to live up here anymore.

Once we got to the Nzhelele Valley, which figures promi-nently in the oral traditions of the Lemba as one of their first places of settlement when they arrived in South Africa from the north, there was no trace of white farming. There were small bleakly modernized African villages, concrete bottle shops, occasional dispensaries, and well-tended small farms. We arrived at Siloam where the first missionaries to be active in the area had settled. These German missionaries from the Berlin Mission arrived in 1872 and were among the first outside witnesses of the Lemba traditions and the traditions surrounding the *ngoma lungundu.*

From the Nzhelele valley we turned up toward the ruins of Dzata—the stone-built town where the Venda and Lemba had first settled in the region, which I had visited frequently in the past with Mathivha, who loved to come here to wander around the stone ruins built, he believed, by his ancestors.

Sure enough, a group of three Lemba, two of whom I knew, were waiting for us. Clapping their hands in the traditional welcome they murmured, "*Mushavi, Mushavi,*" shook my hand in the African way, and embraced me. We spoke of the old days before my first journey north, of my discovery of Senna; of Mathivha and Moeti, of the long-dead Lemba historian Phophi. Our first objective now was to get permission from the paramount king of Venda to visit the more remote areas of his kingdom.

"You must not say what it is we are looking for," I said. "I know that the Venda have been looking for the *ngoma* for a long time. A few years back, the old Venda king set about the task very seriously."

"He's dead," said Norbert. "And the new man doesn't know much about local traditions, history, or anything much else, although he could probably tell the difference between Johnny Walker and Jack Daniels."

We agreed to tell the king simply that we were planning to engage in what we would term, rather vaguely, cultural research.

As luck would have it, the young king was driving his blue Toyota out of the dusty royal compound as we turned in. He was just going off to buy a few bottles of whisky from the bottle shop down the road, but agreed he could attend to this later in the day. He suggested we follow him to the palace, which he used for this sort of official business. And there we could discuss our project, perhaps over a drink. He was an affable and portly young man in his twenties and he was clearly not very interested in our plans. He solemnly gave us *carte blanche* to do anything within his realm that was within the law of the land.

"Don't we need a research permit?" I asked.

"No," he said waving his hand. "Come and have your photograph taken with me."

For a few minutes we posed, one after the other, with the king sitting on his carved wooden elephant throne.

He had a slightly haunted look during the photo session, as if he were fearful that the flashing cameras could somehow do him harm. I learned afterward that his father had recently been poisoned and that his brother, who succeeded him and who had been reared to be king, had died in suspicious circumstances that everyone was convinced amounted to murder. The death of the previous incumbents had solved nothing: there were still a number of people who were after *his* throne. Once the flashes stopped he seemed to pull himself together and ambled out with us onto the steps of his palace, which looked like a modern British villa in a comfortable middle-class suburb. He offered us a drink, which we refused, and then waved us off. We headed for the hills.

Norbert was now totally in charge. Richard knew the name of the village we were bound for. Norbert knew where it was and how to get there. He knew the tracks and the hills better than anyone alive, said Richard. We drove up through fertile fields and orchards until the land grew sparse and forests and fields gave way to great rocky outcrops as we reached the highest points of the Soutpansberg. The scenery was majestic but it hardly made any impression on me. My thoughts were concentrated on what we might find: at last, I thought, I was nearing the end of my quest.

"They love their poison, do the Venda," said Norbert. "In the old days they used to use the sap from the Euphorbia bushes you see everywhere round here." He pointed out a tall clump of Euphorbia serving as a hedge alongside the track. "I believe the poison from the Euphorbia could explain some of the mystery surrounding the *ngoma lungundu.* In many accounts the *ngoma* makes a terrifying sound. Something louder and more fearsome than you can possibly imagine. According to the traditional accounts, when this happened the enemies of the *ngoma* would simply drop dead.

"I think what may have occurred is that the said enemies were invited to the *kraal* to have a drop or two of kaffir beer that had been carefully laced with a small quantity of Euphorbia sap. It's lethal stuff—the sap you get from it is one hundred times more of an irritant than the hottest chilli peppers on the face of the globe. They used to use it for making poisoned arrows. You eat it straight and it perforates your stomach. That would have meant death here. Anyone who drank even a small amount would have been pretty damned ill. When they heard the loud bang, that was it, their heart gave out."

"What caused the bang do you think?" I asked.

"It could be that they had traditional knowledge of low-grade explosives. They certainly had some kind of very primitive wooden guns before the white man got here. The simplest form of gunpowder is just a mixture of saltpeter crystals, added to brimstone and charcoal to create what's called black powder. From the sixteenth century the Portuguese would dig up saltpeter wherever they found it. It occurs naturally here all over the place. That kind of mixture would make quite a bang without doing much damage to the *ngoma*, if it was done right."

"So you think it could it operate as a firearm as well as a drum?" I asked.

"As long as there was an opening opposite the source of the explosion. The explosive will follow the line of least resistance. I've seen men stand behind a sheet of old plastic corrugated roofing material a foot or so from a couple of sticks of exploding dynamite, and nothing happened to them. Nothing at all. The force of the explosion will follow the line of least resistance. But it could be that they had to change the leather pretty often," he added, smiling.

Looking out of the window I recognized a stretch of track that I had walked along five years earlier and then I saw a village where I had once spent the night. From what I could recall this was on the way to Tshiendeulu, one of the most sacred areas in the whole of the Soutpansberg. The higher we rose, the less the imprint of modernity could be seen. All the huts were thatched, there were no concrete buildings at all, and no fences: the small fields of maize were carved out of the wild and forbidding slopes of the mountains and merged into them naturally.

A crowned eagle soared overhead. I felt a strange excitement. Was it possible that after all these years I was finally on the verge of finding the *ngoma*? I recalled the poem of the South African poet Guy Butler about the myth of the *ngoma*:

> The great king, Mwali, like the drum, was never seen,
> No one saw the king or the drum except the old high
>   priest,
> He Dzoma-la-Dzimu, he, the mouthpiece of God.
> The king's dwelling and the drum's dwelling were
>   guarded by plaited fences,
> Where snakes with a head at each end kept slithering
>   watch;
> Also by twelve lions, watchdogs of the king:
> Quiet, quiet, they were, only rousing to roar
> In praise of their lord when the drum beat,
> Drum of the dead, *ngoma lungundu*.

"Are there still lions out here?" I asked Norbert.

"Oh, yes. Toward the east you see lions often enough."

I thought to myself that the Ark had been associated with its guardian lions for thousands of years as the book of Ezekiel reveals.

After a bumpy ride for about half an hour, I realized that my memory had served me well. We were arriving at Tshiendeulu Mountain, famous in the lore of the Lemba and Venda peoples. I was getting increasingly excited. This was more or less the region in which I had imagined the *ngoma* to be hidden. It was one of the areas that both Mathivha and Moeti had frequently suggested as the most likely hiding places of the Ark. And both these men were reliable: Mathivha was by far the most outstanding Lemba of his generation, the spiritual head of the community and its most significant historian. Moeti was a trained anthropologist, politician, and second in importance only to Mathivha. Following their advice, I myself had walked along this very track. If Richard was right, and he professed to have quite incontrovertible evidence of the *ngoma*'s whereabouts, we were now approaching its hiding place.

Richard had been silent for most of the drive. When I glanced in his direction he seemed ill at ease and a little nervous. Hahn told us about the trees we passed, about the wildlife and the traditions of the people who lived here. He pointed out traces of ancient buildings, of stone-built terraces, of non-indigenous tree species that must have been brought up centuries before from the African coast. He knew every stick and stone of this wild and inhospitable region.

As we bumped along the track, Magdel spoke of the Venda traditions surrounding the *ngoma*. The Lemba and the Venda, she said, have somewhat different visions of its function. The Venda revered it essentially as the instrument of the ancestral spirits: it was thought to be the drum of the dead. For the Lemba it had a sanctity all of its own and was primarily the object that had brought them from Senna and from Israel centuries before. It was the object in their lives that symbolized God.

For both the Lemba and the Venda, the *ngoma* was called the Voice of the Great God—the voice of Mambo wa-Denga—the King of Heaven. According to the oral traditions of both tribes it was brought here to the Soutpansberg in times past by the Venda and the Lemba from fertile lands of lakes and groves much farther north.

It was the Lemba priests who carried it. It was the Lemba priests who cared for it, who ensured that it never touched the ground, who hung it up on a specially constructed platform every night, who carried it using the special carrying poles, who prevented the gaze of the uninitiated from ever falling on it. They communicated with God in the *ngoma* and the *ngoma* guided them through the wilderness.

The Lemba priests of the priestly Buba clan controlled the drum and controlled the magic. The Lemba priests were feared universally for their command of the magical gifts. But the king controlled the Lemba priests.

Once the *ngoma* had arrived in the place of the king, the only people to see it were the king and the high priest. The *ngoma* was protected behind plaited fences in the royal *kraal*. The Buba priests protected the periphery of the plaited fences. But it was only the high priest, the *dzomo-la-dzimu*—the mouthpiece of god—who was allowed in its presence. When the priests heard the sound of a trumpet they would gather before the royal *kraal* to see what news would be relayed through the mouthpiece of God. There was always a connection between the trumpet playing and the sound of the drum. The two always went together. When the *ngoma* would sound, all the people would fall flat on their faces saying, "Great king, ruler of heaven, light of the country."

Magdel had written a good deal about the traditions of the *ngoma* in her book and in a number of scholarly articles. Her scholarship was impressive. We all listened respectfully.

"If the *ngoma* was so important for the king, and the king was so intimately involved with it, how come the present-day king does not know where it is?" I asked.

"I have often asked the same question," said Magdel, smiling. "They always give the same answer, isn't it. The traditions have to do with a very distant past. Both the Lemba and the Venda say that the *ngoma* was the central point of the cult in the days before the white man arrived up here. Now it is a different situation. They always say that it is hidden or lost. The reply is always terribly vague, isn't it? Hidden or lost. The king does not know where it is. No one at all knows where it is."

"No one except Richard," I said.

We swung off the stony, rutted track into a small village situated in the shade of the towering peak of Tshiendeulu. This was the village from which Pieter van Heerden had set off with his Venda guide to see the cave where the *ngoma* was hidden some fifty years before. The village was protected by a plaited fence like the plaited, interlaced fence that protected the sacred enclosure of the *ngoma*—its tabernacle.

A dozen or so grass huts huddled around a central square where a couple of villagers were sitting in the shade of a spreading mushava tree. Norbert strode toward them. One of the men, he explained, was Netshiendeulu, the high priest of the Venda Mphephu clan and custodian of the sacred graves and the sacred drums of the Venda. Norbert soon explained our business. Pointing toward the peak of Tshiendeulu, he explained that the cave we could just make out in the distance, in a cleft of the cliff, was what we had come to see. Would there be any objection to our going up there to look at it?

The old man explained that this village had a quasi-autonomous status within the traditional structure of Venda society. The queen of his little village was independent of the king of Venda for many traditional matters. It was only the queen who could give the permission for us to go to the mountain and the queen was off visiting the king of Venda. We must have passed her along the road. In any event, the queen would never grant permission: the side of the mountain where the cave was situated was the burial place of the great king, a place holy to the Venda, holy to the village, holy to the land. There was no holier place than this in the whole Soutpansberg.

The king's name was Dambanyika, the first king of the Venda and Lemba peoples as they streamed in from the north, in their thousands, driving before them their cattle, goats, and the women they had captured on the way, following the priests, following the *ngoma*. Looking for their promised land.

One day Dambanyika was out hunting. He took with him his favorite dogs, Mutshena and Mawilpalile. That night the dogs returned whimpering to the village. The king was missing. Early the next day the dogs led the villagers to the cave at the base of Lwandali. They discovered that the mouth to the cave was filled with giant boulders that had tumbled from above while Dambanyika was inside. The men tried to remove the great pile of rocks but they could not. Through a crack in the rocks their king told them to desist. They should not trouble themselves attempting the impossible. He would die there in the cave. He was a man, a warrior, he was ready to die.

He commanded them to move away to another region. They would not be permitted to grow produce on the mountain, nor could they hunt here. They could not even gather honey. The place was to be taboo. The son of Mbwapenga, the distant ancestor of the old man, was told to remain and to look after the grave.

Magdel started speaking to Netshiendeulu in Afrikaans. She explained that we had no interest in trampling over the bones of their ancestors or desecrating the ancient burial places of the Venda kings. All we were interested in was the *ngoma lungundu*. After all, he, Netshiendeulu, was the high priest and custodian of the sacred *ngoma*.

The old man's face brightened.

"Oh, I can show you that, I think," he said, taking a Yale key out of his pocket. He led us to a large thatched hut thirty yards away from the tree. With his key he opened the wooden door and led us in. In the middle of the space stood a large drum. It was made of a soft, reddish wood and was colored with buffalo hide. It appeared to be about thirty years old.

"Wow! Hey! Just look at that!" said Richard looking at me with a proud grin on his face. "I told you it was here. I've earned my fee. We have found it! This is it. We can get the hell out now before the natives get restless."

"But Richard, this is a modern drum. I have seen dozens like it in Venda villages over the years," I began.

The old man said, "Yes, this is a *ngoma* of the Venda people. But this is not really the *ngoma lungundu*."

"Ah," I said. "Well where really *is* the *ngoma lungundu*?"

"That old sacred *ngoma*," he announced portentously, "is in another hut nearby. But for that hut I must have the permission of the queen to show you."

We filed out of the gloom of the hut into the bright, hot sunlight. Vultures and eagles were circling high above the village. Somewhere, I heard the sound of a cock crowing.

Lawrence, one of the new Lemba men, potentially a successor to the great Mathivha, whispered in my ear, "We must give the old man some food, and then we shall give the old man some drink. Then the old man will tell us what we want to know and because the old man has taken some drink no one will blame him. We never blame a man for his drunken actions. We only blame the beer."

Lawrence and I drove a mile down the track to buy some beer from a small bottle shop and some beef from a traditional butcher. The butcher cut off a few ribs from a carcass covered in flies in the corner of his hut. By the time we had got back, the women of the *kraal* had lit a fire and soon made a sort of beef stew that was served in the hut where we had seen the Venda drum. The women crawled into the hut, prostrate, slithering snakelike toward us on their bellies, their faces toward the floor, their hands raised to one side of their face, bearing aloft the steaming stew and the *sadza,* the maize porridge that is the staple of the region.

Richard brought out his white man's food: some Bodington's beer, some vodka, some Russian sausage, some good wholemeal bread, some biltong, lots of it, and we sat round the modern drum, on plastic chairs, in the cool of the hut, waiting for Netshiendeulu to change his mind and open the second hut. He took his time.

After an hour of desultory conversation, during which time Netshiendeulu drank more than his fair share of beer, we walked over to the car, which was parked in the shade of the *mushava* tree. But before we could get there, the guardian of the grave of Dambanyika pulled at my sleeve and darted behind a hut, his head bent, as he quickly led me and Magdel, who was following close behind, to the hut where the *ngoma* was hidden. He carefully opened the door, looking over his shoulder to see if he was being observed by anyone in the village. Inside there were two more drums. These were significantly older than the first one.

"Which one is the traditional *ngoma lungundu?*" asked Magdel.

He laughed. "These *ngomas* were made in the time of my father. They have always been in the village since I was a boy. They are very old and are used for all our sacred feasts. I was born about eighty years ago. We used these always for the great feasts throughout my life. But there is one that is much older, which we do not use. That one is very, very old. That one we have never used in my lifetime, although it has always been here."

I felt a stab of excitement as the old man pulled a piece of sackcloth from a shapeless object in the corner of the hut. He pointed at a dank pile of rotting wood on the damp earthen floor of the hut. It was dark brown, almost black. The wood was decomposing. It had lost its form. It was anyone's guess what it had once been. It was a rounded pile of rotten, soggy vegetable matter, oozing brown liquid, which had stained the earth around it.

"That is a *very* old *ngoma*," said the old man enthusiastically.

That much was evident. I looked at it again. A portion of it that was not entirely deliquescent was resting on a stone. *It was not allowed to touch the ground.*

"Is this the one?" I asked excitedly. "Is this the *ngoma lungundu?* Is this the magic drum that guided you from the north?"

I touched it and the damp, crumbling wood felt soft and slimy between my fingers. My heart was beating fast.

"No, this is not that old, old magic *ngoma*. That old magic one that the old men used to tell stories about. To know where that old, old *ngoma lungundu* is you must ask the priests of the Lemba. They are the one that carried the *ngoma* when we came together from the north. They are the ones who guard it to this very day. That magic drum you will find among the Lemba priests. They are keeping it, on their side. They are keeping it for us Venda people still now."

I thanked the old man, gave him a small gift, and made my way back to the car. Once again I had failed.

THE DUST OF
ITS HIDING PLACE

I drove down from the mountains with a heavy heart. Mathivha, Moeti, and many of the Lemba elders I had spoken to over the years had been sure that the sacred *ngoma* had been concealed in a cave somewhere in the craggy fast-nesses of the Soutpansberg. I had persuaded myself that they were right. Now I wasn't so sure. I had searched here for years with no luck. Richard's information had looked reliable and I had set great store by it. I had followed the leads I had come up against, and all I had discovered was a pile of rotting wood that in months would be indistinguishable from the rich red Venda earth from which no doubt it originally sprang. I felt I had been duped.

That evening I sat alone, in intense concentration, on the terrace at the Cloud's End Hotel with a pad and pencil and tried to get my thoughts in some order. The last time the authentic *ngoma lungundu* had been seen, as far as I knew for sure, was around 1949 when the German scholar missionary Harald von Sicard had described and photographed it. It was Mathivha who had provided me with this vital clue and subsequently I had come across a rare scholarly book written in German and published in Upsala in Sweden that actually included a black-and-white photograph of the *ngoma*. This much was hard fact.

In around 1949, according to the plate in von Sicard's book, the *ngoma* had been in the National Museum of Southern Rhodesia in Bulawayo, the second city of Rhodesia, and the capital of Matabeleland. This museum, which had been founded by Cecil Rhodes in 1901, had been called the Museum of Natural History since Zimbabwe's independence. I had visited the museum a number of times over the years and never found any trace of the *ngoma*.

In conversations with various Lemba elders I had frequently mentioned the presence in Bulawayo in 1949 of von Sicard's *ngoma*. Both Mathivha and Moeti, as well as others, were convinced that it had been removed long since.

"We know a lot of what happened," Mathivha had told me, "but not everything. Our own precious *ngoma* was hidden for a long time in the Mavhogwe grotto in the MaSenna Mountain near to the Limpopo River. An old Buba high priest was also buried in that cave. A white man called von Sicard took it away many, many years ago and for a while we lost track of it. Then we discovered that it had been placed in a, what d'you call, museum in Bulawayo. But it's no longer there. Our people up there took it away. They could not let the *ngoma* stay in that unholy place."

"The problem is," he lamented, "we do not know *where* they took it."

As far as Mathivha was concerned, the *ngoma* had left Bulawayo, had initially been hidden, he thought, in the Mposi chieftain-ship somewhere near Mberengwe, and had subsequently been smuggled across the border into South Africa by Buba priests.

"We have many Lemba in Bulawayo," boasted Mathivha. "Some of them are important men, like the Lemba everywhere. We *are* the Jews of southern Africa. We *know* how to do things. We have people everywhere in Zimbabwe, in the police, in Zanu PF, in the administration, in the museums. There is *nowhere* we do not have our people. The Good Men are there, spread among the communities, scattered among the nations. Those people did what they had to do to. They took it to a safe place, a holy place. They are guarding that Ark."

Mathivha was convinced, so he had told me, that when I first tried to locate the *ngoma* in the cave at the base of Dumghe Mountain, so many years before, it had been there. That is what he had been told. Subsequently it had been taken away.

"Of course, they knew you went to the cave. Even late that night, late that night when the others were, how d'you call, dancing, and drinking, and waiting for that rain to come, there was always someone *there*. The guardian of Dumghe never *sleeps*. He is always there, watching *out*. They stopped you going there in a kindly way. They might have done it differently. But the *ngoma* was there, all right. You were not far away."

When he first told me that, my heart sank: a moment's cowardice on my part had compromised years of work.

I knew that Mathivha strongly disapproved of my attempt to enter the cave. I had breached the codes. I had gone to a place where the uncircumcised should not go. He agreed that, on the one hand, I had undoubtedly had his authorization to search for the *ngoma*. And he, Mathivha, as the president of the Lemba Cultural Association, was the paramount figure in the tribe at least as far as South Africa went. But, on the other hand, his spiritual, moral, and cultural authority did not fully extend to Zimbabwe and he frequently muttered that I should have had the permission of Chief Mposi before attempting to enter the cave.

Smiling in his most avuncular way he argued that they might have made some special concession or they might have wished to purify me in some way. They might have undressed me and pulled my naked body backward through a hole carved out of a giant anthill in the traditional Lemba ceremony of purification. According to one of the explanations of this arcane ritual, this was to allow the ants to suck out the impure blood of the novitiate. Perhaps they would have circumcised me with the ritually pure knife that every Lemba youth received after circumcision and guards preciously throughout his life.

"Without that ritual purification they would have been in their, what d'you call, their rights to kill you for going on their holy place," he said gravely. "That is the law."

In reality, Mathivha must have known full well that the chief would never have authorized it. The *only* way to go there was secretly. At some level, if he really wanted me to find the *ngoma,* and this was not entirely an assumption I could make, a covert attempt on my part *must* have been what he desired. But was it *true* that the *ngoma* had been there? Was it *true* that it had subsequently been moved? If it was not true, why did he sell me this tale?

That the *ngoma* had once been in the Dumghe area tallies with most scholarly opinion. In 1953 a South African scholar, Moller Malan, recorded the Lemba tradition that it had once been on a mountain somewhere in the north. The Lemba historian

Phophi had told me the same thing. So had Mathivha. In times past the *ngoma* had been there, north of the Limpopo, probably somewhere near Mberengwe, perhaps on Dumghe. Much of the folklore and legends about the *ngoma* is situated in these areas—not far from the mysterious great Zimbabwe ruins.

Mathivha always told me that the sources of his information about the *ngoma,* about the Ark, were very old custodians of the tradition who themselves got it from unnamed members of his own Buba clan, the priests who guarded the *ngoma.* The priests were the only ones who really knew where it was.

"Those old priests," he would say dreamily, "whose forefathers brought us here from Senna, bearing the Ark."

"So it's not lost!" I exclaimed. "They *know* where it is. They are keeping it for the right time. They brought it down here to South Africa from Mberengwe."

"That is right. That *is* right. The Buba brought it down here. No one else would *dare* touch that *ngoma.* Only those Buba priests."

"But where are the Buba priests and what have the priests *done* with it?" I would ask.

"The priests are everywhere. They stay in their own places on their own side. They are keeping it in their *places.* I do not know where. It is hidden until it might be needed. It is out there in the mountains, far, far away. Or in some other place. They have put it in a safe place, where no harm can possibly come to it, and when the right time comes it will be revealed. When the right time comes it will be brought *out.* I do not know *where* it is. But when it is finally revealed there will be singing and *dancing.* The whole people will *celebrate.* The whole *world* will celebrate because they will then see the Lemba as the, what d'you call, the guardians of the Ark, the keepers of the most ancient tradition. The Ark will ring out. It will *shout* out. 'God has gone up with a shout, the Lord with the sound of a trumpet.' The Ark will usher in our redemption and the redemption of Israel."

"But do you still want *me* to find it?" I would ask. "Do I have any chances of finding it?"

"You found Senna. You *will* find the *ngoma,*" he would smile at me in his confident, avuncular way. "If not, the *ngoma* will come to *you*. The Ark will find *you!* That is what we believe. That is what I have been told by the elders, by the old, old men."

These conversations would always end here. It was frustrating. Perhaps he knew more than he was telling me. Perhaps he did not. I had no way of knowing. Perhaps he was deliberately misleading me. Perhaps he had instructions from the Lemba elders to keep me away from the *ngoma* at all costs. I thought back to the day of the armed ambush years before. Were they trying to tell me something? Was this an unsubtle hint? How could I know?

When, so many years before, Sevias had explained that the *ngoma* was lost and had whispered in my ear the rumors he had heard about its possible hiding place on Dumghe, I had believed him. But more and more I felt that the rumors were just that. Rumors, with nothing to substantiate them. The *ngoma*, the Ark, was lost. That was all there was to say on the subject.

One evening as I sat in my room, I jotted down all the likely clues I had amassed over the years, giving a page to each item.

It seemed to me when I had written my last entry, piled the sheets in a neat pile, and closed my eyes wearily, that the most significant evidence was probably that relating to the Mavhogwe cave in the Limpopo valley. This was the only firm point in the morass of rumors, hints, and evasions: in about 1949 Harald von Sicard, the greatest authority on the traditions surrounding the *ngoma*, a man who had spent much of his life living among the tribe and studying their lore, had written that it was in a museum in Bulawayo and he had photographed it. Harald von Sicard was the white man who had found the *ngoma* in the Mavhogwe grotto in the MaSenna Mountain near the Limpopo. The black-and-white photograph of the *ngoma* was in his book. I had seen it. I owned it.

However, the *ngoma* was no longer in the museum. These two facts appeared to be solid ground on which to proceed.

A somewhat less firm base around which to orient my thoughts was the stated opinion of Mathivha, Moeti, and the other elders that the *ngoma* had been taken from the Bulawayo museum by the Lemba themselves, in undisclosed circumstances, at an undisclosed time, and that it had been first hidden in or around Mberengwe, perhaps in the cave at the base of Dumghe and subsequently removed to the Soutpansberg mountains.

Most of the Lemba elders I spoke to said that this or something close to this was what had happened, but no one had any very precise information about the details or the date of its removal from the museum. No one had any idea of the precise identity of the Buba priests who allegedly removed it.

When I had discussed this on the telephone with Reuven he had shrugged and said, "Sounds like a *frommer wunsch* to me—a pious wish. They need it to be guarded by their priests and they would love it to be guarded by their priests so they believe it *is* being guarded by their priests. It's like the people in Jerusalem who would like the Ark to be in the Temple and still believe *beemunah shelemah*—in perfect faith—that it *is* hidden somewhere beneath the Temple Mount. Belief and fact, sadly, are two different things."

To try to find out something of the circumstances of the *ngoma's* initial removal from the museum, I had visited Bulawayo on a number of occasions over the years, hoping to find more information about its provenance and discovery, some trace of its presence, or some information about its departure but the staff knew nothing about it. There was no written record of it having been brought there or taken away. They had no information about the *ngoma* but were quite sure there was nothing in their museum that resembled the photograph in Harald von Sicard's obscure, scholarly book.

On one occasion back in 1999, helpful curators had searched the museum and the storerooms from top to bottom. There was nothing on display in the museum itself and there was nothing resembling the *ngoma* in the storerooms. There was no trace of it.

The last sure sighting of the *ngoma* had been in 1949, some sixty years before. As far as I could ascertain, that was the end of the trail. Richard's well-organized expedition had revealed no more than any of my previous attempts. I was back where I started.

I stayed on for a few days in the Soutpansberg, taking gentle walks in the hills and reliving the exciting times I had had there over the previous decade.

One evening, exhausted, I went into the bar where I had had my last, sad meeting with Reuven. To revive my flagging spirits, I drank a couple of large Laphroaigs on the terrace and then another, and was just about to go to have some dinner when an old man entered the bar behind me, ordered a beer, and came out onto the terrace. Sinking into a chair he raised his glass and muttered *lechyd da*—"good health," in Welsh, the language of my forebears. "Ah—a fellow Welshman!" I said, raising my glass.

David Jones was a former Rhodesian, born and brought up in Wales. He had a mop of white hair and piercing blue eyes. For some forty years he had worked for Rhodesian Railways and in the 1980s had emigrated to South Africa, like many Rhodesian whites. He was now in desperate financial straits. He was owed a pension from Zimbabwe Railways but had not received a penny for fifteen years. He had been to Harare to try to recover something of his railway pension. The black officials he had spoken to just laughed in his face.

I have sometimes been lucky in bars. After a few drinks people open up and reveal things about their life that they hardly know themselves. The Welshman spoke of his bitterness, of his sense of a wasted and frustrated life, of the mistakes he had made, the lost opportunities. He longed to return to Wales and dreamed of the mists and the unique smells of the hills in the early morning.

"You see, mun, Africa is all very well and good, but it's not home. It's Wales I dream of at night. But I'll never afford the flight back now. Anyhow, I've nobody there. They're all gone. Dead, you see. As my mother used to say, 'It's not the cough that carries you off, it's the coffin they carry you off in.'"

I went back into the bar to get us both a drink. When I got back he had cheered up a bit and started telling me about his great love, the passion of his life: the Rhodesian rail network. In his day Bulawayo was the hub of a great rail system—an early link in Cecil Rhodes's vision of a railway line from the Cape to Cairo that would traverse only British territory.

The first line to be built, he told me, had been from Beira, on the Mozambique coast, to Mutare, in eastern Rhodesia. This was begun in 1892 only a few months after Mashonaland had been declared a British protectorate. The line from Cape Province to Bulawayo was completed in 1897 and the link to the capital, Salisbury, was finished in 1902 after initial attempts to build it had been delayed by the outbreak of the Anglo-Boer War in 1899. The old man knew his history. He told me about routes and timetables and gauges and the wild excitement of driving a steam train at night through the moonlit bush. During the black liberation struggle of the 1970s he had driven armor-plated trains from Bulawayo to Salisbury on a regular basis.

"Exciting times," he said. "You never knew when the line would be mined, you see, or when some tree or metal girder had been pulled over the track to derail the engine so the black bastards could cut your throat."

I drank another whisky, then another, and was starting to feel agreeably melancholy. I knew I was drunk but I could see with great clarity that Davie and I had much in common. We had both had great passions and we had both been cheated by life. I bought my new friend and compatriot another drink, put my feet up on the table, and asked the barman to bring the bottle of Laphroaig a little closer, so I could help myself as the need arose, as, I suspected, it soon would. For some reason I thought of the mukhtar of Senna. Perhaps it was preordained that I would never find the Ark. Perhaps I had the wrong guidance, as he had hinted. After all, he had said, "The only guidance is the guidance of Allah." This thought put me in mind of the great Welsh hymn "Cym Rhondda," which I started to sing, quietly at first but with greater conviction as my sense of frustration took over. "Guide me, O thou great Jehovah, pilgrim in this barren land. I am weak but Thou art mighty, hold me with Thy power-ful hand. Bread of heaven, bread of heaven, feed me till I want no more …"

Quite drunk now, I told Dave about Maria and how I missed her, of her passion for me and my passion for her, how she made love like no other woman in the world. I told him how difficult it is to discern the rustle of history's wings and how she had left with no warning when I least expected it. I told him about the Ark, about the *ngoma,* guarded by its twelve lions. I told him about Reuven, about his desire to bring peace to the world, how he had given me every opportunity to undertake his sacred mission properly and how I had mucked it all up. I told him about the brilliant, scholarly, crazed Daud, who had brought so much to the chase, and about the Mossad and its involvement.

I told him that I had been following a will o' the wisp for twenty years.

"You've heard of the will o' the wisp? They were strange lights that led people all over England and Wales from the well-trodden paths into marshes and quagmires. And that's where I am now: I'm in a quagmire, a bloody quagmire. You see Dave," I said, "it's all been a bloody waste of time. That's how I see it now. This *ngoma* was definitely in bloody Bulawayo in 1949 and then it bloody well disappeared. Can you imagine anything disappearing, just *disappearing*, from the bloody British Museum? Something as important, as world shatteringly important, as that. What a bloody useless bloody country."

I reached out unsteadily for my glass.

"Not bloody fair, mun," he said snorting over the rim of his tankard. "You see, there was this little local war we had. Things started to fall apart during the war. Anyway, we did our best, even for the blacks' museums. You see, I never did understand it. The old colonial regime always put a preponderant value on all that African stuff. I can't think why."

He paused and gazed morosely into the bottom of an empty glass. I called for another beer and filled my own glass up to the brim.

"Couple of times, you see, we had loads of junk from Bulawayo piled into the guard's van. Some private collections and some museum stuff. Piles and piles of it going back to the time of Rhodes, I shouldn't wonder. They were protecting the blacks' heritage, you see. Protecting it from the blacks themselves. *They'd* have burned and pillaged anything they got their bloody hands on. To be truthful, mun, there was no history before Rhodes got here, you see. There was just savagery. Unchristian *savagery*. Up here, real history only started with the railways. If you want to see *real* history you should go to the Railway Museum in Bulawayo. That's my museum. That's my life."

He took a sip at his beer and looked down toward the Great North Road, which led up through the Soutpansberg to his adopted country.

There was a longish pause. My head was spinning and I was having some difficulty focusing. Great difficulty focusing. I was also trying to remember what the agreeable old Welshman had just said. There seemed to be something there that resonated rather oddly through the alcohol, something that could perhaps prove to be rather important.

If the Smith regime had arranged for the heritage stuff in the museum to be removed, that meant it was probably taken to Salisbury, capital of Southern Rhodesia, whose name was later changed to Harare. "Did you just say that you took museum artifacts from Bulawayo to Salisbury? Is that what you said? Or did I imagine it?"

I sipped at the Laphroaig to clear my head.

"Yes, that's it. I distinctly remember taking museum stuff up to Salisbury. A mate of mine nicked a giant mask. Gave it to his missus for Christmas. It would have been about 1977. No, I tell a lie, Christmas 1976."

Somehow I missed dinner that night and woke up the following morning only because of the clatter made by monkeys scampering on the corrugated iron roof of the bungalow where I was staying. But something had happened overnight. When I checked my cell phone I saw that I had received a text message from Maria. It was just one word—"Bebé." It was the first word I had had from her in almost a year. I took a long reflective shower and went for a brisk walk along one of the forest paths behind the hotel. As I walked, Dave's potentially critical piece of information flooded back and with some difficulty I put Maria out of my mind.

I had a few days before I needed to get back to London. Maybe I could try one last thing. I put a call through to the

Bulawayo Museum. With what seemed to me unnecessary crispness I was told by a fresh-voiced and articulate young woman curator that there was absolutely no chance at all that the object I was looking for was in her museum.

"Where it is now I don't know but I'm quite sure it's not here because a number of people have asked me over the last few years. It seems a lot of people are looking for it. We've had a good look, but it's not here."

"Let me just ask you a question. If artifacts from your museum had been taken from Bulawayo to Salisbury, I mean Harare, during the liberation struggle, where do you think they would have gone?"

"A lot of state possessions fell into private hands during the struggle. What I mean by this is that they were stolen. They were then smuggled out of the country. But if the people removing the objects had played it by the book probably they would have gone to the ethnographic section of the Victoria Museum in Salisbury, the old Rhodesian capital, or perhaps to one of the regional museums—perhaps in Mutare or Gweru. But I have nothing here to indicate that this *did* happen. There is no record here. You could talk to Everisto Mangwiro in Harare. Maybe he can help." She gave me a number and hung up.

A few minutes later, I telephoned Mangwiro, gave him a brief description of what it was I was looking for, and then booked a flight for the following day from Johannesburg to Harare, the capital of Zimbabwe. I thought of driving, but I was told by the old railway man over a truly splendid breakfast that my chances of finding petrol up in Zimbabwe were nil.

* * *

Moses slid a gin and tonic across the polished surface of the counter. There was no one in the bar except Moses, the barman, and me. On the wall behind the bar was an old framed photograph of the early days of white settlement in what is today Harare. A group of white men recently arrived from South Africa were standing in front of a more or less European-looking hut. They looked proud of the place. It was a corrugated iron building with a wide veranda set in the midst of the as yet untamed bush of Mashonaland.

The photograph was taken in 1893 and the men standing in stiff Victorian attitudes on the veranda were the founder members of the Salisbury Club, which had once been the throbbing hub of the political, commercial, and social life of white Rhodesia. Renamed the Harare Club in 1980, it is still today in the same location as it was in 1893, although a bustling metropo-lis has grown up around it. It is situated at the corner of Third Street and Nelson Mandela Avenue, just opposite the parliament building. The Club showed signs of wear and tear and lack of maintenance. Electrical blackouts were a daily inconvenience and the water supply was erratic.

I dined alone in a colonial dining room where silver table-ware and competition cups from long-forgotten athletic and equestrian events gleamed in their varnished wooden cabinets. I was handed a printed menu but there was not much choice: I ordered pickled fish, some perch, and a bottle of white Zimbabwean wine. I had no real idea what this feast was going to cost me. But I was worried about it.

According to Moses, my drink before dinner cost about $30 at the official rate of exchange; the dinner was going to be close to $350. The black market rate was sixty times better for me than the official rate. Inflation was running at about 1700 percent per annum. But the glazed-eyed touts who crowded around me every time I put my nose outside the Club were just as likely to be police informers or muggers as honest black-market currency cheats. I had not yet figured out how much the entirely average little bedroom in the Club was going to cost—anyway, far, far more than I had ever paid for a hotel room in my life.

Harare was overcast outside; there was a faint smell of jacaranda trees mingled with smoke drifting in from the southern suburbs, and a menacing atmosphere. Hundreds of hungry people were wandering around, some of them pausing to gaze into the Mercedes concession showroom that stood next door to the Club and in whose windows were gleaming top-range vehicles that even Reuven would not have sneered at.

I was advised by the receptionist to stay in the Club until the following day. The muggings and stabbings were so frequent that walking around at night in the center of Harare was asking for trouble. I went to bed and slept fitfully. At some time in the night church bells from the neighboring Anglican cathedral of St. Mary and All Saints started to chime. Then drum beats followed: a big, resonant drum somewhere near the center, not far away.

The drum continued throughout the night. The antiphonal relationship between the drum and the bells interrupted occasionally by what sounded like gunshots filled my sleep like the repetitive nightmare you get when you have the flu. By the time I got up, the drum had finally lost the battle and had given way to the cathedral bells.

The first thing I did was to telephone Everisto Mangwire, the subcurator at the Harare museum whose number I had got from the young woman curator in Bulawayo. He told me that he would be spending most of the day in his Pentecostalist church, with his family, but agreed to come over to the Club later in the afternoon.

After the usual African white man's breakfast of bacon, beef sausages, eggs, and grilled tomatoes, I wondered what to do with myself. I decided to fill in some of the time before Everisto arrived by walking through the gardens of the Square of African Unity, under the jacaranda trees, to the cathedral.

From the outside, it could have been an Anglican church in any British suburb. Not particularly beautiful but not too plain, either. As I went in, I realized in one respect it was different from any Anglican church I had ever attended on an ordinary Sunday: it was full. Everyone except for me was black.

The church service was similar to an Anglican service anywhere. However, the music was radically different. There was no organ music; instead, there were hand-held rattles and two potent drums. The music was explosive.

Two things struck me: the sermon was about the limits of freedom. Absolute freedom meant absolute anarchy. Real freedom meant submission. The day before had been Mugabe's birthday. It had been marked by the banning of peaceful political protests on the part of the opposition following some unrest in the southern suburbs of Harare. The Anglican bishop, Norbert Kunonga, who had been given two splendid, previously white-owned farms to do so, was banging President Mugabe's drum. The drums sounding in the great nave of the church were beating out the tune of oppression. It was difficult, looking at the faces around me, to know whether the congregation was ready to be deceived into believing that corruption and institutionalized abuse were consistent with the message of Christ.

It was the first Sunday in Lent 2007. In the early months of this year, people throughout Zimbabwe were dying slowly of starvation. The World Health Organization had just announced that Zimbabwe, once the breadbasket of Africa, was now the country with the highest mortality rate in the world. The Lenten prayer was advocating to the hungry congregation, many members of which were undoubtedly close to death from unnecessary hunger, that in imitation of Christ's fast they would be well advised not to eat too much over Lent.

I dropped into the Club bar after church and chatted for a few moments with a black rugby-playing arms dealer. I asked him about Bishop Norbert Kunonga.

"He's longing to join this club," he said gleefully. "So is Mugabe. But they're blackballed. Both of them. Won't let them in. They are both criminals."

"Arms dealing must be close to criminal."

"Yes, in a way. You have to cheat to prosper. It's all to do with getting convincing-looking end-certificates. But the truth is that Africa has been a dumping ground for arms for the last three centuries. As soon as stuff became obsolete in Europe it was dumped in Africa. I read a paper about arms dealing here in the nineteenth century—long before the whites got to Salisbury. There were millions of caps imported into Zanzibar, hundreds of thousands of muzzle-loading muskets, tons of gunpowder. Africa has been swimming in the stuff for centuries. I am just carrying on a long and proud tradition!"

THE DUST OF ITS HIDING PLACE

"How about local independent production of firearms?" I asked.

"Yeah. I heard that people here had some kind of wooden guns, very hard wood, and very low-grade gunpowder. They'd have made a helluva noise. But they would never have been half so dangerous as an assegai wielded by someone who knew how to use it."

At four o'clock, reception telephoned to say that my guest had arrived. Everisto was a modest-looking man of medium height, with a shaved skull and ears very close to his head. During the liberation struggle he had been a child and on one occasion had been hit by a stray bullet. He would occasionally rub the thigh where he had been struck.

He now told me, as we sat in the Club lobby, that on the previous Friday he had had a look around the storerooms but had found nothing that really matched my description. There was only one very old, very battered object he had located that had the remains of four wooden rings for carrying poles, although they were broken and only just visible. The object was made of a very, very hard wood.

He thought it was some African hardwood such as acacia.

"The weevil could not eat that wood," he said. "No weevils could even get their fangs into it. But they would not be able to eat it, anyway. Everything in our museum storerooms is sprayed with chemicals. But with this old thing it was not necessary to spray it. No weevil on the face of the earth could ever bite into that wood, not until Jesus comes again."

He smiled at me and added: "Halleluiah!"

* * *

353

Everisto confirmed that there were some things in the store-room that many years before, during the independence strug-gle, had been brought from outlying museums.

"Maybe they did catalogue those old things but probably in the confusion of the war the paperwork was lost or destroyed."

I took von Sicard's book from my briefcase and showed him the photograph.

"Is this the thing you found?"

Everisto looked at it for a long time, holding the black-and-white plate up to the light and then replacing the book on the table of the lobby. After a longish pause he concluded that he could not tell. He was not sure. What he had found was not in good condition and he had not been able to take it out of the storeroom to look at it. The light was not good and the object he had seen was kept on the bottom shelf along with a lot of old, broken objects of uncertain provenance. He had not taken it off the shelf; in order to see it properly he would have had to remove it from the storeroom. This would need special permis-sion from the museum director, Mr. Joseph Muringaniza.

"Mr. Muringaniza is a good man, a fair man. If you have proper credentials he will not hold back with that permission," he said. All he could say about the object he had seen was that it was extremely old, broken in parts, very heavy, and very dense. He would have liked to photograph it but the museum did not have a camera.

He rubbed his hands together nervously and then caressed his thigh.

"You've come a long way to see this object," he said. "I do hope, man, that you will not be too disappointed. How much did that ticket cost from Johannesburg?"

I told him.

He whistled. "That's six months' salary." He paused, calculating. "No, even more. What will happen if this thing is not what you are looking for? Will you have to pay the research money back to your university?"

"No. Don't worry. Even if it's not what I hope it is, at least I shall know that the *ngoma* is not in the Museum of Human Sciences in Harare. It must therefore be somewhere else. It would be a negative result, but at least it would be a result. It will still be pushing forward the frontiers of knowledge," I said smiling.

Everisto smiled apprehensively and told me that he would come and pick me up the following morning.

At eight o'clock, Everisto turned up at the Club. We took a taxi out along Nelson Mandela Avenue to the Museum of Human Sciences, which had started life as the Queen Victoria Museum. In the lobby of the rather attractive modern museum bathed in bright morning sunlight there was a long queue of people waiting at the ticket booth.

"Popular place," I said to Everisto.

"No," he replied, "these are not visitors to the museum; they are workers queuing up in the hope of being paid. They've not been paid for a long time. Neither have we. If *they* get paid today there's some hope that the curators will get paid too."

He led me up to an office on the second floor where the director's secretary, Blessing, told me the director would be able to see me shortly.

My hands felt clammy and my heart was pounding in my chest.

After what seemed like ages, Blessing showed me into the director's office. Mr. Joseph Muringaniza, the museum director, received me uncertainly. He seemed astonished to have a visitor from overseas. He explained why. Very few foreign visitors ever came to his museum; what was more, very few foreign visitors ever came to Zimbabwe. If they did, they were flown straight into Victoria Falls or to one of the game parks. There were only 20,000 whites left in the country and, outside the white suburbs, a white face increasingly was becoming a rarity. He could not remember the last time the museum had received an overseas visitor.

I explained why I had come. I was hopeful that an object that had once been in the Bulawayo Museum might have been brought up to the Victoria Museum in Salisbury during the liberation struggle.

"It's quite possible," he said. "They were difficult times, terrible times, and particularly down there in Bulawayo. A lot of things were brought here for safekeeping but after independence, many things, most things, I think, were taken back to the western part of the country, to Matabeleland. There's no great desire to keep objects from Matabeleland up here. The present regime is really interested only in Shona things. Tribalism, I'm afraid."

He explained that objects not on display in the exhibition halls of the Museum of Human Sciences were kept in storerooms and the storeroom for ethnographic materials was not far from his office.

The corruption of Zimbabwean officialdom has become legendary. There was nothing corrupt about Joseph Muringaniza. He was a tall, gentle man and integrity shone from him. Years before, he had taken a degree at Cambridge in heritage management. The way he talked about those days as a student in England you could see that these were his most precious memories. Now his life was much different. Even teachers could not afford the bus fare into work, he told me. Getting petrol for a car was a daily problem. The buses did not work. The price of foodstuffs was sky high. Starvation, he explained, was not in Harare yet, although there were parts of the country where people were indeed starving to death.

A tray containing a pot of tea and some cups was brought into his office by Blessing.

"Sorry, we have no biscuits," he said, passing me a cup of tea.

He talked about Cambridge and the rigors of its tutorial system for a while, and then he sighed.

"You did not come here to hear me reminisce about my student days," he said with a shy smile. "What precisely can I help you with?"

"I'll try to explain. It's a strange story. Almost sixty years ago a drumlike object called the *ngoma lungundu* was photographed in the National Museum of Southern Rhodesia in Bulawayo. The photograph appeared in a scholarly book written in German, which was published in Upsala in Sweden. Sometime between about 1949 and a few years ago, when I first enquired at the museum and Bulawayo, the *ngoma* disappeared. I am trying to find it."

I showed Joseph the photograph that had appeared in von Sicard's book.

"I have no idea what we have in the store," he said, "but you have my authority to root around as much as you like."

He asked his secretary to call in the head of the ethnographic division of the museum, Mr. Ferai Chabata.

Chabata entered the room with a broad smile. He was carrying a small key.

"We have a dual key system for the storeroom," explained Joseph.

"Ferai has one key, I carry the other. There are no copies. So we both have to be present when the storeroom is opened."

We marched down a bleak institutional corridor to the storeroom. Everistos's office was a glassed-in space between the storeroom and a wide corridor with offices on both sides. In effect, Everisto was the guardian of the storeroom. I was asked to sign a visitors' book. Joseph turned his key in one of the two locks. Ferai did likewise. Gravely, the cheap, flimsy door, set on cheap, flimsy hinges, was pushed open to reveal a treasure house of African artifacts. Everisto and Ferai led the way in and I turned to Joseph to ask if I could accompany them. He waved me in with an expansive gesture and said that if I required further help he would be in his office.

I stepped into the shabby, poorly lit store and paused for a moment for my eyes to adapt to the dim light. I could see that there were stacks of shelves on both sides of a central aisle. The second aisle on the right was reserved for old wooden drums. They were stacked up on metal shelving from floor to ceiling.

Everisto turned and peered into this narrow corridor, slowly edging his way down between the shelving. He looked ill at ease and kept touching his wounded thigh. Toward the end of the drum section he crouched down, turning his head toward me. "This is the thing I was talking about yesterday," he said with a self-deprecating shrug, tugging at a very dusty, very shabby piece of wood to the front of the lowest metal shelf. As he did so, a family of mice, disturbed by the unusual activity, scurried across the concrete floor.

I moved along the aisle and positioned myself behind him. In the dim light it was impossible to see *what* it was. It was simply a dust-encrusted wooden object that looked like nothing on earth. Ferai squeezed past me and crouched down next to his colleague. Together they managed to pull it out and, bearing it between them, carried it out into the light. They placed it on Everisto's desk among his papers and family photographs.

Ferai examined a small cardboard label attached by a piece of wire to the artifact and wrote something into a notebook. Crossing to the other side of the small office, he pulled down a registration book. Flicking through the pages he stopped at the entry Q.V.M. 5218. He explained that Q.V.M stood for the Queen Victoria Museum and that this would date the artifact's arrival to the pre-Independence period, before the museum was renamed. From there he moved to a card catalogue from which he triumphantly produced a subject card. The text read:

Q.V.M. 5218
Name of object: drum.
Material: wood.
Surface decoration
Base only

Ferai wrung his hands in disappointment.

"I am so sorry, man," he said. "It tells us nothing. It says nothing of its provenance, nothing of when it was found, nothing of where it was found."

I turned around and looked back at the object that was now lit by a shaft of sunlight coming through the grimy office window. Everything in the room suddenly took on a hard-edged radiance. A strange sanctity seemed to shine from it. Ferai went over and rubbed off the surface dirt and grime with a black cloth.

"Hey, man," he said, giving me a consolatory African hand-shake. "It's too bad. All this tells us nothing."

I swiveled the *ngoma* around on the desk and aligned it in such a way that what I was looking at was the part of the object shown in the photograph in von Sicard's book. I felt a shiver go down my spine. Without the slightest doubt this was the von Sicard *ngoma*.

I took out the book from my briefcase and showed it to the two young curators. They smiled broadly and nodded in agreement. I looked at it carefully. There was a blackened hole in the bottom of the *ngoma*. If it had been used as a kind of noisy cannon it would have needed a hole of this sort. Half of one side was missing and there were deep and widespread black burn marks along what was left of the rim on the farthest side. It looked like it had been partially consumed in some conflagration. It looked incredibly old. *There went out fire from the Lord.* It was a weapon of mass destruction that had been through the wars. I pressed my nail into the wood on the good side. It was as hard as iron.

The *ngoma* was not covered in sheets of fine gold. There were the shattered remnants of rings on each corner, through which carrying poles would once have been thrust. There is no better description of the object that stood before me on Everistos's cluttered desk than that in the biblical passage from the book of Exodus:

an Ark of shittim wood: two cubits and a half shall be the length thereof
and a cubit and a half the breadth thereof, and a cubit and a half the
height thereof ...

And was this the Ark?

Like the Ark, all the legends represent the *ngoma* as something the tribe had experienced with fear and awe, as the very voice and essence of God.

Like the Ark, it was the dwelling place of God.

Like the Ark, it was never allowed to touch the ground.

Like the Ark, it was associated with trumpets.

Like the Ark, it was connected with death, fire, smoke, and noise.

Like the Ark, it was a lethal weapon of mass destruction.

Like the Ark, it was looked after by priests—by *cohanim* descended from Aaron and Moses.

Like the Ark, Lemba tradition maintained that it had come from Israel.

It was about the same size as the Ark.

Like the Ark, it was carried on poles.

Like the Ark, it was made of very hard wood.

Like the Ark there had been magic things secreted inside it.

It was a drum. And I now knew that the Ark/*ephod* had also been a drum.

I had established that the *ngoma* had come from Senna in Arabia. And there was a mass of legendary material that associated this same area with the Ark.

It was crumbling in places, very badly damaged, and very badly burnt on one side. Was this the original *ngoma* that had led the people from Senna and from Israel, or was it the son of the burnt *ngoma* that had destroyed itself hundreds of years before? I thought of the evening in Jerusalem when Reuven had prophesied that the Ark would be crushed and destroyed— but restored in the fullness of the redemption. My eyes had not left it. Despite Ferai's efforts to clean it, the *ngoma* was still thick with dust. As he rubbed the upper side of the *ngoma*, a carved relief became visible. I approached and peered closely at the carved frieze. *It was the interlaced pattern the book of Exodus had described around the ephod.*

> *Around it there will be an interlaced pattern, around the hole, like the hole of a tahrah.*

I felt a choking sensation that might, I suppose, have been explained by the chemical-impregnated particles that floated in the rays of the sun shining in through the office window. The light and dust gave a fleeting impression that the *ngoma* was somehow alive. I tried to gather my wits and looked around me. I sneezed. Again they laughed.

"The dust of the *ngoma*," said Ferai.

They looked pleased that I had found what I was after.

"This is great," sang Everisto. "You've breathed some life and excitement into these dusty objects we spend our lives with!"

I felt dazed. Grinning idiotically, I went back into the storeroom to see what else there was. There was a remarkable collection of carved stools, ebony head rests, knobkerries, and assegais from around Zimbabwe. There was an impressive collection of drums including a huge, resplendent Venda instrument.

But there was nothing like this, the von Sicard *ngoma*.

I stood at one end of the *ngoma* and Everisto stood at the other. Only a couple of minutes had elapsed since I had found it and recognized it for what it undoubtedly was.

My mind filled with images of Reuven, in Egypt, in Paris, his feet stretched out in the fireplace in the vaulted sitting room of my little Jerusalem house so many years before as he told me of his passions and his quests. I thought of some of the men I had encountered along the way, of Rabin, Doniach, and Patterson, counseling me, warning me, of Daud dancing his lopsided dance in front of his whore's tomb in the City of the Dead. I was overcome by emotion and my eyes misted over. I clenched my hands tightly and looked at the *ngoma*. Was this the end of my quest?

Not wishing anyone to see the tears in my eyes. I looked quickly down at the floor. There was a pool of dark blood spreading around my feet. I felt a terrible fear and thought of the bleeding hemorrhoids the Ark had inflicted upon the men of Ashdod, Ekron, and Gath. I thought of the plague of mice. I examined my hands and felt my face. There was nothing. I felt the operation scar on my stomach. The blood did not appear to be coming from that. I realized that it was Everisto's blood. It was pouring out of his hand. He had ripped a page out of an exercise book and was vainly attempting to staunch the flow. The paper had turned crimson and blood was still dripping onto the floor.

"What's happened? How did you do that?"

"I don't know. It happened all by itself. It started bleeding after I carried the *ngoma*."

We looked to see if there was any metal protruding from it. There was nothing. It was a very bad wound. My first task and duty was to walk with him across to a neighboring shopping center where he said there was a pharmacy. Grudgingly, the pharmacist gave him some bandages and a glass of clean water to bathe the wound. I purchased a tube of antiseptic ointment that he told me represented a week's pay for him. I washed his hand and bound it up. When we got back to the museum we went up to his office for me to have a last look at the *ngoma*.

Ferai was still in the office peering at the accession book and scratching his head. I touched the *ngoma* with some circumspection. I had not told the curators anything about its history or about the search that had finally brought me to their museum. It was clear to them, however, that this was something of great importance to me. Ferai sensed that I was reluctant to leave it and perhaps realized that I was concerned about its future. He was right. The bottom shelf of the shabby ethnographic storeroom of the Harare Museum of Human Science was perhaps no place for the Ark of the Covenant.

I was concerned about it. In addition, I was wondering what my life would be like now, the quest that had filled it, intermittently, but always somewhere beneath the surface, for so many years, was over. It *was* over.

I had no way of knowing how to explain the false leads I had been given by Mathivha, Phophi, and Moeti over the years. Did they know the *ngoma* was here? Was this considered a good and safe hiding place as they awaited better times? Or were the accounts of its removal from Bulawayo and subsequent concealment in the mountains of Zimbabwe and the Soutpansberg so much flimflam?

Smiling at Everisto, I stretched out my hand and caressed the *ngoma*. And what if it were carbon-dated? What would that reveal? And exciting final piece in the puzzle, perhaps. Again I stared at the *ngoma*.

"Don't worry," he said, "don't worry about the *ngoma*. No thieves will ever take the key from Ferai Chabata. Neither will they take the other key from Joseph Muringaniza. While they have the keys, each one his *own* key, this *ngoma* will be safe here in this storeroom. Just don't worry."

Everisto sat on the edge of his desk.

"People do not live long lives in Zimbabwe these days," he said. "We have the lowest life expectancy in the world—just thirty years for men. Statistically, Joseph, Ferai, and me, all three of us are dead! But long after we've all gone, and until Jesus comes again," he said with a broad grin on his face, "your *ngoma* will still be here, quite safe, don't worry, on the bottom shelf with the other old things, there in the debris and the dust."

As I made my way back to the Harare Club there was still fragrant smoke drifting over the city from the southern suburbs.

So that's it, I thought. *I found it. At least my father will be pleased. I can do something else now. Perhaps a trip to Latin America.*

The Ark was here. In the dust of its hiding place.

EPILOGUE

The battered, burnt object that I found in the storeroom of the Harare Museum of Human Science in March 2007 was not dissimilar to the artifact Reuven and I had constructed in our imagination years before in Jerusalem. Reuven had said, "The redemption of Israel will be brought ever closer by the discovery of the Ark. For thousands of years it has been hidden somewhere, probably broken, crushed, worm-eaten. But 'renewed shall be the blade that was broken.' I have a strong sentiment that in my lifetime that blade—the Ark—will indeed be renewed."

Reuven had spoken endlessly of the mystical power of the Ark and the first thing that struck me when I saw it was that I was in the presence of something that exuded sanctity in the same way that some paintings, churches, and mosques exude sanctity even to people without strong religious convictions. But the second thing that struck me was that I was in the presence of something that had been *used* throughout its life for one of its many functions: war. I knew it had been used as some kind of weapon and that it was associated with great noise and fire. I was therefore not surprised to see that some of it had been burnt away in some fashion and other parts had broken off, despite the hardness of the wood.

When I saw it and touched it I sensed that I was in the presence of something of very great antiquity. But was it really possible that a wooden object that had been used in the way that it had been used—as a weapon of war or as an implement of control using fire and possibly explosives—could survive for hundreds or thousands of years? It did seem extremely unlikely. I believed by then that the Ark had been renewed and duplicated at some point over the centuries, certainly from very early times. The priests used it for their own spiritual, martial, and magical purposes and knew its secrets. They could fashion another one at will. Why would they keep something when it was beyond serving their purposes?

I knew the tradition. By now I believed the tradition. The tradition had stated that many, many hundreds of years before, the *ngoma* had been destroyed or destroyed itself and the priests had built another one "on its ruins." The dilemma was clear: should I expose what I had found by such a typically unorthodox means to the unforgiving light of science, or should I leave it alone? As far as I was concerned when I discovered the von Sicard *ngoma* I thought that my quest was at an end. For me it *was* the Ark, the son of the Ark, or the essence of the Ark. Anyway the Ark. Von Sicard had discovered it in the 1940s. Perhaps it was only fifty or so years old when he found it, perhaps more. We do not really know when the original Ark self-destructed—although the Lemba oral tradition puts it in the 1600s.

Doubts began to nag me. Perhaps the period when it was destroyed had something to do with the mid-nineteenth-century period called the *mfecane* when many towns and villages throughout Zimbabwe were burnt and destroyed. If the original *ngoma* had been burnt as a result of these conflicts the replacement would be some one hundred and fifty years old. There was nothing in any of the traditions that I had heard that linked the destruction of the Ark to this period. But who knows?

Years before I had taken a step of faith with the Lemba when I had chosen to believe what was a most unlikely story—that seven of them had arrived in Africa from their original Senna centuries or millennia before. This story had been confirmed by science. We do not know *when* the Lemba people arrived on African soil, although DNA testing using new techniques and particularly more refined subhaplogroup analysis is likely to reveal that in the not-too-distant future. But the broad sweep of the tribe's memories has been confirmed.

Now I was at a crucial stage. Could I accept what their tradition said about the *ngoma*—that it was ancient and that it had replaced something that was even more impossibly ancient, perhaps dating back to the time of the Temple or even to the time of Moses. Mathivha had told me, "Our own precious *ngoma* was hidden for a long time in the Mavhogwe grotto in the MaSenna Mountain near to the Limpopo River. An old Buba High priest was also buried in that cave. A white man called von Sicard took it away many, many years ago." This is the *ngoma* I finally tracked down. We do not know exactly why or when the *ngoma* was hidden in the Mavhogwe grotto or indeed how long it rested there. And we do not know when it was constructed.

Perhaps the small fragment I had taken could offer some answers. With some reluctance and after some time I allowed the precious fragment to be taken for radiocarbon testing.

In October 2007, archaeologists at Oxford University carried out the radiocarbon dating of the piece of wood I prised from the bottom of the Ark/*ngoma*. The results were remarkable. The *ngoma* did not date from the time of Moses nor could it have done given its martial functions over the centuries. According to the radiocarbon dating it was built in 1350 (plus or minus twenty-five years). *It is almost certainly the oldest wooden artefact ever found in sub-Saharan Africa.*

The Lemba people have preserved it for some seven hundred years. Without doubt this is the smaller Ark, referred to in Lemba tradition, which had been constructed by the Buba priests to replace the previous Ark. The previous Ark was probably destroyed—or destroyed itself—around 1350. A substantial hole in the bottom of the Ark seemed to have been deliberately made: I wondered if this Ark had not been constructed on a small core of its predecessor.

We do not know when the Lemba priests brought the Ark to Africa. Was it before 1350 or after? For the moment we cannot say. The fact that the *ngoma* was guarded and cared for so zealously and for so long would suggest perhaps that it was indeed brought from far away—that part of its importance was its association with Senna, which for the Lemba has much the same meaning as heaven or paradise. It was where they came from, and where they hoped to return after death. Mathivha and Phophi had always told me that the Ark had come from Senna, that it had crossed Pusela and that it had finally come to rest hovering above African soil. In this case the Ark that preceded it may have been destroyed in some conflict or natural disaster in south Arabia perhaps some time in the twelfth or thirteenth century. It cannot be said for sure.

In the future the wooden Ark will be more intensively studied and I have no doubt that it has more secrets to give up. But in the meantime science seems to have confirmed the Lemba oral tradition. There can be little doubt that what I found in Harare is the last thing on earth in direct descent from the Ark of Moses.

What will happen when this book is published and the history of the Ark is known?

Will Bishop Norbert Kunonga, the wretched Anglican bishop of Harare, use it for his own unscrupulous ends? Will the depleted, burnt Ark, now of incalculable value, become the center of some great African cult? Perhaps a weapon against tyranny as Reuven had often prophesied? He had always said that his main reason for looking for the Ark was because its discovery would bring strength to the oppressed: The crownless again shall be king.

He had had his eyes fixed upon the tragic history of his own people and upon the End Time that he thought presaged the coming of the Jewish Messiah. He thought finding the Ark would lead to the final redemption of the Jewish people and the construction of the Third Temple in Jerusalem.

But it might impact initially upon the tragic situation of Zimbabwe and much of Africa today, and that seems to me to be a matter of equal concern. If its symbolic authority can be used to force out Mugabe, one of the most cynical dictators the world has seen, my friend Reuven's hopes will in part be realized.

There is no doubt that the discovery of the Ark could have a much more universal application too. The reason that Reuven had first got involved in the Ark and stimulated me to make its discovery my own mission was the impact he imagined it would have upon the Muslim world's attitude towards Israel. How will it affect the Muslim world? I remembered the lines from the Quran, which had first inspired Reuven:

The sign of his kingship is that the Ark of the Covenant will be restored to you ... this should be a convincing sign for you, if you are really believers.

Perhaps it will make a difference.

For Jews, the people who brought monotheism to the world, the Ark was the center of their religious life from the time of Moses until the exile to Babylon in the 6th century BC. They will not ignore its discovery. It is an elemental Jewish icon.

Essentially the Ark was always an African artifact. It may have come with the Hebrews from Egypt, or it may have been constructed, as the Bible suggests, in the Sinai on an African model. But I believe in some sense it came out of Africa and it went back to Africa.

And perhaps it should stay in Africa—but not on the bottom shelf of the storeroom of the Harare Museum of Human Science. Nor in one of Mugabe's private treasure chests.

For more than three thousand years the Ark of the Covenant has been a symbol of the presence and terrifying power of God on earth. Its fate is still a matter of passionate interest to millions of people worldwide. For the last fifty years we know that it has languished, unrecognized, in shabby African museums. Now that the Ark of the Covenant has been discovered, it remains to be seen whether it will be invested with much of the influence and authority its ancestors once enjoyed. One can only hope that its influence will be benign.

INDEX

Aaron 14, 35, 64, 90, 104, 196, 220, 240, 241, 243, 259
Aaron's rod 14, 35, 283, 290
Abbas 35
Abraham 32, 193
Abu Rihana 211
Abu Salih 182–6, 198
acacia wood 63, 135, 195, 221, 353
Achur, Valley of 55
Ad, people of 219
Adam 32
Addis Ababa 179, 186
Aha 137
Ahqaf Islamic library 207, 216
Akhenaten 105, 131, 132
Akkadian 51, 109–10
Aksum, St Mary of Zion Church 184, 186–9, 198
al-Ahbar, Abu Kaab 211
al-Azhar Islamic University 122–3
al-Banyes 226
al-Hawari, Muhammad 170–2
al-Idrisi, Abu Abd Allah Muhammad 225, 226–7, 229, 230, 270
al-Jurhumi al-Harith ibn Mudad 213
al-Mallahi, Abdul Rahman Karim 201–3
Alexandria 161
Alexandrian Church 183
Allegro, John 116–17
Alvares, Francisco 186
Amhara people 190, 194, 198
Amharic 179, 180–1, 188, 193
Anat 171–2

Anatolia 134
Anayer 193, 196
Anba Hadra monastery 172–4
animal sacrifice 2, 70, 240
Anis (Jerusalem antiquities dealer) 24, 73–4, 75
Anthony of Fayyum, St 94, 173
Arab-Israeli conflict 47, 52, 59, 74, 123, 212–13
Arabic 2, 10, 28, 33, 82, 85, 94, 102, 110, 111, 130, 182, 204, 308
Arabs 61, 96, 181, 230, 283
Aramaic 167
Ark of the bulrushes 83–4, 138
Ark of the Covenant
  in Arabia 35, 116, 209–10, 211–14, 218, 219, 220, 221, 226, 228, 229, 245, 253, 361
  Ateret Cohanim excavations 47–8, 59, 77–8
  biblical descriptions 13–14, 32, 63, 133, 134–5, 184–5, 260–1, 326, 360–1
  clues to location 50–7, 113–17, 124, 143–4, 147
  continued existence 48–50, 61–2, 252
  David's dance 6, 66, 265
  dimensions 64, 265, 267
  dualism 42, 93, 109
  Egypt theory 50, 79, 81, 82, 143–5, 150, 154, 155, 159, 162, 163, 165–6, 168–75
  Elephantine theory 153, 155, 159, 162, 165, 168, 169–71, 209
  ephod identified with 217, 263–6, 268

Ark of the Covenant (*continued*)
  Ethiopia legend 43, 129, 151–3, 169,
    173–4, 175–6, 177, 178–9, 181–91,
    190–1, 194–6, 197–8, 199, 214
  fire of God 64, 291
  in Harare Museum 361–5
  historicity 47
  history 30–1, 62–6, 211–14
  importance for Jews 31–3, 47, 49–50,
    61–2, 367
  and Jewish-Muslim relations 33–7, 39,
    41, 71, 74, 123, 273, 367–8
  magical and mystical properties 31–3, 42
  Mercy Seat 32, 63, 70, 163
  multiple Arks 56, 109, 215–16, 267–8,
    275–6
  as musical instrument 112, 260–7
  Muslim accounts 35, 116
  nature of 67, 76–7, 107–12, 137–8, 215–17
  and *ngoma* 13–14, 31, 135, 214, 221,
    252–4, 257–8, 260, 268–9, 279, 313
  Papua New Guinea legend 283, 284–5,
    290, 291, 292, 293, 295, 296, 299–311
  purpose 64
  removal from Jerusalem/Temple 34–5,
    49, 114, 116, 144, 153, 154–5, 158,
    163–4, 165, 182, 210, 257
  in southern Africa 43, 245, 268–72
  in Temple at Jerusalem 31, 38, 41–2, 52,
    66, 154, 163, 164, 165, 184, 257, 342
  treasure hunters 38–9, 46–7, 58,
    69–72, 125–6
  Tutankhamen chests similar 106, 108,
    131, 132, 136, 138
  as weapon 65, 108, 256–60
Arks of Apet 136–7
arms dealing 352
aron 50–1, 108, 109–11, 138, 262
Arrahim 226–7
Ashdod 65, 154
Assyrians 154, 167–8
Aswan 153, 159, 161, 162, 170, 171, 190
Ateret Cohanim (extreme Jewish organi-
    zation) 47–8, 59, 74, 77–8
Auschwitz 40
Avihu 64, 259
Ayn Shams University 170
Azarias 182

ba 94
Babylon 134

Babylonians 34, 49, 61, 62, 69, 114, 165, 210
Baghdad 211–12
Balimo 293–308
Bathsheba 267–8
ben Arieh, Clara 23, 74, 76, 126–8, 146,
    149, 207, 215, 272, 317
ben Arieh, Reuven 23–39, 41, 43, 45,
    57–60, 72–80, 81, 100, 101, 102–4, 117,
    119, 121–9, 140–1, 143, 145–8, 149–53,
    155–6, 157, 158, 161, 179, 181, 188, 199,
    207–10, 213–15, 242, 250, 255–74, 279,
    283, 284, 285–6, 289, 305, 310, 311, 313,
    315, 318, 341–2, 345, 362, 363, 367–8
ben Ezra synagogue, Cairo 83–7, 113
Bey, Azmi 38
Bezalel 32, 63, 107, 184
Bibiato (Gogodala woman) 301–4
Bible 30, 47, 50, 51, 53, 65, 74, 85, 90, 108,
    151, 165, 184–5, 240, 242, 267, 291
  Hebrew 84, 104, 112, 153–4, 158, 263–4
  Vulgate 104
bin Laden, Usama 208
Blue Nile 180, 197, 224
Bodleian Library 99, 100, 101, 114, 115
Bogale (Gogodala Messiah) 281–2, 293–4
Bradman, Neil 239, 241
British Library 236
Brooklyn Museum 167
Brown, Driver and Diggs 154, 264
Bruce, James 187
Buba priests 12, 14, 16, 227, 242–3, 245,
    249, 270, 328, 337, 339–40, 341
Buddhism 119–20
Bulawayo 344
Bulawayo Museum 254, 336, 341, 342,
    345–8, 356, 357–65
Butler, Guy 326

Cairo 81–97, 100, 121, 129–48, 149,
    153–61, 180, 183
Cairo Genizah 83, 113
Camp David Accords 123
Canaan 31, 65, 261
Carter, Howard 132, 133
Cataract Hotel 162, 168–9, 171
Chabata, Ferai 357–60, 362, 364, 365
Challenger 219
Christianity/Christians 26, 53, 71, 96, 124,
    142–3, 190, 197, 206, 270. *See also*
    Amhara people; Coptic Church/Copts
Chronicles 164

Churches and Monasteries of Egypt 182–3
Churchill, Winston 99
CIA 70
City of the Dead, Cairo 87–97, 111, 130, 160–1, 363
Cloud's End Hotel 257, 335
Cohen modal haplotype (CMH) 241, 243
concentration camps 39–40, 127
Constantinople 259
Copper Scroll 53–5, 58, 114–15, 116–17, 125–6
Coptic Church/Copts
    Egyptian 82, 86, 95–6, 130, 131, 137, 141, 142, 156, 157, 173, 175, 180, 181, 183, 186, 188, 229
    Ethiopian 175, 181, 182, 183–4
Coptic language 82, 85, 112, 156
Crotser, Tom 58
Crown, Alan 280
Crusades 38

Dagon 65
Dambanyika, King 330
David, King 6, 31, 66, 217, 265, 267–8
Davies, Philip 268
Dawit (Ethiopian guide) 177–8
de Almeida, Manoel 186
Dead Sea Scrolls 52–3, 57, 99, 100. *See also* Copper Scroll
Deuteronomy 63, 135, 185
Dhimmat al-Nabi (Protection of the Prophet) 28
Dhu Nuwas 206
Diana, Princess of Wales 99
Djerba 61–2, 164
DNA 71, 234, 237, 238, 239, 243, 247, 250, 270, 299, 317
Dome of the Rock 38, 41, 42, 48, 60, 74, 103, 122–3
Doniach, Naki 101–12, 113–14, 115, 117, 119, 121, 124, 131, 140, 145, 210, 314, 363
Dumghe cave 3–4, 15–16, 17–21, 31, 55, 230, 252, 271, 336–9, 340, 341
Dutch East India Company 230
Dzata 321, 322

Eastern Desert 79, 96, 150, 151, 168
Eber 219
Egypt, ancient 50, 82, 94–5, 105, 106, 121, 132, 134, 136–7, 144–5, 154, 155, 165, 167, 258–9

exodus 30, 62, 69, 81–2, 90, 91–2, 261–2
Egypt, modern 81–96, 112, 113, 121–76
Egyptian Museum of Antiquities 131–6
Einstein, Albert 85
Eisner, Shula 59–60, 68, 70, 118–19, 324
Elephantine 155, 159, 162, 165–72, 209, 224
Eliot, T. S. 95, 112, 288
Emek ha-Melekh (Valley of the King) 114
Empty Quarter 200, 219
End Time 47, 125
ephod 66, 216–17, 263–6, 268, 362
Eritrea 188
Essenes 53
Ethiopia 43, 128–9, 151–3, 169, 170, 173–4, 175–6, 177–98, 199, 214, 228, 245, 247, 273, 279
Ethiopian Civil War 194
Ethiopian Jews. *See* Falashas
Etzion, Yehuda 123
Exodus 135, 185, 263, 360–1, 362
Ezekiel 326

Falashas 177–8, 179, 190–1, 193, 194, 196, 197–8, 214, 224, 227, 231, 245, 247–8
Festival of Apet 136
Finks Bar, Jerusalem 57, 59
First Gulf War 39
First Intifada 74
First Jewish Revolt 53
Freemasons 30, 156
Freud: *Moses and Monotheism* 104, 105–6, 108, 131, 132
Funj kingdom 197

Genesis 108, 193
genetics 233–45, 247–8, 249, 280, 299, 315
Gethsemane 68, 71
Getz, Rabbi 77–8
Gideon 217
Gilgal 65
Ginzburg, Carlo 267
Gnostic texts 175
Gogodala people 280–3, 286, 287–8, 289–308
Goha Hotel 181, 197
Goliath 217
Gondar 180, 190, 191
Grañ, Ahmed 187

Great Pyramid 137, 151
Greek Fire 259
gunpowder 258–9, 325, 353

ha-Levi, Jehuda 80
Hadhramaut 200, 201–31, 239, 245
Hahn, Norbert 321, 322, 324–5, 326, 327, 329
Hamas 74, 75, 78, 103, 127
Hancock, Graham: *The Sign and the Seal* 152–3, 156–7, 165, 169, 183, 188
hapax legomenon 111–12
Harare (Salisbury) 237, 343, 347, 348, 349–65
Harare Club 349–51, 352, 365
Harare Museum of Human Science 351, 353–65
Hathor 166
Hawkins, David 134
Hebrew 2, 13, 28, 35, 45, 50–1, 77, 80, 84, 104, 110, 111, 113, 137–8, 141, 154, 158, 263–4, 306, 309
Hebrew University, Jerusalem 45, 52, 60
Hebrews 81–2, 96, 219, 221. *See also* Israelites
Heliopolis 121
Herod the Great 30
Hezekiah, King 163
Himyar (Yemen) 206
Hitler, Adolf 144
Hittites 134
Holland 24
Holocaust 40
Holy Grail 156, 173
Holy of Holies 31, 33, 41, 61, 62, 163, 164, 218
Hud, tomb of 218–23, 225–6, 227
Huldah, Prophetess 52, 164
Hussein, Saddam 40

ibn al-Khattab, Umar 211
ibn Ismail, Hamaysa ibn Nabd ibn Qaydar 213
ibn Munabbih, Wahb 211, 212
ibn Said, Hassan 225, 229
Ibrahim (honey-gatherer) 218
In Search of the Sons of Abraham 244
India 126–7, 149, 269, 292
Iram 219
Isaiah 163
Islam 48, 74, 123, 124, 197, 212, 228, 245

Islamic literature 25–6, 36, 126–7, 143, 146, 161, 207
Islamism/Islamic extremists 39, 74, 162, 208, 211, 215, 222, 223, 291
Ismail, Khedive of Egypt 122
Israel, Ancient 52, 163
Africa connections 128
Falasha origin claims 177, 190, 193, 224
Gogodala origin claims 280, 281, 282, 286, 292, 297, 309
in Jewish mysticism 31
Lemba origin claims 1–3, 7, 11, 12, 14, 200, 224, 230, 249
Qemant origin claims 193
South Arabia connections 206
Israel, modern 24, 25, 40, 125–6, 147, 150, 242
Arab/Muslim resentment 24, 25–6
Daud's opposition 85, 142
Falasha return 177, 178, 190
Gogodala desire to return 289, 297, 308
redemption 35, 36, 37, 273, 340,
Israeli Antiquities department 70
Israelis 59, 70–1, 147, 188
Israelites 30–1, 34, 56, 62–3, 65, 95, 97, 104, 105, 106, 107, 108, 135, 212–13, 215
exodus 30, 62, 69, 81–2, 90, 91–2, 136, 239–40, 261–2
See also Hebrews
Israiliyyat 211–14, 218, 229

Jabès, Edmond 93
Jehovah 134, 169, 171, 215
Jenkins, Trefor 233–5, 236, 237
Jeremiah 34–5, 49, 210
Jericho 31, 65, 262
Jerome 104
Jerusalem 11, 23–43, 45–75, 103, 158, 194, 198, 210, 211, 215, 216, 268, 289
Babylonian conquest (587 BC) 34, 49, 62, 114, 155, 210
as direction of prayer 26, 27, 123–4
Jewish attack fears 39, 40–1
in Jewish mysticism 31
Old City 23, 24, 29–30, 46, 57, 60, 68, 72, 75
Roman destruction (AD 70) 48, 49
Sennacherib's siege (701 BC) 163
Western Wall 30, 47–8, 68
See also Temple at Jerusalem

Jesus Christ 53, 71, 178, 286
  crucifixion site 69, 70
Jewish law 113
Jewish legends 154
Jewish literature 34, 51–2, 60–1, 64, 113,
  147, 151, 164
Jewish-Muslim relations 39
  and Ark 33–7, 41, 71, 74, 103, 123, 273,
    367–8
  Reuven's peace quest 24, 25–9, 33–7,
    123–4, 126–8, 141–3, 207, 273–4,
    367–8
  Reuven's safety fears 72–5, 103, 127–8
  and Temple Mount excavations 38–9,
    48, 59, 74, 78
Jewish religion and culture 25
Jewish Revolt, First 53
Jewish Temple, Elephantine 153, 155,
  166–7, 171–2
Jewish tradition 42, 56, 106, 116, 164, 212
Jews 30, 38, 61, 105, 134, 147, 220, 270
  baal teshuvah (born again) 25
  converts to Islam 124, 211, 213–14
  Daud's attitude 85–7, 142
  Diaspora communities 61, 166, 171
  Gogodala ancestry claims 280, 281–2,
    286, 289, 295, 296–7
  Ethiopian Coptic distrust 188
  European 24
  fear and suffering 40–1
  genetic connection 247
  hatred of 23–4
  importance of the Ark 31–3, 47, 49–50,
    61–2, 367
  Lemba ancestry 1–3, 14, 206, 231, 243–5
  of Medina 26, 27, 212, 221
  priestly genetic markers 239–42
  redemption 29, 37, 125, 367
  of the Yemen 28, 160, 200, 206
  See also Falashas; Israelites; Judaism
Jones, David 343–7
Jones, Steve: In the Blood: God, Genes and
  Destiny 235
Jones, Vendyl 125–6
Jordan 34, 55, 58, 114, 117
Jordan River 30, 65, 210, 261
Josephus Flavius: Antiquities of the
  Jews 107
Josiah, King 52, 164
Judaism 25, 26, 47, 124, 190, 206, 219
Julian the Apostate 38

Jurhum tribe 35, 210, 213
Juvelius, Valter 38

Ka'aba 35
Kabbala 25
Kabbalists 30, 33, 36, 42, 47, 93, 267
Kaplan, Steve 190, 247
Kebra Negast 182
Kings, Book 144, 172
King's Arms, Oxford 101, 103, 111, 112,
  134
Kipling, Rudyard 43, 314
Kiryat Yearim 66
Klopas (Lemba tramp) 9
Knights Templar 38, 78, 173
Kollek, Teddy 59, 68
Kunonga. Norbert 351–2, 368

Labib (Daud's ancestor) 95
Labib, Daud 81, 82–96, 111, 112, 113, 117,
  129, 130–2, 136–44, 145–6, 149, 152–3,
  155–8, 160–3, 172–6, 179–85, 191, 192,
  193–5, 196, 207, 210–13, 215, 217–18,
  219, 220, 222, 224, 227–9, 230, 314,
  345, 363
Lalibela, Saint 184
Languedoc 38, 314
Lawrence (Lemba man) 331–2
Lawrence of Arabia 219
Le Roux, Magdel 239, 315, 327–9, 331,
  332–3
Lemba Cultural Association 321, 337
Lemba people 1–21, 258, 315, 316–17,
  321–2
  ancestral burial sites 318
  astronomy 319
  genetic markers 234–45
  Israelite/Jewish origins 1–3, 14, 200,
    206, 230–1, 234, 242–5
  links to Arabia 214–15, 224–31, 237–9,
    270
  links to Falasha 224, 247–8
  lost city of Senna 2, 3, 7, 11, 15, 16, 197,
    200–6, 215, 221, 224–5, 227, 228,
    230–1, 234, 245, 247, 249, 332, 339
  and ngoma location 15–16, 252, 275–6,
    326–7, 335, 336–9, 341
  and ngoma quest 248–52, 272, 339–40
  ngoma traditions 12–13, 242–3, 253,
    254–5, 259–60, 322, 327–9
  rain ceremony 4–10

Lemba people (*continued*)
Levi, tribe of 30, 84, 240
Lewis, Bernard 26
Limpopo River 13, 255, 256, 269, 336, 339, 341
Limur (scribe) 114
London 117–20, 178, 199, 276, 284
Louis Trichardt (Machado) 238, 250, 319
Luba (convent servant) 68–9, 71, 143
Luxor 136, 144, 162

Maccabees 34, 55–6, 210
Mahdi 35
Malan, Moller 338
Manasseh, King 42, 153, 154–5, 162, 163–4, 165, 167–8
Mandela, Nelson 272
Mangwire, Everisto 348, 351, 353–5, 358–9, 362, 363, 364–5
Mapungubwe 228, 255, 318
Maria (girlfriend) 16–17, 117–18, 119, 128, 160, 285, 288–9, 310, 311, 314, 345, 347
Marquez, Gabriel Garcia 85
Marx brothers 85
Maryam (Cairo widow) 89–90, 90–1, 158, 160–1
Masala, William 249
Mathivha, M. E. R. 11, 12, 13, 203, 236, 238, 242–3, 248–9, 251–2, 256, 275–6, 314, 320, 322, 326–7, 335, 336–8, 339–40, 341
Mavhogwe cave 336, 341
Mbeki, President Thaba 244, 272
Mberengwe 16, 237, 336, 339, 341
Mecca 26, 35, 123, 210, 213, 220, 221
Mena House 122, 123, 130–1, 140, 150, 155
Menelik 43, 182, 198
Messiah, Jewish 47, 114, 123, 367
Messina 255, 256, 258, 319
Micah 217
Michael, Archangel 182
Michal, wife of David 265
Middle East 26, 39, 50, 73, 86, 95, 96, 127, 128, 143, 146, 167, 236, 237, 269, 273
Midrash 64, 213, 265, 292
Mikael, bishop of Ethiopia 183
Miriam, Prophetess 90, 92, 95, 160, 261
Mishnah 151
Moeti, Samuel 248–9, 314, 320, 322, 236–7, 335, 336, 341

Moses (Musa) 10, 14, 34, 35, 67, 86–7, 90, 104–7, 196, 220, 260, 265, 367
Ark construction 32, 63, 97, 107, 135, 184
bulrushes ark 84, 138
Freud's view 105–6, 108, 131, 132
and golden calf 56, 62, 106, 135
"horns" 104
Josephus' view 106–7
receives the Law 30, 32, 62
Moses gene 239–42
Mossad 142, 178, 188, 199, 345
Mozambique 200–1, 204, 228, 230, 344
Mposi, Chief 3, 5, 7, 234, 338
Mposi tribal area 1–16, 95, 237–8, 271, 336
Mubahath al-Dawla (Egyptian Security Directorate) 83
Mugabe, Robert 272, 351, 352, 368
Muhammad (the Prophet) 24, 26, 27, 32, 34, 73, 206, 211, 213, 221
Muringanzia, Joseph 354, 356–8, 365
Muslim-Jewish relations. *See* Jewish-Muslim relations
Muslims 82, 96, 116, 187, 212, 214, 225, 309
Ark narratives 35, 116
See also Islam; Islamic extremists

Nabarro, Margaret 234
Nadav 64, 259
Nag Hammadi 96, 100, 141
Najran 206
Nathan, Prophet 66, 261
National Library in Jerusalem 60–1
Nazis 24, 105, 106
Nebo, Mount 34, 35, 55, 58, 114
Nega Geta, Ato 192–7
Netshiendeulu, High Priest 329–30, 331–4
ngoma 12–21, 51, 249–52, 266
and Ark 13–14, 31, 135, 215, 221, 252–4, 257–8, 260, 268–9, 279, 313
in Bulawayo museum 254, 336, 341, 342, 345–6, 347–8, 357
dangers of discovery 317–18
in Dumghe cave 15–16, 17–21, 55, 271, 336–9, 340
fire of God 12, 254–5
in Harare Museum 357–65
Lemba traditions 12–13, 242–3, 253, 254–5, 259–60, 322, 327–9
links to Arabia 226–7, 253, 270, 329

in Mavhogwe cave 13, 256, 336, 341
multiple *ngomas* 275–6
in Soutpansberg mountains 315, 320,
    326, 327, 329, 331–4, 335, 341
von Sicard's find 13, 252, 254, 335–6, 341
as weapon 12, 257–60, 324–5
Nile 95, 97, 128, 129, 131, 145, 153, 159, 161,
    166, 169, 170, 175
Noah 196, 219
Nubia 166

Obed-Edom the Gittite 66
Operation Moses 178
Origins 235
Osiris 94–5
Oxford 101–117, 134
Oxford Centre for Hebrew and Jewish
    Studies 99–100
Oxford University 41, 45, 99, 102

Palestine 52, 74, 145, 228–9
Palestinians 59, 71, 74, 86, 103, 143
Parker, Montague 38–9
Patterson, David 45, 99, 100–1, 119, 314,
    363
Philistines 31, 65–6, 217
Phophi (Lemba historian) 12–13, 252,
    322, 339
Piatigorksy, Alexander 119–20
Poland 40
Port Moresby 287, 311
Pretoria 239, 244, 315
Psammetichus I 167
Pusela 11, 200, 204, 228

Qasr al-Qubbah 208, 210
Qemant tribe 191–8, 227, 231
Qift 82, 96, 159
Quran 26, 33–4, 36, 87, 219, 223,
    276, 368

Ra 121, 132
rabbinic literature 51–2, 61, 151, 164
Rabin, Chaim 45–58, 61, 62, 99, 100, 116,
    153, 155, 164, 172, 292, 314, 363
Raiders of the Lost Ark 48, 125, 140, 144
Red Sea 62, 69, 90, 92, 128, 159, 160, 261,
    266
Rehoboam, King 144, 165, 172
Rhodes, Cecil 336, 344, 346
Rhodesian Rail network 344

Romans 48, 49, 50, 53, 61, 107, 115
Ronit (Reuven's PA) 150, 151, 158–9, 161,
    162, 214
Russian Orthodox Church of Mary
    Magdalene 68–71

Saba 198
Sadiki (Lemba witchdoctor) 6, 7
saltpetre 258–9, 325
Sana'a 28, 207, 208, 211, 215
Saul 34
Sayhut 203, 205, 228
Sayuna 200–1, 215, 225, 226, 228, 230
School of Oriental and African Studies
    (SOAS) 1, 26, 118, 134, 152, 178, 189, 191,
    285, 314
Second World War 40, 60, 103, 319
Semitic languages 2, 6, 51, 58, 102,
    109–10, 111, 112, 167, 171, 202, 204
Senna 2, 3, 7, 11, 15, 16, 17, 197, 200–6, 215,
    221, 224–5, 226, 227, 228, 230–1, 234,
    239, 245, 247, 249, 322, 339, 361
Senna, Mukhtar of 204–5, 222, 223, 276,
    345
Sennacherib 163
Sennar 190, 197, 224, 227, 231, 247
Sevias (Lemba host) 4, 5, 7, 8, 9, 10–12, 13,
    15–16, 17, 200, 237–8, 340
Sheba, Queen of 177, 184, 198
Shekhinah 33
Sheshonq I 144
Shiloh 31, 65
Shin Bet (Israeli security service) 59
Shishak, King 50, 144, 172
Shona tribe 8, 356
Siloam 322
Sinai, Mount 30, 62, 104, 265
Sinai Campaign 24
Sinai Desert 62, 63, 66, 67, 92, 135, 145,
    160
Singer, Lola 39–41
Six-Day War 24
Skorecki, Karl 241
Sodom and Gomorrah 69
Solomon, King 31, 41, 42, 66, 177, 182,
    190, 198, 212, 292, 293
South Africa 2, 3, 11, 13, 233, 238–9,
    248–76, 315–34, 337, 338, 339, 342–8,
    349
South African Institute for Medical
    Research (SAIMR) 233

Soutpansberg mountains 248–54, 269,
    274–6, 315, 317, 319–34, 335, 341, 342–8
Spencer-Churchill family 99
Sudan 88, 177, 178, 191, 196, 224

tabernacle 30, 31, 36, 55, 64, 240, 261
tablets of the Law 14, 30, 35, 56, 62–3, 135,
    176
tabot 185–6
Tagaruze (police bodyguard) 16, 18–21, 55
tahash 266
tahrah 264, 265, 362
Talmud 25, 41, 78, 109, 151
Tana, Lake 180, 191, 193, 196
Tarim 201, 208–9, 211, 216, 223
Tel Aviv 74, 75–80, 127, 274
Tellez, Balthezar 187
Temple in Jerusalem 6, 261
    Ark in 31, 38, 41–2, 52, 66, 154, 163, 164,
        165, 184, 342
    Ark removed 34–5, 49, 116, 144, 153,
        154–5, 163–4, 165, 182, 257
    Babylonian destruction (587 BC) 34, 81
    First (Solomon's) 31, 41–2, 66, 115, 153,
        154, 163, 165, 182, 184, 257
    in Jewish mysticism 31
    ngoma removed 13
    Roman destruction (70 AD) 240
    Second (Herod's) 30, 115, 116,
        240
    Shishak's ransacking 172
    Third (rebuilding) 47–8, 122, 125, 188,
        242, 273, 367
    treasures 30, 38, 46, 53–5, 113–14,
        114–15, 144
Temple Mount 41, 58, 71, 342
    excavations 38–9, 47–8, 59–60, 77–8
Temple Mount Faithful 59
Temple of Nob 217
Ten Commandments 14, 62–3
teva 84, 138
Thoreau, H. D. 179
Titus, Emperor 240
Tobias, Phillip 233
Tolkien: Fellowship of the Ring 37
Torah 65, 267
Tractate of the Temple Vessels 113–16, 124, 125,
    210
Treblinka 24
Trevisan-Semi, Emanuela 190

Tshiendeulu Mountain 275, 325,
    326, 329
Tutankhamen 136
    tomb treasures 100, 106, 108, 131, 132–3,
        134–5, 138
Typhon 94–5

Ullendorff, Edward 152–3, 189
United States 69, 244
University of Sydney 280
University of South Africa 319
Uriah the Hittite 267–8
Uzzah 66

van Heerden, Pieter 320, 329
Venda people 249, 272, 318, 320, 322, 324,
    326, 327, 318, 329–34
    King of 320, 322–3
Venetia diamond mine 318
von Sicard, Harald 13, 252, 254, 335–6,
    341, 342, 354, 357, 360

Wade, Richard 315–21, 324, 327, 329, 331,
    332, 335, 342
Wade, Thomas 316
Wade-Giles system 316
Waisa, Tony 280–3, 284–5, 287, 288–94,
    298–9, 300, 301, 303, 305, 307, 310
Wales 36, 233, 343
West Bank 117
White Nile 180, 197
Wilbour, Charles Edward 166–7
Windsor 139–40
World Health Organisation 352
Wyatt, Ron 46–7, 58, 69–72

Y-chromosome 234, 235, 240–1
Yassin, Ahmed 74
Yemen 28, 199–223, 224, 282, 308
Yom Kippur War 24, 25, 75, 146

Zambesi River 201, 228
Zanzibar 352
Zena Lalíbela 184
Zimbabwe 1–21, 200, 228, 230, 233, 234,
    238, 239, 252, 255, 272, 315, 318, 319, 336,
    337–8, 348, 349–65
Zion 201, 215, 225, 228, 230
Zionism 26, 207
Zohar 267

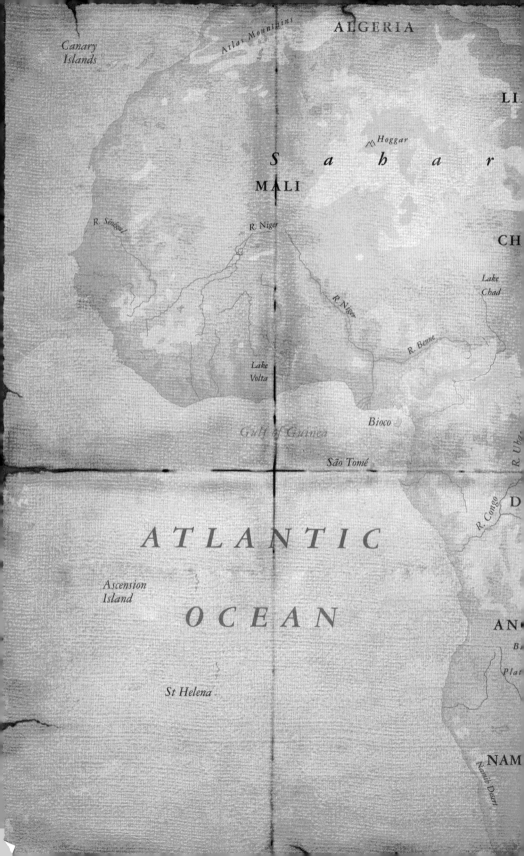